# The London Bombings

# The London Bombings

## An Independent Inquiry

Nafeez Mosaddeq Ahmed

Duckworth

First published in the UK in 2006 by
Gerald Duckworth & Co. Ltd.
90-93 Cowcross Street, London EC1M 6BF
Tel: 020 7490 7300
Fax: 020 7490 0080
inquiries@duckworth-publishers.co.uk
www.ducknet.co.uk

A catalogue record for this book is available
from the British Library

ISBN 0 7156 3583 2
EAN 9780715635834

Typeset by Ray Davies
Printed and bound in Great Britain by
Nørhaven Paperback A/S, Denmark

# Contents

## Dedication

For the victims of the London bombings.

'Dealing with Islamist extremism, the messages are more complex, the constituencies we would aim at are more difficult to identify, and greater damage could be done to the overall effort if links back to UK or US sources were revealed.'

(William Ehrman, Director-General, Defence & Intelligence, Foreign & Commonwealth Office, London, April 2004)

'The policy of guiding the evolution of Islam and of helping them against our adversaries worked marvelously well in Afghanistan against the Red Army. The same doctrines can still be used to destabilise what remains of Russian power, and especially to counter the Chinese influence in Central Asia.'

(CIA analyst, interviewed by Richard Labeviere, Dollars for Terror: The United States and Islam, 2000)

'Terrorism is a part of the dark side of globalisation. However sadly, it is a part of doing business in the world – business we as Americans are not going to stop doing.'

(Secretary of State Colin Powell, Remarks before the Senate Appropriations Subcommittee on Commerce, Justice, State and the Judiciary, May 2001)

# July 2005

On 7 July 2005, London came under attack. Four bombs had detonated in the heart of the city. Three had exploded, almost simultaneously, at separate locations on the London Underground, within 50 seconds of one another, starting at 8.51am. The first went off on the eastbound Circle Line Underground train between Liverpool Street and Aldgate, eight minutes after the train had departed King's Cross St Pancras tube station. 'There was a rushing sound and the blast twisted me and threw me to the ground,' recalled one survivor Michael Henning, a 39-year-old City broker:

> I remember it going dark as I hit the ground and I didn't know whether I would be able to get up. There was a lot of dust and smoke. In my carriage there were four or five people with faces covered in blood and a few people who were hit by debris. But that was nothing to what I saw in the adjoining carriage, part of the side of the carriage was missing and seats were missing. People were screaming in pain, some were trapped and were covered in blood all down their bodies. We tried to open the sliding doors, but they wouldn't budge.[1]

The second bomb went off on a westbound Circle Line Underground train at Edgware Road Station, eight minutes after its departure from Kings Cross. Survivors described how the explosion ripped open a train carriage like a 'can opener', blowing open the floor, sides and roof of the carriage, and shattering the train's windows. A train passing in the opposite direction had its side blown out as it passed by the explosion, hurling one commuter under its wheels.[2]

The third bomb exploded on southbound Piccadilly Line Underground train, after its departure from King's Cross St Pancras towards Russell Square. 'We were only a few minutes out of King's Cross when this thing happened,' according to Gracia Hormigos, a 58-year-old housekeeper from Tottenham, north London. 'I felt like I was being electrocuted. The guy next to me lost his leg. I could see the bone. I was trying to help him, trying to keep him awake. Another guy opposite was slumped over someone else. He was dead.'

Terrified survivors described 'bodies slumped on seats, commuters who had lost limbs, glass tearing through skin and choking smoke'. They could hear endless screams from the adjacent carriage.[3]

It seemed as if the terror was over. For just under an hour, there was no more violence. Then a fourth bomb suddenly exploded on a crowded double-decker bus at 9.47am in busy Tavistock Square, ripping it almost in half and blowing off the roof. Survivors and witnesses spoke of victims and body parts catapulted into the air in a horrifying shower of blood, smoke and wreckage. Other bodies sat slumped in their seats, apparently dead, some with limbs missing.[4]

This was the most devastating bombing in London since the Second World War. Fifty-two civilians had been killed, and more than 700 were injured. It was also, clearly, a carefully planned and sophisticated terrorist operation involving the use of multiple, almost simultaneous, coordinated attacks, designed to paralyse the city through disruption of its public transport system.

But the terror was not over. Two weeks later, on the twenty-first day of the month, there were four attempted bomb attacks in London. The first explosion occurred at 12.26pm on a train at Shepherd's Bush tube station. Four minutes later, there was another explosion on a train at Oval tube station. Then in a further 15 minutes, a third explosion occurred at Warren Street tube station. The final explosion was at 1.30pm on a bus in Bethnal Green.

There were no fatalities as the explosions were very small – in all the bombs only the detonators had exploded leaving everything else intact. Nevertheless, the failed attacks created panic and fear throughout London, as stations were evacuated, tube services suspended, and armed police flooded the streets in search of the culprits and in response to security scares.

The next day, shortly after 10.00am, a Brazilian electrician, Jean Charles de Menezes, was chased and shot to death at Stockwell tube station by undercover police officers. They had been following him from a building under surveillance in connection with the terrorism investigations. Menezes had been shot several times in the head at close range. Police claimed that they believed he was a possible suicide bomber. But it quickly emerged, and police were compelled to admit the following day, that Menezes was an innocent man who had no connection to the terrorist attacks.

The bombings brought terrorism from media coverage of Iraq into the lives of ordinary Londoners. The state's response – in the form of violence against an unarmed man – only heightened the anxieties of Britons and Londoners. As questions about the events of the month mushroomed, the state was on the defensive.

Speaking in Parliament the week after the 7/7 terrorist

attacks, Prime Minister Tony Blair roundly rejected calls for a public inquiry.[5] He explained why:

> I know of no intelligence specific enough to have allowed [the intelligence services] to prevent last Thursday's attacks. By their very nature, people callous enough to kill completely innocent civilians in this way, are hard to stop. But our services and police do a heroic job for our country day in day out and I can say that over the past years, as this particular type of new and awful terrorist threat has grown, they have done their utmost to keep this country and its people safe.[6]

Yet the dedication of individuals is not the central issue here. The bombings raise serious questions about the British state policies, policies that provide the context in which the security services operate. Towards the end of 2005 the Home Secretary, Charles Clarke, confirmed that the government would produce only a written 'narrative' of events surrounding the attacks, authored by a senior civil servant who would quote intelligence sources. There would no public inquiry; no independent scrutiny of government policies or the security environment they created. No attempt would be made to see if more could have been done to prevent the bombings. Sir Ian Blair, Metropolitan Police Commissioner, confirmed that the police 'were consulted' by the government before its decision was made to avoid an inquiry.[7]

The decision is vehemently opposed by victims of the attacks. For example, Colin Ettinger, a lawyer at Europe's leading firm of solicitors Irwin Mitchell, representing 14 victims of the 7 July attacks notes that such a written narrative would not be sufficient to learn lessons and thereby properly improve the necessary safety and security measures.

But Prime Minister Blair and Secretary Clarke justified blocking an independent public inquiry on the grounds that it would divert substantial police and security services resources away from crucial anti-terrorism operations, which would undermine British national security.[8] This is clearly ill-founded. An independent and critical understanding of the specific government policy failures that made it possible for the attacks to proceed unhindered would surely improve national security, if by national security we mean the protection of UK citizens. Pretending that there is no room for improvement is simply to turn a blind eye – a recipe for further disaster.

What then is the status of the criminal investigation into the London bombings, which Blair and Clarke say would be jeopardised by a public inquiry, and in which we should put our faith? A report prepared for Whitehall officials by MI5's Joint Terrorism Analysis Centre (JTAC) in October 2005 was leaked to the *Sunday Times* in early 2006[9]. The largest police and intelligence investigation ever mounted in the UK has discovered almost nothing:

We know little about what three of the bombers did in Pakistan, when attack planning began, how and when the attackers were recruited, the extent of any external direction or assistance and the extent and role of any wider network...

The last few weeks have seen few significant developments ... and we are not that much further on in our assessment ... We do not know how, when and with whom the attack planning originated. And we still do not know what degree of external assistance either group had. Whilst investigations are progressing, there remain significant gaps in our knowledge.

Regarding the possible role of al-Qaeda leaders, the report says, 'We still have no insight into the degree... of command and control of the operation ... How long the 7/7 attack had been planned remains unknown.' Amazingly, the report even suggests that the findings of forensic inquiries at the blast sites remain inconclusive, 'We do not have any conclusive findings from forensic examinations of the group's bomb-making expertise.' Intelligence sources confirmed that by January 2006 when the report was leaked, the status of the investigation had barely improved.[10]

The content of the official Home Office narrative authored by a civil servant is little better. A leaked draft of the report revealed that the official narrative firmly discounts a direct link with al-Qaeda. Instead, the 7/7 bombers were home-grown fanatics who developed their techniques by scouring the internet, and the plot was 'simple and inexpensive.' There was no fifth man, no al-Qaeda 'fixer', and no international network involved. These findings, however, did not pass uncontested. Patrick Mercer, the Conservative spokesman on homeland security, found it 'very hard to believe' that the bombings had no link to al-Qaeda. He warned that the Home Office narrative effectively comes 'from the same sources that provided us with the dodgy dossier over Iraq.'[11]

The government's opposition to an independent public inquiry has been discredited by a former intelligence analyst for the Defence Intelligence Staff, Joint Intelligence Committee and Cabinet Office. According to Crispin Black, who had regularly briefed Downing Street on the terror threat, the attacks were undoubtedly 'discoverable and preventable'.[12] The government 'does not want an inquiry into the events of 7 July because... it does not want to face the fact that its actions put us into danger in the first place'. He argues that an independent public inquiry 'would expose incompetence' in the police's high command and 'complacency and lack of independence' among intelligence services. Although a supporter of the Iraq War, Black highlights British involvement in the war as a pre-eminent cause of the 'anger and alienation' that made 'a small number of our own Muslims more susceptible to the terrorists' message'. In the same vein, he notes that British intelligence services compromise their own remit by operating 'to a political rather than a security agenda'. He points out that the roles of the heads of MI5 and MI6, John Scarlett and Dame Eliza Manningham-Buller in the Iraq dossier fabrications illustrate that they 'allowed their judgement to be corrupted under political pressure'. Black thus sees a full-scale public inquiry as the 'best way to close off vulnerabilities in our intelligence and security services'.[13]

Black hits the nail on the head in pinpointing the role of the *politicisation of intelligence* as a key factor in compromising the ability of intelligence services to perform their statutory obligations to protect the security of the British people. The falsification of intelligence in the service of political interests – in this case, the production of fake intelligence to support the Iraq WMD mythology – was used to justify Anglo-American invasion of Iraq. This is an undeniable example of how the integrity of intelligence-gathering can be subordinated to overarching political objective. This unfortunate track record raises unsettling questions about the integrity of intelligence in relation to the London bombings. We cannot be sure that the failure of the police investigation is a result of simple incompetence. Political pressure of the sort that led to the WMD debacle might also interfere with the work of the police. It is no longer credible to deny that the protection of powerful vested interests play a predominant role in determining the agenda and direction of British state policy, with little reference to the needs or wishes of the majority of the population. It is no longer credible to deny that this has entailed not only massive violence outside the British state, but also the implementation of concerted programmes to manipulate public opinion at home, in order to sanitise and legitimise this violence. Whether or not the Prime Minister and his colleagues were sincere in the drive to war, there can be no question that the state apparatus deceived the British public or that the war made the British people less safe.

Black, and another author, Milan Rai, have done us an outstanding service in demonstrating the direct role of British involvement in the Iraq War in increasing the threat of terrorist attacks on British targets; and facilitating the recruitment of relatively disaffected and disenfranchised British Muslim youths by unscrupulous groups with violent ideologies. However, the Iraq War alone provides an inadequate explanation for the London attacks. The bombings can only be explained through detailed analysis of the political context in which they took place. In this respect the Iraq War was an important factor in the lead-up to the bombings, but only one factor among others. The works of both Black and Rai take for granted the accuracy of the government's official story of what happened. Given the proven mendacity of the British state in the invasion of Iraq, we cannot simply assume that we are being told the truth about matters that touch on matters relating to foreign policy. But what the government did over Iraq, it has effectively repeated in its treatment of the London bombings. Unfortunately, as with the status of intelligence on Iraq prior to the war, much of what the government now claims to be the unquestionable official narrative of the events of 7/7 and its context, is in fact *deeply questionable*. The government's story of 7/7 is at best hopelessly inconsistent, and at worst fundamentally flawed. This is not to say that all or most of the details of the official narrative are untrue. But there is little or no evidence for certain key assumptions and there are many inexplicable contradictions. Above all, the state's version of events systematically suppresses evidence that the bombings are linked to the activities of Islamist groups long tolerated in this country. A more consistent and reliable picture of what really happened that terrifying morning – based on credible public record accounts – strongly suggests that 7/7 was facilitated by a wide array of systematic government, military, financial, security and intelligence policies pursued for several years. Britain has for many years harboured international terrorists linked to al-Qaeda attacks on Western interests in the United States, France, Spain, Morocco, Egypt, and elsewhere. This policy of cohabitation and collaboration with Islamist terrorists created the context in which the attacks took place. The danger is that the overarching need to keep this policy secret will prevent the state from investigating the attacks thoroughly.

The London bombings were a far more sophisticated operation than the government has so far admitted. Furthermore, they were planned and executed by a terrorist network inside Britain that has unambiguous linkages to the international al-Qaeda organisation and leadership. The failure to act on decent intelligence obtained by competent and dedicated police and security officers can only be explained partially by incompetence. The problem goes well beyond that, and relates to the willingness of authorities to tolerate – and in some cases even actively protect – this network to pursue the state's higher policy goals. *7/7 was blowback*, not from earlier, discontinued collaboration with Islamists but from current policies.

In the following analysis, I will show precisely how the government ended up facilitating the London bombings in an embarrassing array of secretive, corrupt and duplicitous policies motivated by vested interests that have compromised national security for decades. The government opposes an independent inquiry because such an inquiry might reveal the extent to which 'national security' policy has endangered British citizens and innocent people throughout the world. For the state's support of special interests in the Middle East and elsewhere created what Black describes as a 'window of opportunity' for the bombings in London. The attacks are inexplicable without reference to Britain's foreign policy, a foreign policy that is rarely acknowledged and to which the British people have never given their consent. This foreign policy not only motivated the bombers themselves, it also permitted the organisers of the bombings to operate freely in Britain for many years. For careful examination of the facts of which we can be certain will show that those who inspired, recruited and trained the bombers themselves have a troubling dual identity as provisional allies of the British state.

I begin by looking at the events of 7/7 itself, examining media reports of police accounts about the 7/7 crime scenes, criminals, and the logistics of the attacks. The shifting nature of the official stories leads us to an investigation of the suspected terrorists and terrorist networks within which the bombers appear to have operated.

This allows me to consider the question of whether these terrorist attacks were foreseeable and preventable. I argue that certainly to some extent they were, and attempt to locate some of the specific intelligence linkages that clearly played a role in paralysing British intelligence services from acting appropriately, in response to escalating warnings of terrorism on British soil.

I then examine the second round of failed terrorist attacks on London on 21 July, as well as the police shooting of Jean Charles de Menezes the following day by armed security officers on a train at Stockwell tube station.

In the final section I explore the geopolitical context in which such a paralysis might have occurred. That context consists of a host of British domestic and foreign security policies which appear to have facilitated the emergence, activities and expansion of these networks for more than the last decade, not only in regions as diverse as the Balkans, Asia and Africa, but also at home. I also present a set of recommendations about how counter-terrorism at home might be served by reform of British and Western policy elsewhere in ther world. In the final analysis, if we want to be safe at home we must stop supporting terrorism overseas.

# A Month Under Siege (Part I)

## 1. 7/7 – Crime Scenes and Criminals

### 1.1 The Bombs

In the early days following the 7 July 2005 terrorist attacks, police and security services were working furiously to understand what had happened, identify the perpetrators, and hunt down their accomplices. The police dedicated a great deal of energy to forensic attempts to uncover exactly what had occurred at the bombsites. As the *Mirror* noted, after the explosions, anti-terrorist officers were 'examining the bus and the wrecked carriages of the bombed Tube trains.' Immediately after the removal of the injured and dead, 'explosives specialists swabbed the scene – including victims' skin and clothes – with chemicals to find out what kind of high explosive was used.' Teams of evidence recovery specialists were sifting through the wreckage to find 'even the most minute bomb parts', in order to develop accurate models of the bombs.[14]

But reports of the conclusions of the forensic investigation have been inconsistent. Multiple, credible reports derived from on-the-record testimonials of forensic scientists, police, government and intelligence officials confirmed in the days after the attacks that the bombs used were military-grade explosives. These reports were repeated and corroborated for a week after the attacks. Yet, by the time another week had passed, the official story had transformed entirely. Suddenly, officials said that the explosives were made from basic household materials.

Forensic investigation of bombsites consists of a standard,

precise and methodical process designed to discover the exact type of explosives and bomb components used at a scene. The process can be divided into a number of key stages:

1. Forensic investigators on the scene look for potential secondary explosive devices that might be placed at the scene to specifically target law enforcement, fire and rescue personnel.
2. After the scene of an explosion is declared safe, specially trained officers conduct the 'post-blast' in search for debris furthest away from the blast.
3. This entire blast area is closedoff and marked into grid squares. Forensic investigators retrieve debris from each grid and document the items found. They are trained to recognise bomb components from bits and pieces of debris. 'They will be able to say, "Oh, that's part of a 9-volt battery, or an antenna lead, or a micro-switch."'
4. Investigators simultaneously gather swabbing samples of explosive residue from surfaces at the scene, which are quickly run through explosive-detection devices. Within minutes, detection devices will gives 'a quick and dirty' of the type of explosive used.

Although it requires a complicated and painstaking system of verification, theforensic analysis of bombsites is nevertheless a reasonably straightforward process, and normally produces decisive results well within 24 hours.[15]

## Military-Grade Explosives from the Balkans

Scotland Yard Deputy Assistant Commissioner Brian Paddick cited technical data from London Underground and witness statements proving that the bombs exploded within 50 seconds of each other.[16] On the same day as the attacks, investigators confirmed that 'the three bombs used in the subway apparently were detonated by timers.'[17] The following day Vincent Cannistaro, former head of the CIA's counter-terrorism centre told the Guardian that police had discovered 'mechanical timing devices' at the bomb scenes.[18] British security officials confirmed the same day to ABC News that:

> Police also have recovered what they believe are the remnants of timing devices on the subway explosions, leading them to believe they were not suicide bombs but explosives planted in packages or bags and left behind. Officials now believe that all the bombs on subway cars were detonated by timing devices.[19]

This discovery indicated that the bombs had been activated automatically to a pre-planned timescale.

Other reports in the ensuing week suggested that the bombs were of military origin. On 12 July 2005, Superintendent Christophe Chaboud, chief of the French Anti-Terrorism Coordination Unit who was in London assisting Scotland Yard with its investigation, confirmed to *The Times* that, 'The nature of the explosives appears to be military, which is very worrying'. According to *The Times*, similar components from the explosive devices found at all four murder sites have led 'detectives to believe that each of the 10lb rucksack bombs was the work of one man. They also believe that the materials used were not homemade but sophisticated military explosives, possibly smuggled into Britain from the Balkans'.[20]

Superintendent Chaboud elaborated that, 'We're more used to cells making homemade explosives with chemicals.

How did they get them? Either by trafficking, for example, in the Balkans, or they had someone on the inside who enabled them to get [the explosives] out of the military establishment.'[21] Chaboud's sources were clearly senior British security officials involved in the investigation. One top British explosives expert corroborated the revelations, telling the *Financial Times* that 'the perpetrators acquired either military or high-quality commercial explosives, possibly from Eastern Europe.'[22] Another senior police official told UPI that investigators had obtained 'concrete evidence' that the 'explosives were not homemade'.[23]

The discovery that the bombs were of military-grade prompted an Europe-wide investigation 'to uncover the source of the military explosives used in the bombings'. So serious was the finding that Scotland Yard had asked its European counterparts 'to check stockpiles at military bases and building sites for missing explosives'.

Citing British forensic scientists involved in the investigation, *The Times* reported six days after the attacks, 'Traces of military plastic explosive, more deadly and efficient than commercial varieties, are understood to have been found in the debris of the wrecked Underground carriages and the bus.' According to one scientist, 'You keep hearing that terrorists can easily make a bomb from using instructions on the internet. You can, but not of the design and sophistication of these devices. These were well put together, and it would appear the bomb-maker has highly developed skill'. Investigators also confirmed that the trigger device was 'almost identical' to those in the rucksack bombs used in the Madrid bombings in March 2004. British miltary sources further noted that this would not be the first time high-quality plastic explosives were used by al-Qaeda. British 'shoe-bomber' Richard Reid, for instance, hid 10 ounces of C4 explosives in each of his shoes when he boarded Flight 63 in Paris on 22 December 2001.[24]

Investigators believed that the European Balkans connection was the key to the conundrum. As UPI reported, Scotland Yard had 'asked for European cooperation' in finding how the London bombers 'obtained military plastic explosives. Traces of the explosive known as C4 were found at all four blast sites.'[25] Although C4 is largely manufactured in the US, experts confirm ample evidence that 'military explosives have been bought by terrorist groups from sources in Croatia and elsewhere in the Balkans, a region heavily imbued with criminal organisations. Islamic militants are reported to have obtained military explosives from sources in Belgrade in recent years.'[26]

British and European counter-terrorism officials similarly told the New York Times that the bombs contained 'military quality' high-grade explosives. One senior official with access to intelligence reports confirmed that new information available on the explosives material indicated that the bombs were 'technically advanced... There seems to be a mastery of the method of doing explosions. This was not rudimentary. It required great organisation and was well put together.'[27]

By 14 July 2005, in an emergency briefing for EU justice ministers in Brussels, French Interior Minister Nicolas Sarkozy confirmed that investigators suspected that 'the explosives used in the bombings came from the Balkans or Eastern Europe, where it is possible to buy the material on the black market after the Balkan wars'.[28] Indeed, one day after the attacks, counter-terrorism sources confirmed that a mere eight hours after the London bombings 'British terror experts were on a special flight from London to the Serbian capital', carrying samples of explosives from the four bombsites. Their intention was to probe their origin and 'find out how the substance was smuggled into the UK'. According to intelligence sources, al-Qaeda is one the biggest customers for illicit weapons in the region.

Jerusalem's intelligence news service DEBKAfile re-ran the story on 13 July.[29] Sources later told DEBKAfile that on that same day, the CIA, MI5, MI6 and the security chiefs of Algeria, Mali, Mauritania and Niger held a top-secret meeting in the obscure capital city of Mauritania, Nouakchott, to investigate 7/7. Al-Qaeda networks in this region are heavily involved in the trafficking of arms, money and drugs, and are exceptionally well connected to the Russian, Central Asian, Balkan and Persian Gulf mafias. The secret intelligence meeting was concerned with ascertaining 'the identities of the masterminds who directed the bomb blasts', who are believed to be based in North/West Africa. DEBKAfile further reports that British intelligence had by then already 'mapped the route by which the explosives used in London reached the British Isles in the last two years', in the following three stages:

**Stage One**: Abu Musab al-Zarqawi, or another senior terrorist planner located in the Middle East, employed Jordanian, Syrian or Lebanese crime mobs to relay the money for purchasing explosives to the Serbian Mafia in Belgrade, which specialises in the acquisition of illicit weapons.

**Stage Two**: The purchased explosives – only a part of the consignment was used, in the view of British investigators – were shipped from the Balkans to North/West Africa and conveyed by local smugglers to al-Qaeda agents in North/West Africa.

**Stage Three**: The explosives were divided into small packages for dispatch to the UK.[30]

DEBKAfile concluded that 'the real investigation' into the London bombings has focused on 'West Africa, the Balkans and the Middle East'. Yet curiously, the British government maintained concerted efforts to prevent the public from grasping this fact:

> The British government is feeding the public with a daily dose of suggestive, diversionary data for two purposes. One is to stop the mouths of Tony Blair's enemies and throw off their efforts to link the attacks to Britain's involvement in Iraq alongside the United States ... The other purpose is to deflect attention from the leads followed by the inquiry to the real source of the attacks.[31]

By late July 2005, DEBKAfile's exclusive story had hit the mainstream press, albeit in a solitary article in Scotland's *Sunday Herald*. Noting that al-Qaeda terrorist networks had 'established links with criminal organisations in Europe and Africa to help them move men, money, weapons and explosives', editors Neil Mackay and David Pratt reported that the MI6 and CIA are increasingly focusing counter-terrorist investigations on 'West Africa as the possible hide-out of some of the most wanted Islamic terrorists in the world – including those suspected of having connections to the London bombings.' They even confirmed DEBKAfile's report that 'US and British intelligence representatives met recently with intelligence officers from Algeria, Mali, Mauritania and Niger' in Nouakchott, 'shortly after the first London bombings.' Investigators reportedly believe that the London bomb team received 'final orders and perhaps even their funding and explosives – from terror leaders operating the West African 'franchise' of al-

Qaeda.'[32] But British officials have consistently refused to publicly elaborate on the progress of these confirmed leads.

## *Or a Homemade Chemical Stew?*

In mid-July, contradicting the coherent picture emerging from independent sources involved directly in the investigation, an opposing version of events began inexplicably appearing in the press. Police were reported to have discovered homemade explosives constituted from acetone peroxide – known as TATP – in a house in Leeds described as a 'bomb-making factory'. They were also hunting a missing Egyptian chemistry student characterised as a possible mastermind of the terrorist attacks.[33] The student, Magdi el-Nashar, who had recently received his doctorate from Leeds University, was reportedly renting the house where the suspicious residue was found, since three works before the attacks.[34] He was also reportedly a friend of bomber Germaine Lindsey, and had helped arrange the lease of a Leeds flat used by the bombers.[35]

Somehow, the purported discovery of TATP residue in Leeds was portrayed as meaning that all the bombs detonated on 7 July 2005 were homemade chemical concoctions. Agence France Presse observed, for instance, that, 'The development suggests that the explosives used in London were homemade, and not of military origin as had initially been thought.'[36] TATP is made from 'commonly available chemicals such as sulphuric acid, which is used to clean drains, hydrogen peroxide, which is used in hair dyes, and acetone'. The process involves evaporating the liquid which leaves behind crystals that constitute the explosive. A large quantity of such residue was said to have been discovered in the bath at the Leeds property. Somehow, security officials said that this isolated discovery made obsolete the decisive conclusions of the past week's forensic investigation, that the bombs used were military-grade explosives. Suddenly, a single find in Leeds had reversed the entire official narrative of the type of explosives used in the London bombings.[37] By 22 July 2005, Janes Terrorism & Insurgency Centre alleged that 'preliminary forensic testing' at the Leeds property as well as at 'the scenes of the 7 July terrorist attacks in London have identified traces of Triacetonetriperoxide (TATP), a powerful homemade explosive'.[38] Then as late as 24 August 2005, senior police sources suddenly told the *Guardian* that the bombs were 'manually activated' using 'a device similar to a button', rather than being automatically detonated by timing devices.[39]

What was happening here? Up to a week after the terrorist attacks, investigators and forensic scientists had already confirmed repeatedly to the press that reliable forensic testing at the bombsites had identified timing devices and traces of military-grade plastic explosives known as C4 to construct technically advanced bombs, originating from organised criminal networks in Europe and the Balkans. How could the decisive identification of military explosives at the bombsites suddenly convert into a finding of traces of homemade explosives put together from household materials? Indeed, how could an alleged finding in Leeds transform the forensic conclusions weeks earlier in London?

Similarly, senior police and security officials had already confirmed the discovery of timing devices in the days immediately following the attacks. Yet in late August police sources simply reversed this story, arguing the bombs were activated manually by a button. In both cases, we seem to have a serious and irreconcilable inconsistency.

Indeed, the second emerging narrative of homemade

explosives – which has entirely eclipsed all mention of the London bombs being of military origin – is difficult to take seriously. How certain was the alleged finding of TATP at Leeds or anywhere? Not very, it seems. A police source who, despite telling the *Daily Mail* that TATP was found in Leeds, had to admit that 'police were still carrying out tests to establish its exact make-up and to see whether there was any link to the substance used by the four London bombers.'[40] In other words, tests had not confirmed whether the substance was indeed TATP; nor that the substance was the same as that detected at the London blast sites. Similarly, the Janes Terrorism & Insurgency Centre which also alleged a forensic discovery of traces of TATP at the Leeds property continued to note that, 'Further testing by explosives forensic experts will still be necessary to confirm the presence of TATP'.[41] Yet if further testing was still necessary to confirm whether or not TATP was really present, then how reliable was this alleged discovery in the first place? How would such a finding change the earlier conclusion that the explosives were of military origin? Not so easily according to a *Times* report which claimed that the ingredients for the London bombs matched al-Qaeda blueprints for hatching explosives found in Kabul, Afghanistan. One document advocates a formula 'using triacetone triperoxide (TATP), also known as acetone peroxide and nicknamed 'Mother of Satan' because of its volatility; and also their own version of C4, the military plastic explosive. TATP is a primer for an explosive device.' Thus, for instance, Richard Reid reportedly used TATP in his shoes, but only as a primer for the main explosive PETN, a version of C4, 'a military-style plastic explosive that can be moulded into any shape'. *The Times* thus observes that the London bombs were 'a carefully balanced mix of commercially available materials and military-style ingredients.'[42] In other words, the alleged presence of TATP is not sufficient to demonstrate the non-presence of military quality explosives – on the contrary, al-Qaeda documents and previous terrorist attacks indicate that the bomb formula included TATP only as a primer for a main military plastic explosive.

Furthermore, the homemade TATP explosives theory is physically inconsistent with the actual nature and impact of the four explosions on 7 July 2005. As the *New Scientist* observes, TATP is an explosive which 'blows up without flames', and 'does not burn when it detonates.' Instead, its molecules 'simply fall apart' without producing heat. Research by scientist Ehud Keinan from the Technion-Israel Institute of Technology in Haifa proves that TATP's explosive force 'comes from a rapid release of gas rather than a burst of energy:

> The TATP molecule sheds acetone units, setting free the oxygen atoms that bound them together to form the gases oxygen and ozone. It also releases just enough energy to spread the reaction to the next molecule. One molecule of TATP produces four of gas, giving TATP its explosive power. Just a few hundred grams of the material will produce hundreds of litres of gas in a fraction of a second.
>
> 'It's different to conventional explosives,' agrees Jimmie Oxley, a chemist at the University of Rhode Island in Kingston, US, who has studied TATP."[43]

Professor Keinan further clarified in the peer-reviewed *Journal of the American Chemical Society*:

TATP is very different from all other conventional explosives in that it does not release heat during the explosion. It explodes by rapid decomposition of every solid-state molecule to four gas-phase molecules. This rare phenomenon, scientifically known as 'Entropic Explosion', is reminiscent of the rapid reaction that produces gas in the safety air-bags of cars during accidents.[44]

As of January 2005, TATP became relatively easy to detect, thanks to the creation of the Peroxide Explosive Tester (PET) which 'looks like a three-color ball-point pen. The device releases three chemical mixtures that change color upon inter-action with the suspected explosive materials.'[45]

Eyewitness testimony and the physical injuries sustained by victims prove that, to the contrary, the London bombs produced immense energy in the form of heat and flames in a manner entirely at odds with the properties of a putative TATP explosion. Jack Linton, who was on the Aldgate train, recalled that, 'Twenty seconds after the train started, there was a massive blast – really, really loud. Outside, sparks and flames burnt up the side of the carriage.' [46] Michael Henning, on the same train, remembers that, 'The blast sent a flash of flame down the outside of the train as the carriages reared up.'[47] Yvonne Madueke, at Kings Cross, describes how 'Seconds after the train pulled out, there was a huge bang, then a flash of light, and I was thrown sideways as the pole exploded in my hand.'[48] Another regular commuter spoke of instinctively knowing a bomb had exploded, 'when the train drew slowly to a halt after a blinding flash and loud bang'.[49] Survivors of the explosion at Edgeware Road described the bombed-out train carriage as 'just black' from burning. 'It was charcoal.' According to Alastair Wilson, clinical director of

Royal London Hospital's Accident & Emergency department, many victims suffered from burn injuries, 'They were typical blast injuries, a lot of burns, burns in the lungs making it difficult for the patients to breathe.'[50] The London Ambulance Service similarly reported that it had treated 'patients with serious or critical injuries including burns, amputations, chest and blast injuries and fractured limbs.'[51] An Associated Press photo captures one injured Tube passenger wearing a burn mask escorted away from Edgware Road Station by a paramedic.[52]

This evidence suggests that the explosions involved a huge release of energy resulting in burning, a phenomenon that is inconsistent with TATP alone. This indicates that TATP, if present, could never account for the full characteristics of the explosions and their impact. It is possible that other home-made explosives were used. But what were they? And why did early reports identify them as C-4?

Finally, as noted above, the actual finding of TATP at the Leeds property seems to remain, as far as Janes was concerned, forensically unsubstantiated. This is also clear from the nature of the investigation into el-Nashar, whose house was where TATP was purported to have been found. Despite being detained by Egyptian authorities for three weeks as a suspected organiser of the London bombings, and apparently wanted by British police, he was eventually released by Egypt on the basis that they 'found no evidence to link' him to the attacks. Despite the huge media fanfare stirred up by British authorities about el-Nashar, he was never interviewed by Scotland Yard investigators throughout the duration of his custody in Egypt.[53] Indeed, it appears that early on in the investigation – that is one week after el-Nashar's arrest in Cairo – British police already knew that el-Nashar had nothing to do with the London bombings. A senior Egyptian security source anonymously told the state-owned Al-Ahram that 'British authorities have concluded that Egyptian biochemist Magdy Nashar was not involved in the July 7 London bombings.'[54] But how could they have been so certain of his innocence when days earlier police claim to have found incriminating traces of TATP explosives at his house? It seems the police did not take their own allegations seriously. Indeed, several weeks later in August 2005 when el-Nashar was eventually freed, the Associated Press noted that, 'The reports linking TATP to el-Nashar were never confirmed.'[55]

The second emerging official narrative that the explosives used in the London bombings were constituted solely of homemade TATP is therefore simply incoherent, cannot be taken seriously, and fails to supersede or obviate the initial official admissions. These admissions confirmed that the explosives were of military-grade, originating from a long-standing criminal arms-trafficking network in the Balkans, which in turn was linked to al-Qaeda's powerful West African terrorist networks. The notion that TATP was really found by police in Leeds and Luton is also deeply questionable, for reasons that are difficult to uncover. By the end of July, police officials were refusing to say anything further at all about the type of explosives used and allegedly discovered. As *The Times* reported three weeks after the 7 July attacks, 'Scotland Yard was still refusing to say exactly what type of explosive was used in the 7/7 and 21/7 attacks on the grounds that doing so might prejudice its investigations.'[56]

Indeed, several days after the London bombs were said to be made entirely of TATP, the military origin of the London explosives was – quietly but authoritatively – confirmed by the Global Information System (GIS), 'a global-coverage, core current strategic intelligence service for use only by governments'.

The GIS is affiliated to the Defense & Foreign Affairs group of publications produced by Washington DC's International Strategic Studies Association (ISSA). Citing its own confidential intelligence sources GIS/Defense & Foreign Affairs reported that it:

> [H]ad already known that the bombs used were based on former Yugoslav National Army (JNA) stocks of Semtex plastic explosive, and that subsequent to the London bombings, UK security officials flew to Belgrade to discuss the matter with Serbia-Montenegro security officials. GIS sources had said that the Semtex had originated from the Bosnian jihadist support network, although it is important to stress that the Bosnia-Kosovo-Albania-Raska (Southern Serbia) jihadist net functions as a single operational zone.[57]

What, then, is the most coherent explanation? In view of the contradictory evidence in the public record, including the recommendations for bomb-making instructions within al-Qaeda documents, it is perhaps most reasonable to infer that that the explosives used a combination of military plastic C4 and TATP, as Richard Reid the shoe-bomber had done. This is consistent with al-Qaeda's modus operandi, and accounts for the possibility that TATP was indeed discovered at the blast-sites. However, it remains unclear whether police really found TATP explosives, bombs, and/or components of bombs in Leeds and Luton.

## Explosions at Floor Level; Bombs Underneath Carriages

Investigators confirmed that the bombs on the London Underground were detonated at the floor level of the train carriages.

According to Andy Hayman, Assistant Commissioner for Special Operations at the Metropolitan Police Service, 'each device on the trains was placed on floor of a carriage, and on the bus a device was placed on the floor or seats'.[58] Similarly, French anti-terrorist police chief Christophe Chaboud noted that 'the victims' wounds suggested that the explosives, which were 'not heavy but powerful', had been placed on the ground, perhaps underneath seats.'[59]

However, reports from survivors and witnesses in the public record largely suggest to the contrary that the bombs exploded from underneath the carriages, rather than from bags placed upon the floor. These accounts emerged in the earliest aftermath of the atrocities, before the police began suggesting that the bombs were planted by terrorist operatives on the floors minutes before the blasts.

*Guardian* journalist Mark Honigsbaum, who interviewed survivors of the blast at Edgware Road Station all morning on 7 July 2005, confirmed that they 'believe there was an explosion this morning under the carriage of the train.' Passengers had heard a 'massive explosion' and some 'described how the tiles, the covers, on the floor of the train, suddenly they flew up, raised up' and the train was 'derailed by the explosion'.[60] Honigsbaum's account indicates that eyewitnesses believed an explosion underneath the train carriage caused the floor to blow upwards. Other reports corroborate this. An off-duty police officer, Lizzie Kenworthy, who survived the train blast at Aldgate, describes how among the victims of the explosion she saw 'a woman... who was on her back trapped in the metal, which had twisted up through the middle of the carriage. The roof was still on, but the lining of the carriage had been blown off. The sides had also come off and there was a big hole in the floor.'[61] The metal from the floor twisted upwards through the middle of the carriage. This is difficult to reconcile with the notion that bombs were placed upon the floor,

In similar vein, according to the *Guardian*, 'witnesses also reported a huge hole being torn in the floor of the carriage' of the train at Edgware Road Station, 'and said one of the men who died appeared to have fallen through the gap.' One survivor, Anita Kinselley, narrates that, 'The tiles on the floor of my carriage suddenly shot up. The next thing I knew there was an almighty crash and the train filled with smoke.' Sean Baran, who had trained as a rescue worker in the US after 9/11 and who helped injured blast victims after departing a bus near the station, recalled that, 'One gentleman told me the floor of the train had blown up.'[62] Another survivor, lawyer Angelo Power, told CNN that seconds after the train departed Kings Cross Station, there was a 'large bang' and passengers were 'physically ejected' from their seats.[63] Bruce Lait, a dancer who works in Cambridge, miraculously survived the blast on the train near Aldgate East Station along with his dance partner, Crystal Main. Lait told the Cambridge Evening News that as they made their way out, a policeman pointed out where the bomb had been. 'The policeman said "mind that hole, that's where the bomb was". The metal was pushed upwards as if the bomb was underneath the train. They seem to think the bomb was left in a bag, but I don't remember anybody being where the bomb was, or any bag.' Lait and his dance partner were reportedly closest in the carriage to where the bomb had detonated.[64]

These eyewitness recollections were issued before a fixed version of events was imposed by the media. They tend to suggest that explosions occurred beneath the floors of the carriages, causing the floors themselves to shatter upwards, with the force of the blast ejecting not only train material but also passengers into the air. The problem for the official narrative is that the notion that the bombs were placed on the floor in bags is simply not supported by the vast majority of eyewitness testimonials in the public record. This gives the official police investigation the appearance of having simply ignored the content of such testimonials made independently by survivors, to the effect that bombs were placed underneath the train carriages. This does not mean that police conclusions are therefore false – however, in the absence of public disclosure, this evidence in the public record certainly does raise questions about the credibility of the official narrative.

It is of course possible that the eyewitnesses were mistaken about what they saw. But in the absence of an independent inquiry, we cannot know the answer to this. This does not imply that the bombs definitely detonated under the carriages. But since there is no clear evidence for another scenario in the public record, there is no clear reason to dismiss these eyewitness accounts. These accounts suggest that the London bombings were a far more sophisticated, carefully planned and synchronised operation than hitherto conceded by authorities. It seems likely that such eyewitness accounts explain the initial assessment of security sources that the London bombers were not suicide terrorists, but 'are still at large and could strike again'. Two days after the attacks investigators were 'convinced that only one bomber – who killed 13 people in the explosion on a double-decker bus – died in the blasts'.[65] Perhaps that assessment was wrong. But if the bombs were in fact planted underneath the carriages as the reports here suggest, rather than on top of the floors, the official police depiction of the bombers' activities is flawed. In this context, the story of the bombers' movements on 7/7, including their operations in the Tube network, needs re-evaluation.

*1.2 The Perpetrators*

*Bombers ID'd*

Within days of the terrorist attacks, police officials claimed to have identified four men believed to be the suicide bombers responsible for planting and detonating the bombs on the three Underground trains and the bus at Tavistock Square. According to *The Times*, police initially had no need of DNA evidence to identify the bombers as they were 'all carrying personal documents ... Documents from one of the group were found on both the bombed-out train at Aldgate and the one at Edgware Road. Police will not say why.' However, they said that 'there was enough documentation found on the bodies of three of the four to lead police to their home addresses.'[66] Sky News terror expert Steve Park observed that 'the documents may have been deliberately planted to 'send police the wrong way.''[67]

Their driving licences and credit cards had been found at the crime scenes. A telephone call from the mother of one of the bombers asking police to trace her missing son had also helped to track them down. Three of the men lived in Leeds: Mohammed Siddique Khan, 30, who planted the bomb at Edgware Road; Hasib Hussain, 19, who bombed the bus in Tavistock Square, and Shehzad Tanweer, 22, the Aldgate bomber.[68] The fourth bomber, reportedly from Luton, who blew up the Piccadilly line train before the first stop at Russell Square, was later identified as Lindsey Germaine.[69] All four bombers were British Muslims from West Yorkshire, the first three of Pakistani descent and the latter of Jamaican origin. About a week after the blasts, authorities reportedly managed to identify Germaine, 'after forensic experts matched DNA samples from a house in Aylesbury, Buckinghamshire, to shreds of tissue retrieved from the Piccadilly Line train that exploded near Russell Square.'[70] No other bombers had yet been identified through their DNA.

In any case, the breakthrough discovery of the four was based on a rough 'profile' created by senior officers depicting the terrorists as 'young men, probably in their 20s and 30s ... carrying rucksacks'. This is difficult to explain – how did senior police officers know to look for young men wearing rucksacks? Given the extensive evidence available to police indicating the sophistication of the operation, the use of military-grade explosives, and timing devices, as well as the abundant eyewitness testimonials that the explosions occurred from underneath the carriages rather than from bags placed upon the floors, it is difficult to understand what in particular could have prompted the police to conjure up this profile. Perhaps they had access to relevant intelligence that has not been revealed to the public.

Guided by the profile constructed by their senior officers, it was not long before detectives viewing thousands of hours of CCTV footage triumphantly discovered 'footage from a camera at King's Cross station in central London ... of four young men carrying bulky rucksacks'. But how could the police justify their conclusion that these individuals were the terrorists? At first, it seemed there was little else except the police's own miraculous terrorist profile of young men carrying rucksacks. But the police later claimed to have substantiated the conclusion in the discovery of explosives in vehicles linked to the four men. The *Telegraph* noted that explosives had been 'discovered in a vehicle left in the car park at Luton station, after a series of controlled explosions to make it safe. Another car, discovered at an undisclosed location, was being examined at Leighton

Buzzard.'[71] Similarly, as already noted, police claimed to have discovered explosives in a bath at a house in Leeds linked to the bombers.

Yet as described above, the Janes account of the Leeds discovery demonstrates its ambiguity and, ultimately, its inconclusiveness. The police decision to cease investigation of the Egyptian chemist who had owned the house where the alleged discovery was made after he had been put forth by police as a suspected mastermind of the attacks, tends to cast doubt on the integrity of the police's claims about the chemist and his property in general. Similar anomalies and questions arise over police claims of having discovered explosives in cars in Luton and elsewhere.

The Scottish *Daily Record*, for instance, reported that apart from the rental car found at Luton, where explosives were found, a second car was also recovered by police to be 'forensically examined in nearby Leighton Buzzard.' Yet curiously, 'Police refused to say exactly where it was recovered. A Bedfordshire Police spokesman said the vehicle was not found at the train station but it was also being linked to the terrorist attacks.' Most relevantly, the spokesman confirmed that senior police in London had somehow already been aware of the car and its link to the terrorists. 'He said they had received a tip-off from the Metropolitan Police and had acted to recover the vehicle.'[72] Yet in the Metropolitan Police Service's official news bulletin regarding the progress of the investigation, no mention was made of the MPS tip-off to Bedfordshire Police concerning the second vehicle, nor indeed was there any acknowledgement of a second vehicle being discovered and examined.[73]

Where was this mysterious second vehicle found? Reports based on police sources say two different things. Some confirm that the vehicle was found at Luton Station and then towed away. Others say that the vehicle was definitely not found at Luton Station, but elsewhere. However, a local report from the Leighton Buzzard *Citizen/Observer* clarified the matter. Police confirmed that 'the vehicle had been routinely recovered from Luton railway station hours *after* [my emphasis] four bombers struck tube trains and a bus in the capital last Thursday.' Yet inexplicably, police had failed to investigate the car for most of the week. The car 'which could hold vital clues to the London bombings stood undiscovered in a Leighton compound' known as J & K Recovery Ltd 'for five days'. Only after having towed the car and left it in a public compound for five days did the police seal off 'a 100 metre cordon around the depot', beginning a long overdue 'painstaking search for evidence and explosives'. But still, 'police would not reveal why the car was towed away or what was inside.'[74]

There is a serious problem here in terms of the relevant public safety procedures concerning possible explosives. The mysterious car had been towed on 7 July 2005 from a previously undisclosed location which now appears to be Luton Station. The Metropolitan Police suspected that the car was somehow linked to the bombers and requested that it be removed. And yet the car was towed without any attempt to conduct the appropriate safety procedures. These would normally include sealing off the area and carrying out selective controlled explosions, The failure to take normal precautions suggests either that the police knew that the car posed no danger or that the police had behaved with incompetence bordering on negligence. Both possibilities raise questions about the police investigation that are unlikely to be answered without a full public inquiry.

Making matters worse for the police narrative, officers involved in the investigation into the vehicles had clearly issued repeatedly mutually inconsistent statements about the explosives purportedly found in the other car at Luton Station. These statements were consistently contradictory about simple matters such as the number and nature of explosives, bombs and/or components thereof, allegedly discovered.

Investigators told the Sydney *Morning Herald* they had 'found another nine bombs in Lindsay's red Fiat, which had been parked at Luton railway station.'[75] Yet police sources told ABC News that the figure was not nine but 'an additional 12 bombs and four improvised detonators' had been found.[76] Then *The Times* reported on the ABC News release of an image of a primed unexploded bomb packed with nails, alleging that, 'In total, 16 bombs were found'.[77] How many bombs had been discovered? Nine? 12? 16? And why such discrepancies? In perhaps the most bizarre report of all, the *Daily Mail* described how, 'Police are *investigating the possibility* that *up to* nine bombs, primed and ready to use, *could have been* [my emphasis throughout] left in the hired Nissan Micra used by the gang'.[78] Still investigating? A possibility? Up to nine? Could have been? Were bombs found or not?

Then *The Times* reported that the ABC News story about the finding of primed bombs including their alleged X-ray images 'contradicts information provided by Scotland Yard. They dismissed the idea that a cache of bombs had been found in the Luton car park.' Instead, senior British police sources 'continued to dispute the US reports ... saying that a number of *components* [my emphasis] for bombs were found in the car', rather than completed devices. Finally, *The Times* concluded by noting that, 'The description of the explosive material recovered in Luton and Leeds varied, but sources have admitted that they cannot definitively identify it'[79] – that is, as late as the end of July 2005, the forensic investigation into material discovered approximately two weeks previously remained, somehow, inconclusive.

Where does this leave the general direction of the police investigation? The conclusion that the four young Asian males seen together at Kings Cross Station on CCTV were suicide bombers responsible for the terrorist attacks is, as we saw above, premised on two things: firstly on a pre-constructed police 'profile' of young men with rucksacks; and secondly on the purported discovery of bombs and/or explosives in properties used or owned by the bombers. The problem is that the evidence of a decisive forensic discovery of such bombs or explosives is lacking – so far, the claims of such discoveries in Leeds and Luton remain unsubstantiated. Looking at the evidence so far made public, the police narrative of the four London bombers appears to be based largely on conjecture.

## Bombers' Movements

I noted previously that police indifference to eyewitness accounts of bombs exploding from beneath the train carriages suggested that the official story of the movements of Sidique Khan and the other men on and prior to 7/7 needs re-evaluation. Indeed, even a quite casual examination of the evidence demonstrates that certain details in the police narrative must be false. This does not necessarily mean that the four were not involved in the bombing operation in some significant capacity. However, it does show that the conventional explanation of the *nature* of their involvement cannot be accepted on the basis of the information that has so far been made public.

Working from hundreds of witness statements and a review of more than 2,500 tapes of CCTV footage, the police had built up a picture of the movements of the four men on the morning of 7 July 2005. The police released CCTV footage of all four men as they were about to enter Luton Station at 7.21am.[80] Citing security sources, the *Mirror* reported that, 'The terrorists bought return rail tickets, and pay and display car park tickets, before boarding a train at Luton for London.'[81] According to Scotland Yard Deputy Assistant Commissioner Peter Clarke, head of the Metropolitan Police anti-terror branch, one of the bombers Hasib Hussain, 'is shown in a CCTV image mounting the stairs at Luton station before taking the 7.40am train to King's Cross' along with his fellow bombers.[82] Police sources told *The Times* that 'A CCTV camera filmed them as they prepared to board the 7.40am train to King's Cross. Near them was another man who might or might not have been an accomplice or even a potential fifth bomber – but he disappeared into the crowd.'[83] The *Telegraph* similarly reported that, 'The four bombers had travelled together on the 7.40am train from Luton to King's Cross before going their different ways.'[84]

Yet bizarrely, on the same day, the same newspaper reported that the bombers had taken the 7.48am train from Luton to Kings Cross.[85] This story was also apparently based on police sources. Newsday for instance states that, 'According to police, the men caught a 7.48 a.m. train in Luton, about 35 miles north of central London, then separated at the King's Cross station.'[86] Channel 4 further reported that the police's 7.48 story was based on credible eyewitness testimony, 'The four terrorists were seen by a witness boarding the 7.48am Thameslink train to King's Cross arriving into the city centre at 8.20am.'[87] Essentially, the police have repeatedly asserted on the public record two different times for the train's departure from Luton.

Moreover, in official statements the police claim to have

obtained CCTV footage capturing all four bombers at Kings Cross Station 'shortly before 8.30am on that morning of July 7'.[88] In another statement, police confirm that the exact time they were photographed in Kings Cross was 8.26am.[89]

The fact that the police have released two contradictory versions of the bombers' travels on the morning of 7 July 2005 raises serious questions about the investigation. Furthermore, its credibility is fundamentally undermined in the light of evidence in the public record confirming that both these contradictory police narratives of the bombers' movements are false, indeed, impossible. Where this leaves the story of the bombers' travels is unclear; yet it does establish that the police stories are incorrect.

The two times variously cited by police, 7.40am and 7.48am, are apparently derived from the official Thameslink timetable for trains which travel from Luton to Kings Cross. The problem is that on the morning of 7 July 2005, no train ran from Luton to Kings Cross at these times due to a number of cancellations and delays in train departures caused by technical problems. Different to the regular Thameslink timetable is a revised schedule of 'Actual Train Times' for train departures from Luton to Kings Cross Station. According to Thameslink's 'Actual Train Times' for the morning of 7 July 2005, there simply was no 7.40am train – it had been cancelled. Furthermore, the 7.48am train did not run at its assigned time within the regular Thameslink timetable; instead, it was delayed and only departed from Luton at 7.56am. It eventually arrived at Kings Cross at 8.42am. There was an earlier train regularly scheduled to depart at 7.30am – however, this too was delayed. It eventually departed at 7.42am, but due to delays similarly arrived overdue at Kings Cross at 8.39am.[90]

So contrary to the police narrative that the bombers took the

7.40am train, this train was in fact cancelled. And contrary to the narrative that they took the 7.48am train, this too was delayed such that the train arrived a total 16 minutes after the bombers were, according to police, photographed by CCTV at Kings Cross Station at 8.26am. Even if they had taken the train whose departure was delayed to 7.42am – very close to the first train time asserted by police – they would have arrived at Kings Cross 13 minutes too late to be caught on the Station's CCTV camera.

Therefore, based on the real train times for that morning, neither police narratives of the bombers' movements can possibly be correct – both of which are supposed to be substantiated by either CCTV footage at Luton Station or eyewitness testimony. This does not necessarily prove that the bombers never travelled to Kings Cross – but it certainly suggests that the official accounts of how this allegedly occurred are wrong. This raises real questions about the integrity of the police investigation. Let us presume, for instance, that the official police accounts – ostensibly based on verifiable CCTV and eyewitness evidence – are correct. In this case, the only possible explanation of the data that the police cite to substantiate their conclusion is that the four men were caught on CCTV waiting at the platform of Luton Station for the 7.40am train. That was cancelled, and an eyewitness account confirms that they had taken the next available train – either the 7.42am or 7.48am. The eyewitness account specifies the latter time; but for either time, the four men would not have arrived at Luton in time to be seen on CCTV at Kings Cross before 8.30am. In summary, by the police's own account, the four men could not have arrived in London in time to mount suicide attacks.

The bombers could have conceivably arrived at Kings Cross via Luton Station on one earlier train. According to

Thameslink's 'Actual Train Times', the train that departed earliest after the bombers' arrival at Luton Station did so at 7.25am. This train arrived at Kings Cross at 8.23am, three minutes prior to all four bombers being allegedly filmed on CCTV there.[91] But if this is the correct account of what happened, why have the police consistently and repeatedly cited impossible accounts – purportedly based on verifiable data – rather than simply amending them?

Could they have arrived at Luton at 7.21, caught the 7.25 and been at Kings Cross at 8.23? Is it possible to get to the platform in time?

In summary, while it is difficult to develop a reasonable alternative account of what happened in the absence of further disclosure of evidence by investigators, this analysis demonstrates that the police account is false. What is particularly bizarre about this scenario is that the police, and with them the media, continue to propagate a very specific, if inconsistent, story of the bombers' movements on 7 July 2005 which certainly never occurred. If a more coherent alternative explanation of their movements might exist, such as the earlier train time departure from Luton, explaining how they were filmed at Luton and Kings Cross at the respective times, it is a mystery as to why such a presumably simple matter has not been acknowledged or resolved up to a year after the terrorist attacks.

In the final analysis, given the inconsistency and inaccuracy of the police narrative about the bombers' movements, the police story concerning the bombers' movements as such becomes deeply questionable. The questions are accentuated in light of the fact that the police have refused to release the alleged CCTV photograph which captures all four bombers at Kings Cross Station at 8.26am – the only photo other than the

Luton Station photo which is described as capturing all four bombers together.

From the perspective of tangible evidence, this leaves us with a significant problem – the only evidence available in the public record that the bombers' travelled from Luton to London on 7/7 to perpetrate suicide attacks is an amalgamation of incoherent and mutually inconsistent police accounts. Once again, this does not necessarily mean that the story is entirely false. But certainly, some of it *is* false, and police sources are clearly telling different stories to different media. Undoubtedly, to some extent this is down to terrible incompetence – and some of it is a deliberate attempt to conceal that incompetence. But incompetence does not excuse, nor sufficiently explain, what amounts here to official deception of the British public, who were the principal victims of the 7/7 terrorist attacks, and who deserve honesty and transparency from authorities. The fact that such deception has gone on without accountability and without any desire to correct the record for public benefit once again raises real questions about the credibility and integrity of the criminal investigation.

Indeed, the proliferation of inconsistent stories about the chronology of the bombers' movements and nature of their involvement throws general doubt on the overall police narrative. In light of the totality of the data available, it is my suggestion that the four men identified as the bombers *were* involved in the operation – but probably not in the exact manner that police have described. Ample evidence indicates that the bombers' actual movements occurred in the context of a wider British-based terrorist network capable of pulling off a far more sophisticated operation than police wish the public to understand.

## 2. Networks and Covenants

### 2.1 Londonistan

*Al-Qaeda in Europe?*

British investigators are exploring the links between as many as 30 people and the London bombings. MI5, MI6, Scotland Yard and GCHQ identified these people on the basis of 'phone taps and reports from foreign agents and police forces'. According to Lord Stevens, former Commissioner of the Metropolitan Police, 'We believe that up to 3,000 British-born or British-based people have passed through Osama bin Laden's training camps over the years.'[92] Current Met Commissioner Sir Ian Blair confirmed that there are 'connections in other countries' to the bombings.[93] In other words, initial assessments strongly supported the notion that the organisers of the July 2005 terrorist attacks were part of a much larger terrorist network.

The attacks certainly bore resemblance to al-Qaeda terrorist atrocities elsewhere in Spain, Turkey, Saudi Arabia, Morocco and elsewhere that had involved 'multiple bombings aimed at unguarded, civilian targets that are designed to scare westerners and rattle the economy'.[94] On the same day as the London bombings, a claim of responsibility was purportedly made by al-Qaeda in the form of a statement posted on an Islamist website by an organisation calling itself 'The Secret Organisation Group of al-Qaeda of Jihad Organisation in Europe':

Rejoice for it is time to take revenge against the British Zionist Crusader government in retaliation for the massacres Britain is committing in Iraq and Afghanistan. The heroic mujahideen have carried out a blessed raid in

London. Britain is now burning with fear, terror and panic in its northern, southern, eastern, and western quarters.[95]

One expert on MSNBC questioned the authenticity of the claim due to purported errors in the statement's Arabic terminology and citation of the Qur'an. But Middle East expert Juan Cole confirms that no such errors could be identified. Germany's *Der Spiegel* pointed out, 'in recent months, authentic bulletins and claims of responsibility from different terrorist groups, including the Iraqi al-Qaida affiliate, have been posted to the 'al-Qala'a' website where today's posting was found,' apparently run by London-based Islamist Dr. Saad al-Fagih.[96] As the *Guardian* notes, Al-Qaeda in Europe had also claimed responsibility for the previous major terrorist attack in Europe: the multiple, simultaneous coordinated bombings of commuter trains in Madrid in March 2004, just over a year before the London bombings.[97]

There was another distinct clue to this effect in the phrase used in the statement, 'Qaeda al-Jihad' which refers to the decision by Ayman al-Zawahiri to merge his Egyptian 'al-Jihad' terrorist group with Osama bin Laden's al-Qaeda. The joint organisation formalised al-Zawahiri's 1998 alliance with bin Laden's. 'The group claiming responsibility for the London bombings represents itself as a secret, organised grouping or cell of "Qaida al-Jihad in Europe," ' observes Professor Juan Cole. 'It is significant that they identify themselves as "in Europe", suggesting that they are based on the continent and have struck from there into London. This conclusion is bolstered by their description of the attack as a "blessed raid". One raids a neighboring territory, not one's own.'[98]

Once again, the Europe connection arises, this time through

al-Zawahiri. The al-Zawahiri connection was apparently reaffirmed in the release of Khan's videotape on 1 September 2005, in which he criticised British foreign policy and described himself as a soldier fighting a war. Khan's message was recorded on the same tape as a message from al-Zawahiri, now Osama bin Laden's right-hand man, in which he made the first direct claim of responsibility for the 7 July terrorist attack.[99] Although the claim does not prove that al-Zawahiri had any direct contact with Khan – as the two appeared in the tape in edited shots – it does indicate that Khan and his fellow bombers were operating within a wider network with links to al-Qaeda and al-Zawahiri.

## Omar Bakri Mohammed and Al-Muhajiroun

Compelling evidence corroborates the above conclusion. London-based cleric Sheikh Omar Bakri Mohammed, founder and spiritual leader of the radical Islamist group Al-Muhajiroun, had warned publicly that a terrorist attack was being prepared in London by an organisation affiliated to al-Qaeda. Bakri gave the warning in April 2004 in an interview with a Portuguese magazine, *Publica*, 'It's inevitable. Because several (attacks) are being prepared by several groups.' One 'very well organised' group in London calling itself 'al Qaeda Europe has a great appeal for young Muslims. I know that they are ready to launch a big operation.' The term 'al Qaeda in Europe' appears to be a rough abbreviation for the al-Qaeda group that claimed responsibility for the 7 July attacks. Bakri then went on to explain, as if to identify himself and his organisation with the London terror group, 'We don't make a distinction between civilians and non-civilians, innocents and non-innocents. Only between Muslims and unbelievers. And the life of an unbeliever has no value. It has no sanctity.' Bakri also confirmed the existence of several 'freelance' militant groups in Europe, such as 'al Qaeda London' which was actively preparing to conduct operations similar to al-Qaeda's.[100]

Then in January 2005, using live internet broadcasts urging British Muslims to join al-Qaeda, Bakri claimed that the 'covenant of security' under which Muslims agree to live peacefully in the UK had been 'violated' by the British government's anti-terrorist legislation. He asserted that consequently, 'I believe the whole of Britain has become Dar ul-Harb (land of war).' In such a state, he added, 'the kuffar [non-believer] has no sanctity for their own life or property.' He also urged his listeners to participate in al-Qaeda's worldwide jihad:

> Al-Qaeda and all its branches and organisations of the world, that is the victorious group and they have the *emir* and you are obliged to join…. These people are calling you and shouting to you from far distant places: al jihad, al jihad. They say to you my dear Muslim brothers, 'Where is your weapon, where is your weapon?' Come on to the *jihad*.[101]

Who is the *emir*? Is it bin Laden?

These statements were an unambiguous call to arms to British Muslims to consider that any obligation to abide peacefully by British laws was over; that Britain was now a legitimate theatre of war; that non-Muslim British citizens were legitimate targets; and finally that jihad in the form of military action must be embarked on under al-Qaeda's umbrella.

Bakri's statements clearly suggest that he had advance warning of the plans to conduct a domestic terrorist attack in London by a British-based group, al-Qaeda in Europe. This, in turn, suggests that he was in a position to be directly acquainted with the relevant terrorist planning; and by implication that being so acquainted, he must have had sufficient contact with the planners and/or their terrorist associates. In either case, Bakri's statements raise the question of his own involvement, the involvement of his organisation, or the involvement of members of his organisation, in the London bombings.

According to British counter-intelligence operative Glen Jenvey, who worked as a spy for the British government as well as with military attaches of foreign governments covering terrorist groups, Bakri is a likely candidate for direct responsibility for the London bombings. Jenvey was directly involved in British counter-intelligence efforts against Bakri's colleague Sheikh Abu Hamza al-Masri, the Imam of the notorious Finsbury Park mosque, and is thus exceptionally well acquainted with their connections. In an interview on the same day as the bombings, when asked about what is known about the al-Qaeda in Europe group that had claimed responsibility, Jenvey confirmed that, 'The group is linked directly to terrorists associated with Abu Hamza', who was jailed in February 2006 largely due to Jenvey's operations for British intelligence. 'The group is also tied to other clerics in Britain. They have taken an oath to Osama bin Laden, if not in person, then at places like the radical Finsbury Park mosque... One of the organisations tied to the London bombing is Al-Muhajiroun,' the organisation headed by Bakri (which was officially disbanded in 2004, but in fact continued to operate under other names). Jenvey noted that Abu Hamza had met regularly with Bakri, and that 'his organisation is known to share the same platform.' Indeed, Bakri 'took over Hamza after the arrest' at Finsbury Park mosque.[102]

According to *The Times*, 'Mohammad Sidique Khan, Shehzad Tanweer and Germaine Lindsay, who detonated rucksack bombs on London Tube trains, all heard him [Abu Hamza] exhort Muslims to kill unbelievers in the name of Islam.' Khan and Tanweer 'heard the cleric's sermons inside the North London mosque.' They were with Lindsay, 'among crowds that heard Abu Hamza preach on the street after the building was closed in a police raid in 2003.'[103]

It was not long before other reports surfaced pointing to a connection between Bakri's network and the London bombers. One of the earliest indications that something was seriously wrong with the government's position on the bombers – i.e. they had never ever entered the radar of the intelligence services – came when the French Interior Minister Nicolas Sarkozy spoke at an emergency terrorism briefing for EU justice and home affairs ministers.[104] Sarkozy confirmed that 'some of the suspected suicide bombers who attacked London on 7 July had been arrested about a year ago, but freed in a bid to catch a wider network.'

Section
removed for
legal reasons

Section
removed for
legal reasons

Bakri himself seemed to be aware of the potentially incriminating implications. After the London bombings, he had gone into hiding 'as police intensified efforts to discover who radicalised the London bombers', and had not been seen at his Edmonton home for several days. His wife denied knowing his whereabouts, and he himself 'failed to answer his telephone'. Even his 'closest associates have switched off their mobile phones.' *The Times* further noted that:

> Bakri Mohammed has a strong following in Luton, Bedfordshire, where the bomb gang met last Thursday morning before catching a train to King's Cross. He is also known to have preached in Leeds and other parts of West Yorkshire. In the 1990s his organisation was banned from the campus of Leeds Metropolitan University where Mohammad Sidique Khan and Shehzad Tanweer, two of the suicide bombers, were students.[111]

Further firm evidence of a direct connection between the bombers and al-Muhajiroun came in the form of a confession made by al-Qaeda suspect Muhammed Junaid Babar, detained in New York for attending an al-Qaeda terror summit in Pakistan. Babar admitted to US authorities that he knew the chief London bomber, Mohammed Siddique Khan. Babar was a member of the Queens branch of al-Muhajiroun.[112] Reportedly part of a terrorist network in Pakistan, Babar was also connected with the March 2004 plot uncovered by the police. After pleading guilty in June 2004, he turned informant for the security services.[113]

As one investigator who tracks Islamic extremists noted, al-Muhajiroun's worldwide leader is Bakri, but the group in London is also closely linked to the Finsbury Park mosque run by Abu Hamza al-Masri, who was arrested in June 2005 and finally jailed for incitement in 2006.[114] Indeed, Mohammed Siddique Khan reportedly 'frequented the mosque before it was seized by the authorities and its radical imam, Abu Hamza Masri, charged with encouraging his followers to kill non-Muslims.'[115] Khan's Queens connection was corroborated when ABC News reported that authorities cited telephone records proving that he had 'made a direct phone call to a suspected recruiter for an extremist group in New York', associated with the Islamic Center, a local mosque.[116]

Section
removed for
legal reasons

Section removed for legal reasons

Section
removed for
legal reasons

Section
removed for
legal reasons

## 2.2 Our Pact with the Devil

*The Covenant of Security*

One explanation of the failure to pursue the organisational network and terrorist planning uncovered in Operation Crevice, according to former Cabinet Office intelligence analyst Crispin Black, was the prevailing British doctrine of terrorist appeasement known as the 'Covenant of Security'. According to Black, 'This refers to the longstanding British habit of providing refuge and welfare to Islamist extremists on the unspoken assumption that if we give them a safe haven here they will not attack on these shores.' The problem is that the policy 'pervades every aspect of our intelligence apparatus', to the extent that 'nearly everything we do or plan for our security takes place within this doctrine'.[124]

Black's admission is the first of its kind from a former senior British military-intelligence official. As Mohamed Sifaoui observes in his *Inside Al-Qaeda*:

[I]t has long been recognised by the British Islamists, by the British government and by UK intelligence agencies, that as long as Britain guarantees a degree of freedom to the likes of Hassan Butt [an overtly pro-terrorist Islamist], the terrorist strikes will continue to be planned within the borders of the UK but will not occur here.[125]

The *New Statesman* thus concludes that the Covenant of Security implicitly assumes that 'the presence of vocal and active Islamist terrorist sympathisers in the UK actually makes British people safer, while the full brunt of British-based terrorist plotting is suffered by people in other countries.'[126]

The existence of the Covenant of Security, and its fundamentally detrimental impact on British counter-terrorist policies, is indisputable. Even the Royal Institute of International Affairs, in a briefing paper on 'New Security Challenges' published after the London bombings, confirmed that:

> By the mid-1990s the UK's intelligence agencies and the police were well aware that London was increasingly being used as a base by individuals involved in promoting, funding and planning terrorism in the Middle East and elsewhere. However, these individuals were not viewed as a threat to the UK's national security, and so they were left to continue their activities with relative impunity, a policy which caused much anger among the foreign governments concerned.[127]

However, it is worth noting that it is not merely individuals, but fully-fledged networks, that have benefited from the Covenant. The Covenant of Security, in other words, had one fundamental implication for Britain's relationship to international terrorism. For more than a decade, due to the deliberate policies of successive governments, the United Kingdom has been a state harbouring terrorism.

Section
removed for
legal reasons

Section
removed for
legal reasons

Section
removed for
legal reasons

Section
removed for
legal reasons

Section
removed for
legal reasons

*Al-Muhajiroun: Inciting to Violence and Terror*

Under the Covenant of Security, Bakri and al-Muhajiroun have been tolerated, indeed actively protected, by the British government, regardless of their involvement in terrorist activity. Bakri boasted in a 2002 interview, 'The British government knows who we are. MI5 has interrogated us many times. I think now we have something called public immunity.'[144] In an interview with Al-Sharq Al-Awsat, when asked why Islamists do not attack Britain, Bakri responded, 'I work here in accordance with the covenant of peace which I made with the British government when I got [political] asylum ... We respect the terms of this bond as Allah orders us to do.'[145]

Al-Muhajiroun spokesmen, including Omar Bakri himself, have openly incited violence – even against Muslims who disagree with them – and incited acts of terrorism abroad. Reporting on an al-Muhajiroun meeting in Birmingham less than a week after 9/11, the *Telegraph* noted that, ' a group of 50 young men and women was encouraged to travel to Afghanistan and give their lives in the defense of Islam. "Martyrdom operatives will be rewarded in heaven," one speaker declared.' Another speaker said:

> I am a Muslim first and foremost. We will never be accepted by the Kufr [the West] so we should not pander to their whims or support their actions like some so-called Muslims have been doing. If they continue to do so, it is our duty to persuade them not to. But if they do not listen, they are Kufr too and so it is our duty to fight and even kill them.

Leaflets for the meeting contained brazenly pro-terror symbolism, stating, 'The final hour will not come until the Muslims conquer the White House' upon a background with a picture of the Pentagon in flames.[146]

Omar Bakri himself has issued several fatwas (religious rulings) inciting international violence and terrorism. His 'Jihad Fatwa Against Israel' dated October 2, 2000, reads:

> O Muslims, this Fatwa is a call to fight against Israeli forces, their government, Israeli Embassies, military airports and jets etc.... as they are legitimate targets for Muslims wherever they may be... any aggression against any Muslim property or land by any Kuffar or non-Muslim forces whether American, British or the Jews of Israeli makes Jihad [fighting] against them an obligation upon all Muslims. ... The Fatwa is therefore JIHAD against the Jewish occupiers, their government, army, interests, airports and institutions and it has been given by the most prominent scholars of Islam today

because of the occupation of Muslim land and aggression against the Muslims of Palestine. The only Islamic Fatwa against this explicit aggression is Jihad.[147]

The fatwa contains only one qualification, that 'it is prohibited to target any non-military or innocent Jews because this would be considered to be murder and therefore aggression against the sanctity of Human life.' But as counter-terrorism expert Ely Karmon rightly observes, the fatwa amounts to:

[A] call to all Muslims to perpetrate acts of terrorism, not only in Palestine against Israelis, or against Israeli military forces, but also all over the world against 'Israeli embassies and companies ... interests, airports and institutions.' This call to arms in fact contradicts the prohibition not 'to target any non-military or innocent Jews because this would be considered to be murder.'[148]

A week later, al-Muhajiroun issued a press release titled 'Advice and Warning to All Jews and Muslims in the UK,' claiming that 'it is an Islamic obligation upon Muslims everywhere to support the Jihad against those who fight Muslims anywhere in the world or who occupy Muslim land and that this support must be financial, physical, military or verbal.' While adding a similar qualification as above that 'civilians' should not be targeted, the document went on to describe all Jews expressing even verbal support for Israel as legitimate targets, 'We urge Jews in the UK and elsewhere not to show any support for the Israeli regime whether verbal, financial or physical or they may allow themselves to become targets for Muslims everywhere.' The press release also quoted Omar Bakri inciting Muslims worldwide without exception to launch a violent uprising against all governments, including his own British government, and to ignore all national and international laws:

> I call upon Muslims around the world to march toward their government buildings, parliament and presidential palaces, to occupy them and to depose their leaders as a step forward and to take charge and send the Muslim armies to fight the aggressors and occupiers and to establish the Khilafah [the Islamic State] [...] I call the Muslims world-wide to resist all man made law wherever they are and to introduce Islamic law.[149]

In the same vein, al-Muhajiroun has published a variety of other fatwas issued by Omar Bakri, inciting acts of violence and terrorism against foreign governments, including for example a death threat against Pakistani military ruler Gen. Musharraf.[150] Omar Bakri also issued a similar wider death threat in December 1999 to Russian President Boris Yeltsin over the war in Chechnya. According to al-Muhajiroun spokesman Anjem Choudry, 'Russian embassies ... government buildings, ministers, [and] personnel' around the world, including in London, 'are legitimate targets' of the fatwa. This broad category therefore would include a large number of civilians by definition.[151]

After the coalition invasion of Afghanistan, another al-Muhajiroun spokesman and leading member Abdel Rahman Saleem characterised the UK as a legitimate target of terrorist violence:

> Because the allies, the British and the Americans, have started bombing the Muslims of Afghanistan, for those

people over there, the government buildings here, the military installations, including 10 Downing Street, become legitimate targets ... if any Muslim wants to assassinate [the Prime Minister], wants to get rid of him, I am not going to shed any tears for him and from the Islamic point of view this person is not going to be chastised, this person is not going to be punished for that act, this person will be praised.[152]

These selected citations are only a small representative sample of hundreds of inflammatory anecdotes, documents and speeches made by Bakri and other leading members of al-Muhajiroun.Inciting people to violence breaks existing UK law and under normal circumstances would lead to arrests, charges, prosecution, and in appropriate cases, deportation. After the London bombings bombings, the government called for new legal powers to tackle terrorism. But this only highlights the question of why the government failed to use the powers it already had?

*Britain's Terror Trainers*

Bakri and his associates have never really attempted to conceal the extent of their involvement in terrorist training activities for British Muslims in support of al-Qaeda operations abroad. Less than two weeks after the 9/11 terrorist attacks, Bakri boasted to his al-Muhajiroun supporters outside the Pakistan High Commission that his brother had joined al-Qaeda fighters in Afghanistan, 'Like me he has received training in Texas and in the north of Scotland where he undertook a one-year course in weapons and evasive vehicle ma-noeuvring.' By the end of the month, he commanded activists in Birmingham that they 'had an obligation to help and support Afghanistan and to fight with them.'

Al-Muhajiroun member Mohammed Jameel, wrote an article for the Arabic daily *Al-Wassat*, entitled 'Yes, we have camps for the training of the mujahidin', in which he admitted having supervised the training of over 150 Britons, including members of Abu Hamza's Supporters of Shariah at the Finsbury Park mosque, and others sent to camps in Pakistan and Afghanistan. Abu Yaya, who after 9/11 acted as a spokesperson for al-Muhajiroun, was interviewed by Radio 4's *Today* programme in June 2000, and was quite happy to talk about his four months of military training in Kashmir where he learned how use artillery, fire a Kalashnikov, and make bombs. Only two weeks after 9/11 he announced, 'My allegiance is to Islam, not to Queen or country – if I have to shoot British soldiers, then so be it … There is no law in the UK that can stop us going. I have already had military training, I know the area and I am ready to return to Afghanistan.' Another al-Muhajiroun member, Omar Brooks, told a newspaper a week after 9/11 that, 'There are a sizeable number of Moslems undergoing military training in the UK … If America decides to bomb Afghanistan, then we'll wake up. If they're going to attack Afghanistan then what's my duty? It's going to be a new chapter.' His colleague, Zahir Khan, addressed a meeting in Birmingham the day after, vowing that, 'If Britain helped attack Afghanistan, it would be allowable for Moslems to attack military targets in Britain.'

In particularly brazen speeches at two mosques in Burnley – broadcast on Channel 4's *Dispatches* programme – Abu Hamza ordered British Muslims to:

Get training … What are you training for? So you can get

> the kafir [non-believer] and crush his head in your arms,
> so you can wring his throat, so you can rip his intestines
> out … Forget wasting a bullet on them – cut them in half
> … if you could put a balaclava on your face and walk
> down the road and stick one on somebody then do it. As
> long as you're going to get away with it.

Much of the training advocated by Bakri, Abu Hamza, and
others, was conducted by a company called 'Sakina Security
Services', which was closely affiliated to both Omar Bakri's
al-Muhajiroun and the Supporters of Shariah group led by
Abu Hamza at the Finsbury Park mosque. Sakina, which has
run training sessions in the UK, once advertised a two-week
course in the United States designed to train potential terrorists
in 'live fire engaging multiple targets; live fire concealed carry;
combat jungle run; live fire sniper; live fire shooting at,
through and from vehicles', among other skills. Sakina also
organised training in many different sites in the United
Kingdom. Bizarrely, although police were forced to shut down
the operation after a number of MPs protested the training
programme, the Department of Trade and Industry had still
not closed the company.

These anecdotes and reports are shocking. How could British
authorities have allowed these terrorist training operations to
continue on British soil for so long without any sanction? It is
not as if these individuals were even slightly worried that they
might one day come under the long arm of the law. To the
contrary, they were fearless, if not boastful and proud, about
their terrorist training activities, and made no effort to conceal
it from the public – to the extent that they regularly gave
interviews to the British press about their exploits. Indeed, all
the information cited in this subsection was gleaned directly

from a concerned address given by Labour MP Andrew Dismore in the House of Commons on 16 October 2001. 'Surely it is time to take action against such extremists', he urged, noting anxiously that, 'The Crown Prosecution Service and the Director of Public Prosecutions have not adopted as aggressive an approach as they should have in dealing with these individuals.'[153] As a result of this inexplicable reluctance to take action these individuals operated with increaing boldness, even after 9/11.

## Al-Qaeda's Recruiting Sergeant for Future British Terrorism

Al-Muhajiroun member Abdel Rahman Saleem has even admitted to undergoing military training with al-Qaeda camps in Afghanistan and Pakistan, and has declared his intent to fight 'on the front line.'[154] He also confessed to actively recruiting British Muslims to participate in such training abroad.[155] 'My support for my brothers in the Taliban ... will be verbal, financial and physical,' he confirmed.[156]

Al-Muhajiroun has in fact been deeply involved in material support of al-Qaeda terrorism. They have recruited naive Britons to join the ranks of al-Qaeda abroad. Representative of the group's Pakistani wing, Briton Hassan Butt, was in Lahore as the war on Afghanistan began. He 'claims to have recruited hundreds of fellow Britons to the cause of Osama bin Laden,' some of whom later died in the conflict.[157] Butt claimed that 60 per cent of foreigners fighting on behalf of al-Qaeda and the Taliban were from Britain, and that he was among 40 Britons in Lahore recruiting fighters, 'I've been in contact with a thousand British Muslims who are going to the holy war. Hundreds have passed through here on their way.'[158] The most disconcerting element of this sequence of events is

the consistently inadequate response of British police and security services. While al-Muhajiroun spokesman such as Butt
were loudly and triumphantly advertising its terrorist recruitment programme to every media outlet who would speak to
them, British authorities did nothing to disrupt the network.
The al-Muhajiroun recruiter even warned that the British
al-Qaeda volunteers 'may return to Britain to launch terrorist
attacks against government and military targets,' a veritable
' "new phase" of terrorism in their British homeland.' In a
BBC interview from Pakistan, he remarked, 'If they do
return, I do believe they will take military action within
Britain,' targeting 'British military and government insti-
tutes, as well as British military and government
individuals... I have always been in favour of this.'[159]
Al-Muhajiroun had coordinated an international terrorist
training and recruitment drive on British soil, under the
nose of British authorities.

Butt's claims regarding the size of al-Muhajiroun's program
seemed outlandish at first glance. However, they were subsequently verified by British military intelligence in Afghanistan,
which concluded that, '1,200 British Muslims trained with
Osama bin Laden's al-Qa'eda terrorist network in Afghanistan.
... The names, addresses and other details of the Britons were
found by British military intelligence during searches of bin
Laden's cave complex at Tora Bora in eastern Afghanistan.'
Apart from those who died in combat, the recruits 'are now
thought to have returned to Britain ... Special Branch detectives
fear that some of the men who cannot be traced could be
plotting terrorist attacks in Britain.' As for those who can be
traced, it seems they have not been interviewed or investigated
by British authorities.[160] Butt was detained under the Terrorism
Act 2000 toward the end of 2002 for his role in recruiting

Britons to join al-Qaeda, but for unexplained reasons was almost immediately released.[161]

Al-Muhajiroun was involved in inciting violence and physically supporting al-Qaeda's international terrorist network. There is also no doubt that in some cases, little effort has been made to conceal such activities, not only from the security services, but from the wider public. According to one US government security and defense analyst, al-Muhajiroun's and Omar Bakri's connections to al-Qaeda are well known in the intelligence community:

> Sure, [the Al Muhajiroun] are a major recruiter for terrorists. It is common knowledge among counter-terrorism operatives and agents that they are a front for bin Laden. There are clear al-Qaeda ties by way of religious, criminal and foreign mujahideen links. Al Muhajiroun, being the bin-Laden front in the UK, essentially connects all the dots.[162]

In other words, contrary to British government denials which have continued into the post-7/7 period, al-Muhajiroun's position as a UK-based front organisation for al-Qaeda is well documented and widely known in the international intelligence community. There is no possibility that the British government is in the dark about what has occurred on its own territory. As noted by Steve Atkins, spokesman for the British Embassy in Washington DC:

> The police and security services are fully aware of this individual and his organisation, al-Muhajiroun. The Home secretary has already made it clear that his and their activities are closely monitored. Anyone breaking the law,

whether provisions of the Terrorism Act, the Race Relations
Act or the Public Order Act, will be prosecuted.[163]

The security and intelligence services knew that al-Mahajiroun
was recruiting aggressively and successfully in the UK. They
knew that individuals radicalised by the group had fought
and died in Afghanistan. By consistently refusing to arrest and
charge members of al-Muhajiroun for their post-9/11 terrorist
training and recruitment programme, which by their own
proud admission allowed British Muslims to be trained in
al-Qaeda camps in Afghanistan in preparation for future
terrorist operations on UK soil, British authorities left intact
the networks that radicalised Sidique Khan and his companions.
We have had no explanation for this apparent lapse and are
unlikely to do without an independent inquiry.

## The Finsbury Division

The network coming under the jurisdiction of the Covenant of
Security, although distinctly marginal and unpopular in relation
to the wider British Muslim community, spans a large number
of hundreds, now possibly thousands, of hardcore followers
ideologically subordinate to an inner circle of closely linked
radical Islamist leaders of various persuasions, united however
by their basic military-political principles.

As already noted, Bakri was closely linked to his extremist
peer, Abu Hamza, at the Finsbury Park mosque, which chief
bomber Khan is known to have frequented. In the mid-1990s,
Bakri was able to use the mosque as a platform,[164] and once
again when Hamza was arrested. Both Bakri and Hamza
controlled the mosque to varying degrees until its trustees
shut it down temporarily after a police raid in January 2003.[165]

Another close associate of both Bakri and Hamza is Sheikh Abu Qatada, who has spoken at al-Muhajiroun events alongside both.[166]

Like Bakri and his al-Muhajiroun network, both Abu Qatada and Abu Hamza were very well known to British authorities, and closely monitored by security services. Bakri's associate, Abu Qatada, is largely believed by the international intelligence community to be the leader of al-Qaeda's European networks. Linked to a large number of terror suspects throughout Europe, Spanish national High Court judge Baltasar Garzon accused him of masterminding al-Qaeda operations in Spain and described him as the 'spiritual head of the mujahideen in Britain.'[167] A US Executive Order identified Qatada as a 'specially designated global terrorist' after 9/11,[168] while the British Treasury confirmed that he was 'believed to have committed, or pose, a significant risk of committing or providing material support for acts of terrorism.'[169] Intelligence on Qatada's terrorist connections is, in other words, well established. As the *Guardian* reported in May 2002, he is 'at the centre of a global web of terrorist conspiracies that runs from Washington to Amman and from London to Madrid. Police in America, Britain, Belgium, Spain, France, Germany, Italy, and Jordan want him.'[170]

An extraordinary *Sunday Times* report two months after 9/11 revealed that British intelligence had been fully aware of Abu Qatada's terrorist activities at the notorious Finsbury Park mosque for several years, but had declined to take action against him. 'MI5 was warned more than two years ago that an Islamic cleric said to be Osama bin Laden's "European ambassador" was using his mosque in London to raise money for a Muslim holy war in Afghanistan and to issue decrees justifying the murder of women and children,' reported

*Sunday Times* correspondent David Leppard. 'A former MI5 agent claimed last week that intelligence chiefs failed to act after he told them that about 20 members of a group with links to bin Laden's al-Qaeda network were operating inside the mosque.' The MI5 informer, Reda Hassnaine, had infiltrated Qatada's Finsbury network and witnessed first-hand how 'several of the men were engaged in a counterfeit credit card ring that raised tens of thousands of pounds to fund terrorist activities abroad.' Proceeds from the cards, sold by Qatada for £150 each to dozens of Qatada's supporters, were used to buy electrical goods, furniture and clothes which he resold on the black market. Hassnaine found that Qatada's profits were invested in 'communications equipment such as satellite telephones, computers and, it is believed, weapons in eastern Europe. The goods were then shipped to Islamic fighters in Algeria and Afghanistan.'[171]

The former British intelligence informant recorded his findings in 'a series of written reports to MI5,' documenting that 'Qatada was the "spiritual leader" of a banned Algerian terror organisation called the Salafist Group for Call and Combat, known as GSPC,' affiliated with al-Qaeda according to security officials. Hassaine recalled that when Qatada issued a fatwa, 'he said that it was legitimate for fighters waging the holy war in Algeria and other Arab countries to kill the women and children of members of the security forces.'[172]

Qatada is also closely linked with the other principal al-Qaeda-affiliated Algerian terrorist group, the Armed Islamic Group known as the GIA, with which the GSPC is closely associated as a splinter organisation. Algerian newspapers identify him as 'the mastermind of the GIA',[173] and he was also editor-in-chief of the GIA's principal ideological voice, the London-based journal *Al-Ansar*. In this capacity,

Qatada worked hand-in-hand with *Al-Ansar*'s managing director, fellow arch-terrorist Mustafa Setmarian Nasar, a Syrian-born confidant of Osama bin Laden.[174] Police believe that Nasar could be a key figure involved in the organisation and planning of the London bombings. Nasar had moved to London in June 1995 when he was already under surveillance by Spanish police, accompanied by fellow operative Abu Dahdah. French authorities implicated him in the 1995 Paris Metro bomb attacks apparently orchestrated by GIA operatives. Nasar was reportedly arrested by British police in connection with the attacks, but later inexplicably released. He left for Afghanistan in 1998. According to the US Justice Department, during his tenure in London, Nasar had 'served as a European intermediary for Al-Qaeda'.[175] Nasar's link to the Finsbury division points to the wider North/West African connection. In a MSNBC interview, leading US terrorism expert Steve Emerson cited British intelligence officials who informed him that the London bombings 'might be tied to the North African-based terrorists who carried out the strikes in Madrid last year.' He noted the existence of 'an interconnected network of Algerians, of Moroccans, of Saudis operating throughout Europe.'[176]

Qatada was also linked with at least seven al-Qaeda operatives detained by Spanish authorities in connection with international terrorism and 9/11. The local al-Qaeda group's leader, Abu Dahdah – who headed the cell responsible for the Madrid bombings – visited Qatada at least 17, and up to 20, times in the UK. The meetings were closely monitored by MI5.[177] On one occasion, Abu Dahdah sent $11,000 to Abu Qatada for Abu Mohammed Al Maqdari, a terrorist arrested in Jordan for his links with al-Qaeda.[178] The terrorists involved in the Madrid bombings, 'also attempted to call Abu Qatada in

London's Belmarsh Prison' before blowing themselves up in the apartment in which they were hiding from Spanish police.[179]

According to Moroccan authorities, one of Abu Qatada's students,[180] Mohammed Guerbouzi – now a British citizen residing in London for over a decade – is a leader of the al-Qaeda affiliated 'Group of Islamic Combatants of Morocco' and is a key suspect in organizing the Casablanca bombings for which he was convicted in absentia for 20 years. British police have refused to question him,[181] although his organisation is on the United Nations list of banned terrorist groups.[182] The *Observer* reported in March 2004 that "Security forces in Britain have confirmed that Al Guerbouzi has been living in Britain for more than a decade, but say that, while they were aware that the Moroccan authorities 'take exception' to Al Guerbouzi, the authorities have not been presented with sufficient evidence that he was involved in any terrorist attack ... The authorites here are yet to be convinced he is a terrorist".[183] Guerbouzi is reportedly 'a member of the Supporters of Shariah, the Finsbury Park group' founded by Hamza, and according to French and German officials is 'connected ... to Abu Musab al-Zarqawi'. Spanish counter-terrorism experts allege that 'strong evidence' indicates Guerbouzi's complicity in the Madrid bombings as well as the London 7 July attacks.[184] According to the MIPT Terrorism Knowledge Base sponsored by the US Department of Homeland Security, 'British authorities are investigating Guerbouzi's connection to the July 2005 train bombings in London' although 'they are not explicitly mentioning him as the man behind the bombings'.[185] Wanted also by French and Spanish authorities, a Brussels-based police official revealed on 7 July 2005 that shortly after the bombings, British authorities 'made an urgent plea to their European counterparts to track [Guerbouzi] down "in relation to the attacks on London" ', as he had disappeared since April 2004.[186] But British police chiefs appear to be playing an odd double-game. Three days after the attacks – the same day that British authorities' had called for European help in tracking him – Guerbouzi himself told the *Washington Post* that although he was keeping a low profile in Britain due to fear of harassment, 'Scotland Yard investigators knew of his whereabouts.'[187] If they knew his whereabouts already, why were they pretending to the Europeans that they could not locate him and needed help to do so?

According to a 700-page dossier produced by Spanish anti-terrorist judge Baltasar Garzón, Abu Qatada made direct contact with Osama bin Laden in 1998.[188]

Another of Hassnaine's findings while spying for MI5 was that Qatada was recruiting directly for al-Qaeda terrorist operations, 'He saw a lot from the inside. Abu Qatada recruited the shoebomber Richard Reid and the "20th hijacker" Zacarias Moussaoui, Hassaine says. "I saw them. Abu Qatada is the best brainwasher there is." '[189] Yet still, British authorities refused to prosecute Qatada and his associates.

In a number of other interviews, Hassnaine – an Algerian Muslim who infiltrated al-Qaeda networks for secret services in Algeria and France, for Scotland Yard's Special Branch and for M15 – has disclosed further crucial details of his investigations into al-Qaeda's London network. Not only had he witnessed and documented for MI5 Abu Qatada's direct links with and material support to the al-Qaeda terrorist network, he also uncovered similar detailed information on Abu Qatada's Finsbury Park colleague, Abu Hamza.

At the beginning of 1999, Special Branch asked him to infiltrate the Finsbury Park mosque to 'gather as much information as he could on Abu Hamza.' He spent the next weeks at the mosque, every night writing a report for his handlers 'detailing Abu Hamza's associates, his speeches and the attitudes of those around him.' Later, under MI5 instructions, he burgled the offices of Abu Hamza and senior militant figures at the Finsbury Park mosque and elsewhere. For weeks, Hassnaine repeatedly 'stole scores of documents' describing what police believed to be al-Qaeda cells in the UK planning terrorist attacks. The documents included communications from al-Qaeda affiliated terrorists in Algeria.[190]

As European law-enforcement officials confirm, reliable intelligence proves that the Finsbury Park mosque had 'functioned openly as a centre of recruitment, ideological incitement, and even support of terrorist acts.' Investigators say that it constitutes 'a crossroads connecting European ideologues to Afghan training camps and Islamic battlegrounds in Chechnya, Bosnia-Herzegovina, and the Middle East.' Nevertheless, European experts have been alarmed that 'British authorities were slow to move against Abu Hamza or Abu Qatada.'[191]

## The Saudi Dissidents

That reluctance applies to other radical Islamists still operating in the UK. One of Bakri's prominent colleagues is Dr Muhammed al-Masari, head of the Committee for the Defense of Legitimate Rights (CDLR), a Saudi opposition group. Al-Masari has been a central figure in al-Muhajiroun's activities and a close associate of Bakri, who has lectured at the latter's 'School of Sharia'. He is also a close associate of Abu Hamza, and led the congregation at Finsbury Park mosque on the first anniversary of 9/11.

One of the websites run by al-Masari is 'al-Qala'a' – the same website where the first claim of responsibility for the London bombings was issued by al-Qaeda in Europe on the same day as the attacks.

Al-Masari has openly admitted both previous support of al-Qaeda and willingness to continue such support. BBC News reported six months after 9/11 that:

> Al-Masari admits he has talked with and helped Osama bin Laden in the past and would do so again, telling [BBC Radio] *Five Live Report*: 'Yes, why not?' The program asked Al-Masari why he had helped Osama bin Laden in the past, he said: 'It's the same cause.' When asked if he would still help him he replied: 'Yeah, if we can help anything, why not?'[192]

Al-Masari was also a close associate of Khalid al-Fawwaz, Osama bin Laden's alleged European spokesman, who is now in a British prison awaiting extradition to the US for planning and supervising the 1998 embassy bombings. As the *Telegraph* reports, al-Masari 'helped Fawwaz establish bin Laden's London office.'[193] In an interview with journalist Nick Greenslade, he candidly confessed that 'when Khalid al-Fawaz arrived here from Sudan [in 1994], we helped him get set up with an office. Osama subsequently phoned to say thank you.'[194]

This was a valuable logistical and financial assistance to Bin Laden's activities. According to the official indictment for the 1998 US embassy bombings, bin Laden worked together 'with KHALID AL FAWWAZ, [...to] set up a media information office in London, England.' The office was:

> [D]esigned both to publicise the statements of USAMA

BIN LADEN and to provide a cover for activity in support of al Qaeda's 'military' activities, including the recruitment of military trainees, the disbursement of funds and the procurement of necessary equipment (including satellite telephones) and necessary services. In addition, the London office served as a conduit for messages, including reports on military and security matters from various al Qaeda cells, including the Kenyan cell, to al Qaeda's headquarters.[195]

One of al-Masari's close associates is Dr Saad al-Fagih, another Saudi dissident based in London who heads the Saudi opposition group, Movement for Islamic Reform in Arabia (MIRA). Al-Fagih has worked closely with al-Masari, campaigning to stop the latter's deportation by then Conservative Home Secretary Michael Howard. He, too, has a documented connection to al-Qaeda. Telephone records from the New York trial of four al-Qaeda operatives behind the 1998 bombing of US embassies in Kenya and Tanzania reveal that al-Fagih purchased the satellite phone that was used by bin Laden and his military commander Muhammed Atef to direct al-Qaeda's operations from 1996 to 1998. Citing the records, BBC News notes that, 'On 30th July 1998 one of the suicide bombers who blew up the US embassy in Nairobi telephoned the satellite phone number: 00 873 682 505 331. Eight days later the suicide bombers struck in Nairobi and Dar-es-Salaam killing 247 people.' Saad al-Fagih had bought the phone for bin Laden in November 1996.[196] The *Sunday Times* further reports that:

Bin Laden and his most senior lieutenants made more than 260 calls from their base in Afghanistan to 27 numbers in Britain. They included suspected terrorist agents, sympathisers and companies.... The records, obtained by the *Sunday Times*, show that the terrorist leader made more calls to Britain than any other country in the two years that he used the phone. ...

According to trial documents, the satellite telephone was bought in 1996 with the help of Dr Saad al Fagih. ... It was al Fagih's credit card which was used to help buy the £10,500 Compact-M satellite phone in the United States and it was shipped to his home in north London, according to American court documents. His credit card was also used to buy more than 3,000 minutes of pre-paid airtime ... [He] has not been arrested or charged in connection with any of these actions.[197]

Moreover, court records show that al-Fagih's provision of the satellite telephone to bin Laden was conducted through the latter's key London lieutenant, Khalid al-Fawwaz, who has been indicted for complicity in the 1998 US embassy bombings.[198]

Khalid al-Fawwaz and his co-workers Ibrahim Eidarous and Adel Abdelbary – all of whom reportedly ran bin Laden's London office whose front name was the 'Advice and Reformation Committee' – were monitored extensively by British security services before the US embassy attacks. Al-Fawwaz in particular, who was personally assisted by Dr Al-Masari and Dr Al-Fagih, was an MI5 informant. 'There is no doubt that security services here were aware of what they were doing', reported the *Guardian*. Al-Fawwaz's lawyers showed that from 1994 when he arrived in the UK to 1998 when he was arrested:

[H]e was in regular contact with the security services ...

Summoned to Room 030 of the old war office building in Whitehall, al-Fawwaz would tell his handlers, one of whom he names, what he was up to. The meetings often lasted three hours or more, he says. MI5 would have made its own discreet checks. Al-Fawwaz's phone was probably tapped, his correspondence intercepted.

Despite this, there was a surprising 'lack of concern about the danger posed by al-Fawwaz.'[199] Indeed, the British government remains reluctant to expedite the long drawn out proceedings, which have already cost millions of pounds, to extradite al-Fawwaz to the United States where he is wanted for trial as a conspirator in the 1998 terrorist attacks.

## Immunity from the Law

Despite the roles of al-Muhajiroun, Bakri, and Hamza in inciting and supporting international terrorism, they faced no legal sanctions from British authorities, although they had apparently violated UK anti-terrorism (and other) laws. Under the Terrorism Act 2000, they appear to have at least breached:

- Part II, section 11(1), by 'furthering the activities of' a proscribed terrorist group, al-Qaeda.
- Part II, section 12, by organizing or addressing a meeting with full knowledge of its aims to support or further the activities of a proscribed organisation, al-Qaeda.
- Part IV, section 59, by 'inciting terrorist activity' overseas.
- Part VI, Section 56, direct the activities of a terrorist organisation, al-Qaeda 'at any level'.

Although British officials have repeatedly claimed that they do not have the legal power to pursue such individuals and groups for their documented involvement in the support of al-Qaeda, this claim is patently false. The UK government has specific powers to combat terrorist groups.

Far from being powerless, the UK government's powers are so wide-ranging and arguably draconian that they practically invite abuse. For example, under the Anti-Terrorism, Crime and Security Act 2001, the British government has the power to indefinitely detain without trial any asylum seeker on the pretext of a mere 'suspicion' that they are involved in terrorist activity. Taking the legislation at face value, the state has demonstrated a bewildering inconsistency in its application.

Under the Prevention of Terrorism Act, the government has detained more than 7,000 people. The vast majority, however, were released without charge. Only a small fraction of this number has ever been charged with offences related to terrorism. Indeed, rather than targeting genuine terrorists, in Liberty's assessment, 'Current anti terror laws are being used to quell peaceful protest, to detain foreign nationals without trial, and are fostering discrimination against the Muslim community in Britain.'[200] Meanwhile, unscrupulous operatives with documented and often admitted, even widely broadcast connections to al-Qaeda, who certainly do fall under UK anti-terrorism legislation, have been permitted to continue their activities unsanctioned.

This apparent immunity continued even after January 2005 – six months prior to the London bombings – when Bakri told his followers that the Covenant of Security was broken, violated by the British government. The violation, Bakri announced, justified Britain's conversion into a 'land of war' requiring British Muslims to join al-Qaeda and participate in 'jihad'.

British authorities should have taken this as a clear warning that 'Londonistan', the burgeoning network of radical Islamist supporters of terrorism, no longer viewed the Covenant of Security as a functioning or binding agreement. Operation Crevice had revealed the existence of an active plan to bomb London. A key Islamist had made it clear that the threat was escalating. Why did British police and security services, instead of raising the threat level and intensifying counter-intelligence operations to foil an impending domestic terrorist attack, fail to take action at this point? Is it just that the authorities could not escape the 'groupthink' mindset shaped by the covenant of appeasing terrorists on British soil to stay safe? Or was there something more going on that prevented the security services from pursuing the logic of surveillance and arrest?

Before looking at these questions in detail, however, I will complete our examination of the two other major events of July 2005 connected to 7/7: the attempted terrorist attacks on the London transport system conducted two weeks after 7/7, and the shooting of an innocent civilian, Jean-Charles de Menezes, by police officers the day after those attacks.

# A Month Under Siege (Part II)

## 3. Two Weeks After

### 3.1 21/7 – Failed Criminals

*The Devices*

Almost before the 7/7 criminal investigation got off the ground, on 21 July 2005, London was hit again by a series of small explosions in a coordinated attack that almost replicated the events of 7 July. According to Met Police chief Sir Ian Blair, the failed attacks were clearly designed to kill. A Home Office source on the same day claimed that the attacks 'were linked to al-Qaeda', although he admitted that the obvious incompetence with which they had been conducted raised questions.[201]

Reliable information on the 21/7 attacks in the public record is difficult to find. Police and security services have been even less forthcoming about the progress of their investigation than they have been in relation to 7/7. A BBC News analysis cited officials saying that the 21/7 devices 'were put together in a way very similar to those used two weeks ago.' They were, in fact, 'so similar to those used two weeks ago that they may even have been part of the same batch.'[202] One day after the 21/7 attacks, 'Officials refused to describe the explosives used, although they said they were investigating whether the materials were similar to those of the July 7 attacks.'[203] Several months later, despite media speculation about the composition of the explosives, 'the authorities [were still] remaining tight-lipped on the detonators and explosive type used.'[204]

Investigators moved fast in narrowing their focus on four

individuals who had planted their devices and fled the scenes, as well as an additional fifth man who had abandoned his device before attempting to detonate it. When it emerged that one of the suspects, Hamdi Isaac also known as Hussein Osman – who had allegedly performed the Shepherd's Bush attack – had managed to escape the UK, catching an Eurostar train to Rome, Italy, it became clear that British authorities were also being tight-lipped about the explosives material with their Italian counterparts. After Osman had been captured by Italian police, he told his interrogators in Rome that he and his accomplices 'had not sought to kill anyone, not even themselves. He claimed the "bombs" were only supposed to make a "bang" and were intended to sow terror.' Angry at the treatment of Muslims in Iraq and the UK, Osman described the coordinated operation as a 'demonstrative action' rather than an attempt to cause mass casualties. But British officials were adamant, and refuted him outright, insisting that 'the July 21 bombs were designed to maim and kill.' While still withholding the precise nature of the explosives material, Metropolitan Police Commissioner Sir Ian Blair and his senior aides stated their conviction that 'the devices, had they detonated properly, would have caused death and destruction on a level comparable to the July 7 attacks.'[205]

In the context of the previous analyses of the 7/7 explosives, it is difficult to take this claim seriously. During his interviews with Italian police, British investigators, and his own Italian lawyer, it quickly emerged that according to Osman, his backpack bomb was made only 'from nails, flour and a liquid hair product', and according to his lawyer Antonietta Sonnessa, 'were not meant to harm, just to make noise.' It was supposed to be an 'attention-grabbing' action to convey to the public 'the state of fear in which one lives in countries afflicted by wars, including Iraq.' Notwithstanding the insistence of British officials that the bombs were of the same calibre as those used on 7/7, they did not dispute Osman's description of their simple components. One and a half months later, Sonnessa was still waiting for the conclusions of the British forensic analysis of the bag's contents, 'I'm waiting for the technical material, I would like to see the legal report. It would be good for the objective checks to be brought to the attention of the Italian authorities.'[206] Indeed, Sonnessa argued that the failure of British authorities to provide the analysis provided grounds for an appeal.[207]

So far British authorities have refused to say exactly what the 21/7 bombs were composed of, or whether they were bombs at all. Further details, however, were provided in the report of the ruling by the Italian judges panel which authorised Osman's extradition to the UK. The panel confirmed that the bombs were created 'using plastic containers, putting flour, hair lotion, nails, nuts and bolts.' This bizarre concoction – which lacks any explosive properties whatsoever – was attached to what the panel described as 'a primitive device featuring a battery, which included a powder to act as a detonator once it had been manually attached to some electric wires.' More oddly, the panel noted that the European arrest warrant for Osman included a 'preliminary assessment' of the bombs alleging that 'TATP or HMTD explosive material was used for the detonation mechanism'. A sample of white powder discovered on the detonator of an abandoned non-exploded bomb 'was identified as TATP, which, as HMTD, is often used for bombings.'[208]

But there are serious inconsistencies in the account of the Italian court. The investigation, as late as mid-August, was inexplicably unable to confirm the precise nature of the detonation mechanism. Was it TATP or HMTD? Although the latter are both derived from hydrogen peroxide, they are still chemically distinct materials. The clear chemical distinction between these two types of explosives materials and their properties makes it difficult to see why the Italian court could not be more specific.

More significantly, the ruling concedes that these materials were confined to the detonation mechanism, and therefore did not constitute the main explosives material used in which the detonator was supposed to trigger an explosive reaction. Chemical explosives consist of two elements, a primary and a secondary explosive. The latter, although powerful, is less easy to detonate. The function of the primary explosive is therefore to detonate more easily, although its explosive properties are generally more limited. TATP and HMTD largely function as primary explosives, that is, as a detonation mechanism, and thus lack significant explosive power in a loose powdered form (the form in which the material was purportedly found in the bombs). In the case of the 21/7 bombs, while there are reports inconsistently suggesting – though never conclusively confirming – that the primary explosive material used in the crude detonator devices was either TATP or HMTD, the secondary explosive which was meant to be subsequently detonated consisted of a maximum of five components: flour, hair lotion, nails, nuts and bolts. These were deposited in plastic containers. The problem here is that a simple mixture of flour and hair lotion forming a lacklustre sludge in which are dumped miscellaneous bits of metal, simply does not constitute a chemical explosive of any kind.[209]

The bombs failed to detonate because they lacked a proper secondary explosive content. Given the contradictory reports about the material used in the detonator, it is not even clear whether TATP or HMTD was actually present therein. Even if so, in the loose powdered form in which it was applied, the primary material was too unstable and had very little explosive potential – as evidenced by the nature of the blasts that occurred. It is difficult to avoid the conclusion, in this context, that Osman's claims about the bombs are plausible. The silence of the British authorities on the bomb components, simultaneous with their hysterical insistence that the explosives used were capable of replicating the scale of mass death, destruction and injury that occurred on 7/7, only discredits the official position further.

Whatever the intentions of Osman and his terrorist associates, the nature of the bombs as described by the Italian court and other reports could never have produced anything like what happened on 7/7. This means that either Osman was telling the truth when he claimed to have never intended to cause deaths and injuries, or that his team were extremely incompetent, and therefore had received insufficient terrorist training.

## The Cell

The identification of the alleged members of the cell behind the 21/7 attacks was completed swiftly. By the end of July five men had been arrested and detained, including the man who is alleged to have abandoned his device. They were Muktar Said-Ibrahim, Yassin Hassan Omar, Ramzi Mohamed, Hussein Osman, and Manfo Kwaku Asiedu. Unlike the 7/7 bombers, who were all British-born, they had come to the UK from various East African countries as child asylum seekers.

A number of factors lend credence to the notion that 21/7 was not intended to kill – although it certainly was intended to instil fear and terror in London. Firstly, the inclusion of the bus bombing in the targets indicates that the planning was indeed supposed to mirror that of the 7/7 bombings, as reports suggest that Hasib Hussein had boarded the bus in a panicked last minute decision when the pre-planning was foiled by the suspension of the Northern line that morning. Secondly, Asiedu's alleged decision to abandon his device before attempting to detonate would suggest an operation hatched and executed by amateurs who were not fully indoctrinated. Thirdly, neighbours reported 'no suspicious activity prior to July', suggesting again that if the group were involved, the planning for the attack was put in motion hastily in order to mimic 7/7. Whoever was responsible the attacks did not occur at peak hours, when they might have incurred maximum casualties, but rather just after midday at the least busy period in the London transport system. For instance, there were only three passengers on the upper deck of the bus targeted on 21/7, as opposed to the bus crammed with commuters on the morning of 7/7. It is more plausible therefore that the projected effect 'was not mass casualties but rather to create a state of lasting fear.'[210]

The arrested men do hold extremist views, and appear to have gone through some sort of indoctrination process. During his interrogation in Italy, Hussein Osman told officials that 'he and his associates attended Finsbury Park mosque in north London,' which was run principally by Sheikh Abu Hamza al-Masri. According to other newspaper accounts they had also been members of the radical Muslim group al-Muhajiroun.[211] They were thus radicalised by the same extremist networks to which the 7/7 bombers were closely connected.

Many of those involved in the bombings escaped the

clutches of the law. Muktar Said-Ibrahim, the alleged bus bomber received a full British passport in September 2004 after applying for naturalisation in November 2003. However, to gain citizenship, applicants are required to show that they have no criminal record and that they are "of good character." At the age of 17, Ibrahim was arrested with four other youths after a street robbery. At that time, they were jailed by Luton Crown Court in 1996 for terms ranging from two to four years, after admitting five robberies. Ibrahim, however, received a five-year sentence for having carried a knife. As a matter of law and routine procedure, Ibrahim should not have been able to receive British citizenship due to his criminal record. The fact that he was is difficult to explain, as checking an applicant's criminal record is an essential condition of the process of assessing applications for naturalisation. As the *Telegraph* notes, 'questions will be asked about how his record did not come to light.' Unfortunately, the reality of the matter is that in the absence of an independent public inquiry, such questions not only remain unanswered, they have not even been asked of government.[212]

Yet another alleged bomber fell under the radar of the intelligence services. The individual, whose identity has not been revealed, was tracked by MI5 and MI6 on a trip from the UK to Pakistan 'months before the attempted bombings'. Secret documents leaked to the *Sunday Times* record MI6 chief John Scarlett admitting that the suspect had been monitored by MI5 in the UK. The agency allowed him to travel to Pakistan 'after he was detained and interviewed at a British airport. Once in Pakistan he was monitored by SIS [MI6], which gathers intelligence overseas', launching 'a low-level short-term investigation' into the suspect. Scarlett claimed that British intelligence ceased monitoring him because 'the Pakistani authorities assessed that he was doing nothing of significance'.[213]

This account raises several crucial issues. If MI5 and MI6 were conducting a surveillance operation against one of the alleged bombers months before the attack, this will have been launched in the context of substantive information suggesting the suspect's involvement in terrorist activity, most likely due to associations with suspected terrorists already under surveillance within the UK, in the course of which his own activity will have been sufficiently suspicious so as to warrant further investigation. At face value, any such surveillance could never have simply occurred spontaneously in a vacuum. It must have been initiated on the basis of a UK-based background of specific prior intelligence. That the decision to cease the surveillance operation was prompted not by an internal assessment by either MI5 or MI6, but simply on the blind acceptance of the advice of Pakistani intelligence services, is damning. Declassified US Defence Intelligence Agency (DIA) documents dated two weeks after 9/11 record in detail that, 'bin Laden's Al Qaeda network was able to expand under the safe sanctuary extended by Taliban following Pakistan directives.' Bin Laden's camp, for example, located on the border between Afghanistan and Pakistan, 'was built by Pakistani contractors, funded by Pakistan's Inter-Services Intelligence (ISI) Directorate.' The Taliban regime 'was created, imposed and recognised by Pakistan in pursuit of its own interests', and under its jurisdiction, al-Qaeda was 'able to grow unmolested inside Afghanistan.' After 9/11, the Pentagon agency continues:

Pakistan's goals are simple, the continuance of the policy they have always demonstrated regarding Afghanistan...

In Islamabad, they have tried to ignore or bury the evidence for some time. It must be a deeply troubling period for General [Musharraf] in Pakistan, who is asked to help hunt down the culprits that he helped to establish and supported. Not to support the US invites trouble and to assist the US to their aims also presents problems to Pakistan. The quandary leaves the Pakistanis confused as to how they might be absolved without permanently shattering their regional aspirations or their Government.[214]

Given this background of al-Qaeda sponsorship, it is difficult to understand how MI6 chief Scarlett could justify the failure to continue the investigation into the would-be 21/7 bomber with reference to a claim from Pakistani intelligence as to his innocence.

*Scotland Yard Knew*

One day after the attacks, British authorities 'acknowledged that, as with the previous [7/7] bombings, they had had no intelligence warning of the attacks.'[215] Despite the government's official insistence that it had no prior knowledge of the attacks of 21 July 2005, anonymous British security sources revealed that Scotland Yard had obtained precise advanced warning of replica bomb attacks on the Tube network that would almost certainly be executed on Thursday of that week. 'Certain information was received that pointed to another round of explosions this week, but the informant couldn't name exactly where and when,' said one intelligence officer, who confirmed that police chiefs independently 'deduced the attack would probably be on a Thursday', as was the case with the 7 July attacks. 'After that', he added, 'we just knew it was going to happen and if it was going to happen it would be on Thursday.'

Scotland Yard, in other words, was not simply anticipating – but *knew* of –another bomb attack in London for the 21 July. Indeed, only two hours before the terrorist strikes, Home Secretary Charles Clarke 'warned senior cabinet colleagues the capital could face another terror onslaught' in a confidential briefing. A senior Downing Street source confirmed that Clarke had made 'very clear there would be further attacks.' Most surprisingly, the Home Secretary had specifically 'hinted at fears there could be copycat attacks in the wake of the July 7 atrocities'. In light of the existing urgent intelligence available to police chiefs that week about an imminent terrorist attack for that very day, it is highly unlikely that Secretary Clarke would have been uninformed.

Indeed, police were racing on the morning of the 21 to locate at least one of the bomber suspects, several hours before the detonations. 'Scotland Yard knew the Tube would be bombed yesterday after being tipped off there would be an attack this week,' reported the *Mirror* the day after the attacks. 'At 9.29am an armed unit raced to Farringdon station as they closed in on one suspected bomber – but narrowly missed him.'[216] The incident indicates the extent of the detail apparently available to the police. How did they know he would pass through Farringdon? If they had information of such precision, did it extend to other elements of the plot? Although the *Mirror* states that there was a visible increase in the presence of armed police at selected areas in London, this was simply insufficient as a preventive measure given the scale of the potential threat. In view of the fact that security sources confirm that warning of an attack 'this week' was based on 'certain information', such that security services 'just knew it was going to happen

... on Thursday', London should have been on the highest state of alert.

If police were chasing one of the bomber-suspects on his way through Farringdon, they clearly had sufficiently precise intelligence to know that the London Tube network specifically, and transport system generally, were again the principal targets – an inference given credence by Secretary Clarke's confidential Downing Street warning hours earlier of the probability of copycat attacks. But there have been no reports to suggest that the alert status on 21/7 had been raised in response to the specific intelligence available. Nor was the public informed in any manner. On the contrary, official pronouncements to the effect that the attack happened entirely without warning tended to confirm the opposite, that the government was taken entirely by surprise. Why did authorities fail to raise the alert level appropriately? Given the imminent possibility of further mass casualties in London, an immediate shutdown of the London Tube and transport systems for that day would have sufficed to prevent the attacks from proceeding.

## Al-Qaeda or Not?

Two principal problem facing investigators purportedly remain unresolved. The first is the question of the connection between the 7/7 and 21/7 attacks. Were they conceived jointly by the same masterminds, or were they executed independently by different groups? The second concerns the sophistication of the group responsible – was the group connected to al-Qaeda, or was it simply a homegrown network of self-inspired extremists? MI5 and Scotland Yard have not provided any decisive resolution of these issues; moreover, spokesmen have repeatedly claimed that this is because no such resolution has been provided in the course of criminal and intelligence investigations.

On the first issue, circumstantial evidence has already been discussed indicating that it is likely that the 21/7 attacks constituted a copycat operation executed by amateurs. In light of this evidence, it is difficult to find any compelling reason to believe that both attacks were conceived by a single mastermind, or a single group. On the other hand, it is worth noting that at least four of the 21/7 bombers were indoctrinated at the Finsbury Park mosque, led principally at that time by Abu Hamza, and secondarily by Omar Bakri. While this does not show that there was any contact between the 7/7 and 21/7 bombers (there is no decisive evidence of this at all), it does show that the two different cells were inspired, and possibly activated, within a common network of radical ideologues. This obvious fact appears to have escaped the attention of the police and intelligence services, at least in their public statements.

On the second issue, the amateurish copycat nature of the attacks, in particular the ineffectiveness of the devices, effectively rules out the idea that this was an operation planned and directed by al-Qaeda. It is far more likely that the 21/7 cell, although radicalised for a shorter period of time within a similar environment to that of the 7/7 bombers and by some of the same ringleaders, was nevertheless largely conducted without the supervision of veteran terrorist operatives. Al-Qaeda operatives themselves have confirmed much the same thing. For instance, senior al-Qaeda terrorist Laui Sakra, the number five leader in the network, told his interrogators in Turkey's Anti-Terror Department Headquarters in Istanbul that he had prior knowledge of the 7/7 attacks – but knew nothing about 21/7.[217] Sakra is suspected of involvement in the November 2003 bombings of UK and Jewish targets in Istanbul which killed 63 people, and was arrested in Diyarbakir, south-east Turkey.[218] The Turkish daily *Zaman* reported that, 'Sakra, who confessed that he talked with bin Laden both face to face and via a courier very often, said he gave information to Laden about the London attacks.' He admitted to personally sending 'many people to the United States (US), Britain, Egypt, Syria and Algeria for terrorist activity.' Sakra noted that many 'militants have the operational initiative' and that there are several autonomous groups 'organizing activities in the name of al-Qaeda. The second attack in London was organised by a group, which took initiative. Even Laden may not know about it.'[219] The 21/7 attack, therefore, did not involve senior planners and trainers from al-Qaeda. The same is not the case for 7/7, for which there is extensive evidence of an al-Qaeda connection (see Chapter 2.1).

### 3.2 22/7 The Criminal State

#### The First Casualty

On 21 July 2005, despite a coordinated, if amateur, operation in which five extremists attempted to terrorise Londoners by detonating four devices, the latter did not so much as explode, as self-implode. Consequently, thankfully, there were no casualties. But the following day, in the course of police operations purportedly targeted at pursuing the terrorists, an innocent man was shot and killed – not by Islamist terrorists, but by officers of the law.

The initial police account as contained in the first post-mortem report of the shooting was straightforward. The man, later identified as a Brazilian electrician, Jean Charles de Menezes, was followed by police on the morning of 22 July. Originally, officers stated that Menezes had 'walked from a property in Stockwell to the local Tube station. But later the statement was changed to say he had been under surveillance during a three-mile bus journey from his home' in Tulse Hill, south London, 'to the station.' The officers were under the control of Gold Command, Scotland Yard's major incident centre. Police also claimed that they believed Menezes might have been concealing a bomb underneath his heavy, 'quilted jacket' which he was wearing on a summer's day. When he entered Stockwell station, armed officers intervened. Witnesses cited in initial press reports claimed they saw Menezes bolt, leap over the ticket barrier and run down the escalator, 'pursued by the plainclothes officers.' Menezes either tripped or was pushed to the floor, after which one police officer with a black automatic pistol 'held it down to him and unloaded five shots into him.' No explosives were found on the body.[220]

Within hours, police announced that they were 'very confident' that Menezes had been one of the four 21/7 bombers. When it became clear that this was inaccurate, police insisted that he was nevertheless linked to the bombings. On the same day, Met chief Sir Ian Blair described the shooting as 'directly linked' to UK anti-terror operations. The next day, hours before his real identity was confirmed, British security sources claimed that he had been 'known to police from a recent counter-terrorist investigation'. But on the 23 July, the Metropolitan Police Service issued an official statement as follows, 'We are now satisfied that he was not connected with the incidents of Thursday, July 21, 2005. For somebody to lose their life in such circumstances is a tragedy and one that the Metropolitan police service regrets.'[221]

In the following days and weeks, however, it quickly emerged that the police explanation of how they had managed to shoot an innocent civilian was full of contradictions. Secret police documents and photographs obtained by ITV News showed that at 9.30am on 22 July, 'Surveillance officers wrongly believed he could have been Hussain Osman, one of the prime suspects, or another terrorist suspect.' According to the new evidence, Menezes 'was not carrying any bags, and was wearing a denim jacket, not a bulky winter coat, as had previously been claimed.' Moreover, his behaviour was entirely normal. Contrary to police statements, CCTV footage shows that Menezes entered Stockwell station at a 'normal walking pace.' He had not vaulted the barrier, and even stopped 'to pick up a free newspaper,' after which he 'descended slowly on an escalator.' He only ran 'when he saw a tube at the platform.' After entering the carriage, he sat in an available seat. 'Almost simultaneously', the document confirms, 'armed officers were provided with positive identification' depicting him as a terrorist. The document cites the testimony of a member of the surveillance team:

> I heard shouting which included the word 'police' and turned to face the male in the denim jacket. He immediately stood up and advanced towards me and the CO19 officers. I grabbed the male in the denim jacket by wrapping both my arms around his torso, pinning his arms to his side. I then pushed him back on to the seat where he had been previously sitting. I then heard a gun shot very close to my left ear and was dragged away onto the floor of the carriage.

In other words, Menezes had not tripped, but was grabbed and pinned down to his seat by officers before being shot at close range. According to the post-mortem examination, Menezes was subject to a total of not five, but *eleven* gun shots – seven in the head, one in the shoulder, and three which missed.[222] In a statement to the Independent Police Complaints Commission (IPCC), witness Sue Thomason, a freelance journalist from south London, confirmed that, 'The shots were evenly spaced with about three seconds between the shots, for the first few shots, then a gap of a little longer, then the shots were evenly spaced again.' Thomason noted that the IPCC excluded the crucial details about the number of shots (she had confirmed 11) and the intervals between them from her final statement until she repeatedly insisted that the omission be rectified.[223]

Further contradicting initial police accounts that they thought Menezes was a suicide bomber about to detonate a device on the Tube, senior sources in the Metropolitan Police further revealed that members of the surveillance team who followed Menezes into Stockwell station did not believe he posed 'an immediate threat'. On the contrary, they concluded that 'he was not about to detonate a bomb, was not armed and was not acting suspiciously.' Sources confirmed that the surveillance team only 'wanted to detain de Menezes, but were told to hand over the operation to the firearms team.' Indeed, one police source observed, 'There is no way those three guys would have been on the train carriage with him [Menezes] if they believed he was carrying a bomb. Nothing he did gave the surveillance team the impression that he was carrying a device.'[224] Indeed, a British soldier involved in the surveillance operation who was staking out the block of flats where Menezes resided, identified him as IC1 – police terminology for ethnic white; yet none of the 21/7 bombers were white, and the Stockwell bomber Hussein Osman had been 'captured on CCTV and was known not to be white.' Rather, the footage depicted an Asian/north African male.[225]

## Senior Culpability

A confidential IPCC report found that undercover detectives altered a Special Branch surveillance log to avoid blame for Menezes's murder. The logbook describing Menezes's last movements 'had been altered to hide that he had wrongly been identified as a suspect' by a single member of the Special Branch surveillance team shadowing him on his way to Stockwell station. Although 'one of the team identified Mr de Menezes as the terrorist suspect [named Hussein Osman] … the IPCC also found that elsewhere in the log there were "degrees of doubt" raised by the team.' In view of the previously cited revelation that the surveillance team had concluded that Menezes was not an immediate threat, was not carrying a bomb, nor behaving suspiciously, it is clear that the early positive identification was effectively erased in the minds of the other officers. Nevertheless, the fact that at some point a positive identification of Menezes as a terrorist was made by one surveillance officer, was considered incriminating enough for someone to try to erase it from the record. 'The log was changed at a debriefing meeting at 8pm that night, about ten hours after the shooting. … The log originally said that there was a positive identification but the word 'not' was then added.'[226]

Who was ultimately responsible for the positive identification? Although the IPCC speculated that the culprits were members of the surveillance team trying to pin the blame on their counterparts in firearms, there is no specific evidence of this available in the public record; all members of the surveillance team deny having altered the log. Moreover, the available evidence suggests that according to the firearms team itself, the culprits were not among the surveillance team, but were among senior officers coordinating both teams in the overall operation.

Elaborating on this, senior sources in the Met and Downing Street said that it was likely that the two police marksmen who shot Menezes dead would not be charged with murder or manslaughter. This was due to indications that culpability lay elsewhere. Prosecutors, sources said, would accept the marksmen's principal defence, that they 'honestly believed' Menezes was a terrorist and used 'reasonable force' to prevent him endangering the public in an imminent attack. Their defence is reportedly based on 'accounts of radio communications between their unit, part of the Yard's elite CO19 firearms team, and officers higher up the chain of command.' Indeed, citing the radio communications, the marksmen 'say they were *led by senior officers* to believe that he was a terrorist, that he was a suicide bomber.' According to a Whitehall official, it was 'those responsible for passing on the *false intelligence* that de Menezes might be a suicide bomber' who could be at fault. 'The possibility arises that someone *higher up the chain of command* [my emphasis throughout] could have acted unlawfully.'[227]

On the same day as the shooting, Sir Ian Blair wrote to Sir John Gieve, Permanent Secretary at the Home Office, to say that he had decided not to refer the Stockwell shooting to the Independent Police Complaints Commission but instead to hold an internal inquiry which would 'be rigorous but subordinate to the needs of the counter-terrorism operation'. As Menezes was believed to be a suicide bomber at the time, the IPCC's disclosure obligations was thought to create a risk to further lives. However, was there another reason more suited to 'the needs of the counter terrorism operation'?[228]

A glimpse of an answer was provided in revelations that the Special Reconnaissance Regiment (SRR), a British Army Special Forces counter-terrorism unit established in April 2005, was involved in the operation that culminated in the shooting of Menezes. The Regiment, trained by the SAS, is 'modelled on an undercover unit that operated in Northern Ireland.' Indeed, it reportedly 'absorbed 14th Intelligence Company, known as '14 Int', a plainclothes unit set up to gather intelligence covertly on suspect terrorists in Northern Ireland.' On 22 July, the Regiment was deployed in the surveillance operation that tracked Menezes from his flat to Stockwell station.[229] Regiment personnel were also 'on the tube train when [Menezes] was shot.' One of the SRR soldiers at Scotia Road monitoring the apartment block 'used equipment which sent realtime pictures of all who came and went... Those receiving the pictures could check them against footage of who they were looking for.' The police account confirms that the SRR soldier 'sent out a message calling the man who left [Menezes] an 'IC1' – a white northern European.' According to one security source familiar with the SRR, the Menezes shooting was not a police operation, 'This take-out is the signature of a special forces operation. It is not the way the police usually do things. We know members of SO19 have been receiving training from the SAS, but even so, this has special forces written all over it.'[230]

The SRR's Northern Ireland connection raises a number of disturbing questions. The Regiment unit is 'formed from members of a highly secret surveillance agency – the Joint Communications Unit [JCU] Northern Ireland – which has worked in Ulster for more than 20 years.' The JCU worked with the SAS, MI5 and Special Branch in 'covert surveillance' of urban and rural areas. One of its predominant functions was to create 'a network of double agents who supplied the British security forces with intelligence on terrorist attacks.' The SRR's primary mission in turn is 'to infiltrate Islamic terrorist groups such as al-Qa'eda… to penetrate groups, either directly or by "turning" terrorists into double agents.' In doing so, the Regiment is tasked to provide the intelligence necessary for SAS and other agencies to conduct covert military operations effectively.[231]

The SRR thus employs the same personnel, methods and objectives as its predecessors in Northern Ireland, which on behalf of the British state fought a protracted covert war against the Republican movement in Northern Ireland to maintain British control of the six counties. Among the agencies participating in this covert war were the ultra-secret wing of British military intelligence, the Force Research Unit (FRU), and the 22 Squadron.

According to Detective Sergeant Nicholas Benwell, member of the Scotland Yard team (the Stevens Inquiry) that had been investigating the activities of the FRU, the team found that 'military intelligence was colluding with terrorists to help them kill so-called "legitimate targets" such as active republicans… many of the victims of these government-backed hit squads were innocent civilians.' Benwell's revelations were corroborated in detail by British double agent Kevin Fulton, who was recruited to the FRU in 1981, when he began to infiltrate the ranks of IRA. In his role as a British FRU agent inside the IRA, he was told by his military intelligence handlers to 'do anything' to win the confidence of the terrorist group. 'I mixed explosive and I helped develop new types of bombs', he told Scotland's *Sunday Herald*:

I moved weapons... if you ask me if the materials I
handled killed anyone, then I will have to say that some
of the things I helped develop did kill... my handlers
knew everything I did. I was never told not to do something
that was discussed. How can you pretend to be a terrorist
and not act like one? You can't. You've got to do what
they do... They did a lot of murders... I broke the law
seven days a week and my handlers knew that. They
knew that I was making bombs and giving them to other
members of the IRA and they did nothing about it... The
idea was that the only way to beat the enemy was to
penetrate the enemy and be the enemy.

Most startlingly, Fulton said that his handlers told him his
operations were 'sanctioned right at the top... this goes the
whole way to the Prime Minister. The Prime Minister knows
what you are doing.'[232] Police chief Sir John Stevens, head of
the Scotland Yard inquiry, described the relationship between
British army intelligence and Northern Irish terrorist groups
as 'institutionalised collusion'.

What was an organisation such as the SRR, employing
personnel and methods with such a track record, doing in the
British capital one day after the 21/7 attacks leading to the
unlawful execution of an innocent civilian on the London
Underground?

*Operation Kratos*

The guidelines for the police shooting of Menezes on 22/7
were officially stipulated under the secretive jurisdiction of
'Operation Kratos', which encapsulates a set of procedures
designed to facilitate a 'shoot-to-kill' policy against potential

suicide bombers. Operation Kratos was initiated after the 9/11 terrorist attacks on US soil. Under its guidelines, developed with assistance from Israeli Defence Force advisers, 'a senior officer is on standby 24 hours a day to authorise the deployment of special armed squads, who will track and if needs be, shoot dead suspected suicide bombers.' According to one senior Metropolitan police source, the Menezes shooting 'was an intelligence-led operation, within the parameters of Kratos.'[233]

Kratos was initiated without public consultation. One of the architects of the Kratos strategy, Barbara Wilding, Chief Constable of South Wales Police, revealed that 'members of the Association of Chief Police Officers (ACPO) advised against a national debate when the new [Kratos] guidelines were drawn up' in 2003. Indeed, 'top-ranking officers' ridiculed the proposals who told her 'that the public would not accept it.' Although the Home Office was aware of the Kratos guidelines, 'they were not publicised or discussed in Parliament before being introduced.'[234]

ACPO's guidance to police under Kratos as of February 2005 stipulates:

> You may open fire against a person only when absolutely necessary after traditional methods have tried and failed, or must, by the very nature of the circumstances, be unlikely to succeed if tried. To sum up, a police officer should not decide to open fire unless that officer is satisfied that nothing short of opening fire could protect the officer or another person from imminent danger to life or serious injury.

Firearms are to be used only when the threat to life is clear and present, in which case 'police officers need to shoot to stop an imminent threat to life. The imminence of any threat should be judged in respect to the potential loss of life… and consideration of necessity, reasonableness and proportionality.'[235] Kratos instructs that the most effective way of stopping a suspected suicide attacker from detonating their bomb is to target the head. In Wilding's words, 'If you go for the body mass, what is going to happen to those explosives? It's likely to go off,'[236]

Yet such procedures were clearly violated in the Menezes shooting, in relation to whom there was no evidence of any suspicious activity, nor any firm conviction that he was a suicide bomber or suspected terrorist. Officers who from the original police account thought Menezes could be a suicide bomber, nevertheless chose not to arrest or detain him after his departure from his home, but instead allowed him to walk away, board a bus (although a bus was targeted on 7/7 and 21/7), walk into a tube station, and then board an underground train. Throughout this period, armed SRR soldiers were alert and on hand, yet they did nothing. After Menezes had boarded the train, he was approached by an officer, grabbed, and pinned down *before* being shot, while as many as seven other officers and some civilians were also on board. This act was in stark breach of Kratos procedures, whereby a suspected suicide bomber is deemed to be such a threat that multiple shots to the head are advocated as the only viable means of disabling him in a manner that prevents him from detonating his bomb. If the Brazilian had indeed been a suicide bomber, the assault could easily have triggered the detonation of his device. Thus, police and SRR conduct on 22 July is inconsistent with the idea that officers were convinced Menezes posed a clear, present and imminent threat to life as a suicide bomber. More precisely, police and SRR conduct was in breach of Kratos guidelines. Therefore, Kratos neither absolves nor explains the shooting of

117

Menezes. In any case, in the words of John Gardner, Professor of Jurisprudence at Oxford University and Visiting Professor at Yale Law School, whatever the 'guidance' self-adopted by the police:

> There are special police powers to arrest and search. But there is no special police licence to injure or kill. If they injure or kill, the police need to rely on the same law as the rest of us. The necessity and proportionality of the police use of force is to be judged on the facts as they [reasonably] believed them to be... It is no defence in law that the killing was authorised by a superior officer. A superior officer who authorises an unlawful killing is an accomplice.[237]

Despite such legal difficulties, most unnervingly the 'shoot-to-kill' policy was unilaterally widened by police chiefs, once again without public consultation, in October 2005 'to include other offences such as kidnapping, stalking and domestic violence'. Despite the caveat that 'the decision to shoot a suspect in the head without the marksman giving a warning would only be used under exceptional circumstances', the principal problem of the new guidelines is that the pivotal decision-making factor is officers' perception of the imminent threat to life posed by the circumstances.[238] As such, the 'shoot-to-kill' policy inherently overrides all legal rights and procedures designed to safeguard the impartial execution of justice (where the innocent are protected and the guilty are punished proportionally). It purports to permit the army, police and intelligence services to use extreme force to kill suspects – to act as judge, jury and executioner – based solely on the threat perceptions of officers.

At its inception, the IPCC confirmed, the investigation was resisted by the police. The body was prevented from 'investigating the shooting of Mr Menezes until three days after his death, where they should usually be at the scene immediately.' The prevention of IPCC access to the Menezes crime scene was a violation of standard mandatory procedure, and opens the question of whether evidence at the scene was altered or tampered with (as was the case with the surveillance log for that day). In November 2005, IPCC lawyers confirmed that the police had breached their statutory duty by failing to immediately permit IPCC to begin its investigation, as 'vital evidence' could have been lost. By March 2006, 'well-placed' sources told the *Sunday Times* that 'Metropolitan Police had turned down "repeated requests" from the Independent Police Complaints Commission (IPCC) watchdog to disclose hundreds of internal papers.' The documents reportedly contain the Met's 'private assessment' of the Menezes shooting, including 'discussions about how much compensation de Menezes' family should receive, whether [Sir Ian] Blair or the Met could face civil action for damages and possible criminal charges against officers.' In view of the Met's continuing lack of cooperation, the IPCC investigation was fundamentally compromised largely due to insufficient access to the key evidence.[239]

In the Menezes case, the bulk of the evidence available in the public record strongly suggests that the threat perceptions of officers on the ground were manipulated by senior officials for reasons that so far remain difficult to fathom. While the weight of the evidence shows that Menezes was certainly a marked man, the conventional explanations of why he was targeted in this manner are riddled with inconsistencies. Although much clearly remains unknown about the shooting, one thing is certainly apparent: purported anti-terrorist operations conducted in the name of 'national security' without sufficient democratic accountability can backfire drastically, to the extent that the 'security' of an innocent civilian who should have been subject to the state's protection instead became its victim. The Menezes debacle was the last major tragedy of that month illustrating the extent to which the British national security system was behaving dysfunctionally. But the clearest evidence of such a dysfunction was in the occurrence of the London bombings, and the failure of the national security system to have prevented them.

# 7/7: Paralysis of the National Security System

## 4. The Intelligence Failure

### 4.1 What We Knew, When

*No Specific Intelligence?*

On the same day as the terrorist attacks, London's most senior police officers stated that they had received no sign of an imminent terrorist attack on the city. In an interview with Sky News, Metropolitan Police Commissioner Sir Ian Blair said, 'We are not aware of any warning at the moment.' Later on in the day, Deputy Assistant Commissioner Brian Paddick reiterated that there had been 'no warning'.[240]

But this was untrue. In the following weeks, abundant evidence emerged in the public record demonstrating unambiguously that British intelligence services had received reasonably precise advanced warning of a terrorist attack. The data, from different sources, provided a clear picture of the attack's probable date, method and targets.

*Internal Threat Assessments*

As early as May 2004, secret Whitehall documents leaked after the London bombings revealed that the government had been 'warned of a thousand-strong groundswell of al-Qaeda sympathisers in the UK, actively engaged in terrorist activity.' According to the joint Home Office and Foreign Office dossier prepared for Prime Minister Tony Blair, al-Qaeda has established a network of 'extremist recruiters' targeting 'middle-class Muslims in British universities and colleges', particularly those with 'technical and professional qualifications' such as engineering or IT degrees, 'to carry out terrorist attacks in this country.' But also targeted are 'under-achievers with few or no qualifications, and often a criminal background'.

The report, drawing on over 100 pages of letters, papers and other documents, corroborated the statement by former Met police chief Lord Stevens two days after 7/7 that 'up to 3,000 British-born or British-based people had passed through Osama bin Laden's training camps.' It cites MI5 intelligence data suggesting that 'the number of British Muslims actively engaged in terrorist activity, whether at home or abroad or supporting such activity, is extremely small and estimated at less than 1%.' However, the number of people actually prepared to commit terrorist attacks runs into hundreds.

> They range from foreign nationals now naturalised and resident in the UK, arriving mainly from north Africa and the Middle East, to second and third generation British citizens whose forebears mainly originate from Pakistan or Kashmir. In addition … a significant number come from liberal, non-religious Muslim backgrounds or (are) only converted to Islam in adulthood. These converts include white British nationals and those of West Indian extraction.

In its discussion of specific extremist organisations in the UK, the dossier also repeatedly mentioned al-Muhajiroun as a radical group which has openly endorsed terrorist activity in its recruitment, preaching and public relations programmes – including such gestures as the glorification of the 19 alleged hijackers on 9/11. The group was targeted for specific concern.

Contradicting Prime Minister Blair's public denial of a connection between the Iraq War and terrorism, the dossier identifies British involvement in the war as a principal cause of the rising tide of extremism among British Muslims. 'It seems that a particularly strong cause of disillusionment among Muslims, including young Muslims, is a perceived "double standard" in the foreign policy of western governments, in particular Britain and the US.' The Iraq War has thus become a 'recruiting sergeant' for terrorism. 'The perception is that passive "oppression", as demonstrated in British foreign policy, e.g. non-action on Kashmir and Chechnya, has given way to "active oppression". The war on terror, and in Iraq and Afghanistan, are all seen by a section of British Muslims as having been acts against Islam.'[241]

Six months later, MI5 chief Eliza Manningham-Buller warned that the intelligence services had strong grounds to believe that Britons faced a 'serious and sustained' threat of terrorist attacks at home and abroad, 'There might be major attacks like Madrid earlier this year. They might be on a smaller scale. The terrorists are inventive, adaptable and patient. Their planning includes a wide range of methods to attack us.' Despite success in apprehending some al-Qaeda figures after 9/11, al-Qaeda 'retains the capability to mount terrorist attacks on Western interests', including British interests. She also noted the danger that 'other terrorist groups or networks that, inspired by Al-Qaeda's successes, and in imitation of it, are now planning attacks against Western interests.'[242]

## Pakistani Warning

Manningham-Buller's public warning came hot on the heels of the latest intelligence on al-Qaeda planning for attacks on

British and American targets. In September 2004, Pakistani intelligence officials warned that al-Qaeda's third in command, Abu Faraj al-Libbi, had 'taken charge' of al-Qaeda sleeper cells in the US and UK. Over the previous 10 months, al-Libbi had 'sent coded messages to "several" Islamic militants in Britain,' including some among the eight Britons arrested under the Prevention of Terrorism Act. According to one investigator:

> The coded messages deciphered recently have revealed to us that he was not only co-ordinating pre-election terrorist acts in the US, but had sent several messages to several militants in the UK in the last eight to 10 months … to share notes with them about future terror attacks in the UK.

At least two British-based militants reportedly travelled from London to Pakistan 'and met Abu Faraj to finalise details of attacks.'[243] As other reports suggest, despite the eight arrests, British police were well aware that at least five other members of the cell – four of whom were the 7 July bombers – were still at large.

## French Warning

In late June 2005, a classified 20-page report by French intelligence services (DCRG) to the French Interior Ministry warned of the growing threat of terrorism by elements of Pakistani communities in both France and the UK. It noted that 'in recent years, we have observed more and more trips to France by Pakistani activists from southern Asia or London, as well as the establishment here of clandestine or official representations of the principal extremist movements', such as Lashkar-e-Taiba and Jaish-e-Muhammad. In particular, the report noted the threat of an imminent al-Qaeda terrorist attack being planned within the UK. Britain 'remains threatened by plans decided at the highest level of al Qaida [sic] ... They will be put into action by operatives drawing on pro-jihad sympathies within the large Pakistani community in the UK.' Intelligence services on both sides of the Atlantic have refused to clarify further the implications of the report. When the *Guardian* contacted the French Interior Ministry, an official spokesman in Paris 'declined to comment on the report and refused to say whether or not the DCRG's warning had been passed to London.'[244]

In all likelihood, the report would probably have been passed to London as a matter of routine. But the key point is that even in France, firm indications of an impending al-Qaeda terrorist strike in the UK mobilised through ethnic Pakistanis, were intercepted by the intelligence service. If France was aware of what was imminent in the UK, what were British intelligence services doing? The idea that France knew more than the British government what was going in its own backyard is implausible. It is difficult to avoid the conclusion that in all likelihood, British intelligence services which closely monitor radical groups such as al-Muhajiroun, the Finsbury network, and so on, must have received similar warnings around the same time.

This assumption receives corroboration from the fact that investigations made by Western European intelligence and security agencies after the 2004 Madrid blasts 'revealed that the Al Qaeda had a large number of supporters in the Muslim diaspora of West Europe.' This was noted in the European Union's annual report on counter-terrorist initiatives in Europe, which pointed out that 'Morrocans and Pakistanis constituted the largest number of terrorist suspects arrested

and questioned in West Europe' in 2004. British sources estimated that about 70 Muslims from the UK, many of Pakistani
origin, travelled to Iraq in 2004 to participate in al-Qaeda
operations led by Abu Musab al-Zarqawi. One of these British
Muslims reportedly participated in a suicide mission, prompting
British police to make some arrests of unidentified terrorist
suspects in the UK that year. There is therefore little doubt that
'British authorities were apparently aware of the presence of
suspected Al Qaeda sleeper cells in the Muslim diaspora in the
UK and had been closely monitoring their activities for nearly
a year.'[245]

## US Warning

In May 2005, senior al-Qaeda operative Abu Faraj al-Libbi,
described as the terror network's number three man and
operations chief, was arrested and detained by Pakistani
authorities, who quickly gave US investigators access to him.
A US intelligence official confirmed that, 'There was some
intelligence that they wanted to do another Madrid in Europe.
This came from al-Libbi's secret notebooks.' Another US security
source corroborates the revelation, noting that 'US intelligence
had picked up warnings recently that the al-Qaida terror
network or its followers were seeking to duplicate the dramatic
3/11 Madrid train bombings in another European city',
although the information 'lacked details on what city might be
the target or when the attacks might occur.'[246]

However, a number of other US officials were more forthcoming, and admitted that although the precise details were
still open, certain targets were named in al-Libbi's interrogation.
'A captured al Qaeda leader warned United States interrogators
that the London mass transit system was a likely target for an

attack', the officials told ABC News. Al-Libbi had specifically 'detailed plans to target London and selected US cities, but did not specify a time for the attacks' in the interrogations.[247] The warning of a 'Madrid-style' attack on London was passed to Britain two months before the 7 July attacks.[248]

Prior to his capture in Pakistan, al-Libbi had extensive contacts with a British terror network planning operations in the year leading up to the 7 July attacks – essentially the same network to which the London bombers were affiliated. These contacts were already known to US and British investigators. The information on a terrorist strike potentially on London's public transport systems culled directly from al-Libbi himself pointed directly to the need to intensify surveillance of that same network, and of all individuals linked to it.

## Saudi Warnings

In December 2004, Saudi intelligence provided MI6 with details of an imminent terrorist plot to bomb the London Underground. The Saudis even confirmed that the terror cell involved would consist of four people. Senior Saudi security sources told the *Observer* that the plot 'involved a Saudi Islamic militant who fought with insurgents in Iraq and was financed by a Libyan businessman with links to Islamic extremists in the UK.' The militant was arrested after returning to the Gulf kingdom from Iraq on a false passport in the name of a fellow insurgent known to have been killed.

Under interrogation he told Saudi intelligence officers that 'he was on a mission to fund a plot to target the Underground or a London night club within six months' – in other words, by July 2005. He also gave his interrogators a Syrian telephone number 'for the contact who would give him orders'. The operation was funded by a Libyan businessman with close links to Islamic extremists in Britain, who is already known to the international intelligence community. Although the latter was reportedly in the UK prior to the bombings, his location is unknown. As one Saudi source remarked, 'When we heard about the bombs in London we immediately recalled the warning we had given Britain – in particular the fact that four individuals carried out the attack and that it happened almost in the timescale we were told about.' The warning was passed immediately to British authorities in Riyadh, as well as the CIA and FBI, who 'are understood to be trying to trace the businessman.'[249]

Remarkably, it contained very specific information alerting British security services to the threat of an imminent strike: it revealed the target – the London Underground; precisely established a maximum time-scale for the operation's execution – July 2005; and confirmed the size of the cell involved, four men. During that six-month period, authorities knew exactly what was in preparation on UK soil.

The Saudis specified that the cell consisted of four individuals and this is crucial. At first glance, the casual observer is inclined to wonder how British authorities might be able to focus intelligence operations to discover a cell of four terrorists. However, British officials were already well aware from the successes – and failures – of Operation Crevice, that out of a network of 13 terrorist suspects, eight had been arrested, and five escaped. Out of these five, four apparently consisted of the would-be London bombers, whereas the fifth man with apparent foreign connections had escaped abroad, reportedly to Pakistan, at least for the time being. This left the cell of four London bombers, who were already under MI5 surveillance. The idea that British counter-terrorist officers had no idea where to look is simply wrong. Given that British officials had already expressed 'concern that they didn't get everybody'[250] in Operation Crevice – a reference to the escaped would-be London bombers – the Saudi warning about a four-man cell planning a future London attack on the Tube network pointed straight back at the same network within which exactly that plan had been actively hatched; and thus at the four individuals still at large. Why were they not re-investigated?

The Saudis did not stop there. Just weeks before the July attack, Saudi Arabia 'officially warned Britain of an imminent terrorist attack on London… after calls from one of al-Qaeda's most wanted operatives were traced to an active cell in the United Kingdom'. The phone calls were intercepted from a mobile phone owned by Kareem al-Majati and 'revealed that an active terror group was at work in the UK and planning an attack'. There were similar calls to the UK from al-Majati's lieutenant, al-Qaeda logistics expert Younes al-Hayari. Both operatives were killed in shoot-outs with Saudi police shortly before the London bombings. The contact also included emails, text messages[251] and even highly sophisticated 'money transfers'. According to Prince Turki al-Faisal himself, Saudi Ambassador to the UK, 'his country had warned Britain less than four months ago that such an attack was pending.'[252]

In another official statement, Prince Turki confirmed that, 'There was certainly close liaison between the Saudi Arabian intelligence authorities and the British intelligence authorities some months ago when information was passed to Britain about a heightened terrorist threat to London.' One Saudi official further told the *Observer*:

It was clear to us that there was a terror group planning an attack in the UK. We passed all this information on to

both MI5 and MI6 at the time. We are now investigating
whether these calls were directly to the London bombers.
It is our conclusion that either these were linked or that
a completely different terror network is still at large in
Britain.

In reality, the choice is not that simple. The London bombers
were embedded in an entrenched al-Qaeda affiliated network
consisting of a number of recruiters, groups and planners. The
terror network that remains at large is the same one within
which the 7/7 cell operated. Al-Majati, for instance, 'is believed
to have masterminded the May 2003 attacks on Casablanca
and has also been named in connection with the March 2004
Madrid bombings.'[253] The unavoidable fact is that the local
al-Qaeda groups responsible for these two attacks are
inextricably linked to a single terrorist network centralised in
London, revolving around the Finsbury Park mosque. The 7/7
operation in its planning, recruitment, logistical and executional
stages was initiated from within this network.

The two Saudi warnings to MI6 – as well as confidential
liaisons between the two intelligence services – coming
months and weeks before the 7 July bombings, provided detailed
information of an imminent strike on the London Underground.
Saudi intelligence specified that four bombers were in the
team; four individuals had been left at large after Operation
Crevice. Did the British make any connection? If they did,
what action if any did they take?

## Spanish Warnings

In March 2005, Spanish security services also warned British
intelligence that Mustafa Setmarian Nasar, alleged mastermind

of the Madrid bombings, 'had identified Britain as a likely target' for an imminent terrorist operation according to a *Sunday Times* investigation. In the flat raided after the Madrid attacks, Spanish police found coded commands from the al-Qaeda operative, widely believed to be al-Qaeda's European operations chief, which 'included threats to other European countries including Britain'. Spanish investigators also cited evidence that Nasar was linked to the establishment of a 'sleeper' cell of terrorists in Britain, and 'believed he was planning an attack to coincide with the British general election in May.'[254] In the aftermath of the London bombings, Nasar's name has been widely mentioned in press reports citing security sources speaking about the investigation into the July 7 bombings.[255]

The Spanish warning had made its way into the British press in the months prior to the Tube bombings. Reporting in March 2005 *The Times* noted that 'security sources believe that [Nasar] may be planning an attack in Britain during the general election.' British security agencies took the warning seriously, concerned 'that Nasar lived in North London in the mid-1990s and has a record of leaving handpicked "sleeper" cells to await his instructions.' The warning had prompted Sir Ian Blair, the new Metropolitan Police Commissioner, and Charles Clarke, the Home Secretary, to speak publicly about the prospect of an imminent al-Qaeda terrorist strike occurring around the time of the general election.[256]

Two months later, the Spanish national intelligence centre had intercepted an al-Qaeda internet message posted on 29 May 2005, ordering attacks on Europe. The message in Arabic was signed by the 'Abu Hafs al-Masri Brigade – European division'. Spanish intelligence did not send the message to their British counterparts until the weekend after the London bombings.[257] However, if the Spanish secret services had intercepted the message, it is difficult to imagine that British and American intelligence failed to do the same. Neither has commented on this issue, but the surveillance centre at London's GCHQ which works in liaison with its American counterpart, the National Security Agency, is one of the world's most powerful electronic communications eavesdropping systems. It monitors emails, internet messages, faxes, telephone conversations, using massively sophisticated technology. It is almost certain that the 20 May al-Qaeda attack order intercepted by Spain was also intercepted by the GCHQ/NSA surveillance system.

## Scotland Yard and Israeli Warning

On 7 July 2005, the Associated Press quoted an anonymous source in the Israeli Foreign Ministry stating that Scotland Yard had warned the Israeli embassy in London of imminent terrorist attacks in London. The information was then passed to the embassy 'minutes before' the first bomb struck at around 8.50am, on the basis of which the embassy promptly ordered Israeli Finance Minister Benjamin Netanyahu to remain in his hotel on Tavistock Square, where the last 7/7 bomb detonated. Netanyahu was slated to attend an Israeli Investment Forum Conference at a hotel next to Liverpool Street Station where the first bomb went off that morning. No sooner had the AP story hit the press, official denials were issued by British and Israeli authorities, including Netanyahu himself, insisting that no advanced warning had been given by any party.[258]

But the story cannot be dismissed out of hand. Terrorism expert Thomas L. Preston – a former US Army counter-terrorism officer who now heads the corporate crisis prevention firm, Preston Global in Frankfort, Kentucky – confirmed the original

AP report citing his own 'sources in the intelligence community'. He noted that, 'Just before the first blast, Netanyahu got a call from the Israeli Embassy telling him to stay in his hotel room. The hotel is located next to the subway station where the first attack occurred and he did stay put and shortly after that, there was the explosion.'[259]

Even Israeli military-intelligence officials contradicted the official retractions of the British and Israeli governments. According to the Israeli national news service, Arutz Sheva, Israeli Army Radio quoted 'reliable sources' confirming 'that Scotland Yard had intelligence warnings of the attacks a short time before they occurred.' How far in advance British intelligence had warning is not clear. However, the Israeli Embassy in London was also 'notified in advance' by Scotland Yard – but only minutes before the attack, 'resulting in Finance Minister Binyamin Netanyahu remaining in his hotel room rather than make his way to the hotel adjacent to the site of the first explosion... Israeli officials stress the advanced Scotland Yard warning does not in any way indicate Israel was the target in the series of apparent terror attacks.'[260] The Israeli *Insider* similarly considers credible the confirmation by Mossad sources of this sequence of events to the German newspaper *Bild am Sonntag*. 'The Mossad office in London received advance notice about the attacks, but only six minutes before the first blast', and therefore 'too late for us to do something about it'.[261]

Multiple intelligence sources, including Israeli, have confirmed that advanced warning of the blasts was received by the Israeli embassy from Scotland Yard, minutes before the first explosion. The British security services had some degree of precise advanced warning of the London bombings, not only in terms of the exact date – the morning of 7 July 2005; but also in terms of the specific time – minutes before 8.50am; and the probable target – in the heart of London at Liverpool Street Station, the site of the first blast, exactly adjacent to which Finance Minister Netanyahu was due to speak. It is of course possible that this warning to a 'high value' target such Netanyahu came about as a result of a last minute tip-off. On the other hand, given the context of warnings discussed previously, it is more likely that Scotland Yard's warning to Mossad derived from the emergence of specific intelligence produced on the basis of a long-term counter-terrorist operation. This suggests that substantive and precise information on the 7 July London bombings was available to British security services well in advance of the bombings, indeed, well in advance of six minutes before the first blast.

My analysis here is supported by that of the respected American private intelligence agency, Strategic Forecasting (Strafor), although Stratfor's perspective is slightly different. Stratfor cited persistent claims by different sources 'in intelligence circles [which] indicate that the Israeli government actually warned London of the attacks "a couple of days" previous.' Strafor's assessment was that as Israel has previously provided warnings about possible attacks that turned out to be 'aborted operations', the British government was reluctant to disrupt the G-8 summit in Gleneagles, Scotland, 'hoping this would be another false alarm'. Perhaps British reluctance then rebounded on to Mossad, which decided that if UK intelligence services were unconcerned the threat need not be heeded. According to Stratfor, 'The British government sat on this information for days and failed to respond. Though the Israeli government is playing along publicly, it may not stay quiet for long. This is sure to apply pressure on Blair very soon for his failure to deter this major terrorist attack.'[262]

Although from Stratfor's perspective it is not clear whether

Israel warned Britain first, or the other way round, given that multiple Israeli intelligence sources have independently corroborated reports that Scotland Yard gave the first warning to Mossad minutes before the attacks, this appears the more likely explanation. Stratfor's confirmation that some intelligence sources believe a warning of the London attacks had been circulating 'a couple of days' earlier is, in this context, more likely to be in relation to the intelligence already developed by British security services – as opposed to Israel or anyone else. It is also possible that Israel might have provided a warning days before the attacks and received a separate tip-off from the British as well. The details of this matter cannot be known without the disclosure of the facts through a public inquiry.

*Bomb Scares*

Days before the 7 July attacks, there were inexplicable major bomb scares in two major UK cities which, given the context of repeated intelligence warnings of an imminent terrorist strike on the London Underground by July 2005, should have set off major alarm bells for British security services in light of the G-8 Summit.

The first bomb scare occurred in Cardiff city centre, 3 July 2005, when a high-street retail store received a bomb-threat call. Staff subsequently spotted a suspicious package 'deliber-ately wrapped to look like a potential bomb'. Large areas around the city centre were immediately evacuated, cordoned off and blockaded, as Army disposal units investigated the package. After several hours, the scare turned out to be a hoax. Investigat-ing officers 'had no idea for the reasons behind the prank'.[263]

Only two days later, another bomb scare occurred in Scotland, where the G-8 Summit was being hosted, reportedly due to another suspicious package. The small town of Auchterarder, where journalists, protestors, tourists had gathered 'was cut in two' by police cordons as swarms of officers patrolled the area for several hours from morning to midday. Gleneagles, where the Summit occurred, is a mile south of the Auchterarder. 'Diversions were set up around residential roads and pedestrians were prevented from walking up the short stretch of the High Street.'[264] This scare also seemed to be a hoax.

In any case, the occurrence of two bomb scares as the G-8 Summit approached should have heightened security concerns around the country. In view of the specific intelligence already clearly available about an impending strike on the London Underground, bomb scares occurring during this particular time period coinciding with the Summit were indications that an attack could be looming at any time.

## 7 July 2005: Terror on Trial

Perhaps one of the most striking prior indications of the date of the planned terrorist attacks on London is the role of radical terror preacher Abu Hamza, who preached to the 7/7 bombers. In a little-noted report, *The Times* pointed out that, 'On the morning of July 7 Abu Hamza was in the dock at the Old Bailey about to stand trial. But his case was postponed for six months.' The schedule of the trial 'raises a possible new explanation for the timing of the attacks.'[265] If Hamza had been originally due to stand trial on the morning of 7 July 2005, this would have been scheduled several months in advance. Indeed, according to British spy Glen Jenvey, whose evidence has helped to jail Hamza, the primary reason for the timing of the 7/7 terrorist attacks was their coinciding with 'the beginning of the court trial of Abu Hamza'.[266]

Given that Hamza's close associate, Omar Bakri, had first

publicly warned in April 2004 of terrorist attacks being planned in London by al-Qaeda in Europe, and secondly told his followers in January 2005 that the Covenant of Security with the UK was annulled due to new British anti-terrorist legislation, the connection becomes quite clear. At that time, Bakri's colleague, Hamza, was under arrest under the very anti-terror laws that Bakri had criticised. His January sermon thus alluded to the fact of Hamza's detention and future trial, at that time scheduled for the morning of 7/7, while simultaneously announcing that Britain had as of then become a 'land of war'. Together, this information provided perhaps the most pristine example of advanced warning of a terrorist strike that intelligence services could ever hope for. British intelligence services intensively monitored Bakri and his organisation. They would hardly have missed a sermon that had been reported in *The Times*.

Indeed, terrorist trials are a traditional 'watch date' for security services. The 9/11 attacks, for example, were on the same date as the conviction of al-Qaeda operative Ramzi Yousef in the United States for his coordination of the 1993 World Trade Centre bombing, 11 September 1996. Given Bakri's open threats of a terrorist attack in London, and fearless incitement to British Muslims to participate in murder and terrorism, the date of Hamza's trial should have been a watch date.

*Intelligence Overview and Threat Assessment by July 2005*

British security services were aware in early 2004 that several thousand British Muslims were actively engaged in either terrorist activity, or the support of terrorist activity. Out of these certainly over 100 were prepared to participate in a terrorist operation, at home or abroad. Al-Muhajiroun was active in recruiting and radicalising British Muslims. Toward the end of that year, MI5's chief publicly warned that the threat of a terrorist attack against Western, and British, interests had increased; and that an operation could easily be conducted either by al-Qaeda itself, or by disparate groups and networks inspired by and imitating al-Qaeda. That view was seconded a few months later by both Home Secretary Clarke and Met chief Sir Ian Blair, who warned the public of the danger of a 'Madrid-style' attack on London.

During the period in between, British intelligence in liaison with US and several other intelligence services successfully intercepted terrorist plots against Western targets, including key structures in Washington and New York, as well as specific plans to detonate bombs in London at West End nightclubs and/or on the London Tube network. The four London bombers were already under surveillance at this time, and chief bomber Khan on a Scotland Yard 'target list', for their connections to the network involved. Indeed, it seems that they along with an unidentified fifth man with clear foreign connections (certainly to Pakistan) had evaded arrest in Operation Crevice, a fact that concerned British investigators on the ground – but apparently not the senior echelons of UK intelligence who, for reasons unknown decided to ignore them.

To recap, by the end of 2004, Saudi security chiefs were warning MI6 with specific intelligence of an imminent terrorist attack on the London Underground to be carried out by a cell of four individuals at any time up to July 2005. The information supplemented what British intelligence already knew – that a partially apprehended British terror network was already involved in just such a terrorist plot, and four individuals under MI5 surveillance linked to the network, including an unidentified fifth man, were at large. Instead of intensifying the surveillance of these four individuals, MI5 officers were told not to bother on the grounds that they were not a potential threat. This notion flatly contradicts specific and credible indications that the four men at large were involved in the plot described by the Saudis.

In March 2005, Spanish intelligence had warned its UK counterpart of an increasing threat of a Madrid-style attack on London, which was taken seriously by both Met chief Sir Ian Blair and Home Secretary Charles Clarke. The warning was linked to plans belonging to senior al-Qaeda operative Mustafa Setmarian Nasar, closely linked to British terror networks, particularly the Finsbury division in London.

Then in May 2005, the Saudis warned again that an imminent terrorist attack was being prepared against targets in London by a cell with links to the network implicated in the Madrid and Casablanca bombings. That network was well known to British security services, and centred on al-Qaeda's Finsbury division. In the same month, US intelligence warned its British counterpart that a network controlled by al-Qaeda's number three, Abu Faraj al-Libbi – the same network partially apprehended under Operation Crevice – was planning an attack on London's mass transit systems, as well as on targets in the US. Once again, al-Qaeda's Finsbury division was implicated. This network had already been implicated in trying to target London, including the Tube.

By June 2005, French intelligence had picked up information of an imminent attack being prepared in the UK by elements of the Pakistani community. Whether or not that information was passed to the UK, a matter which both the British and French authorities refuse to disclose, British intelligence on its own territory would in all likelihood have intercepted the same information.

Two bomb scares in the UK provided signs in the run-up to the G-8 Summit, within the first week of July 2005 that something seriously untoward was in the air. The first scare occurred on the 3 July in Wales. Two days later, on the fifth, a second scare occurred in Scotland. Two days later, as if in sequence, a real terrorist attack occurred in the English capital. Given that the United Kingdom consists of three regions on the mainland, the sequence had moved from Wales, to Scotland, and then to England. The sequence is obviously quite curious, and perhaps only discernable in hindsight. Nevertheless, the scares were warning signals occurring at the beginning of the last month that the Saudis had warned was the deadline for attacks on the London Underground.

Finally, on the morning of 7 July 2005, multiple Israeli intelligence sources confirm that Scotland Yard contacted the Mossad office at Israel's embassy in London six minutes before the first blast at Liverpool Street Station. The warning prompted the embassy to immediately order Finance Minister Netanyahu to stay away from the conference at the Grand Eastern Hotel adjacent to that very station, where he was due to speak at the same time. The warning indicates undoubtedly that British security services at some level had achieved very specific intelligence on the 7 July London bombings. Precisely when this intelligence had come together is unclear. From the standpoint of the procedures and methods of intelligence collection and analysis, it is problematic to argue that it all instantaneously came together minutes before the attacks, unless by way of a last-minute tip-off. As Stratfor suggests citing unconfirmed reports in intelligence circles, it is more likely that British security services had developed this intelligence at least several days in advance of the attacks.

According to standard operating procedures, the multiple

warnings coming in from allied foreign intelligence agencies and elsewhere would pass automatically to MI6 liaison officers assigned for the respective regions. After assessing the reliability of the respective warnings – and the documentation here indicates that the warnings were credible and grounded in verifiable data – they would be immediately passed on to MI5's Joint Terrorism Analysis Centre (JTAC) for integrated analysis in order to gauge the intentions and capability of the terrorist group under consideration.[267] All the separate intelligence warnings received by British intelligence services since early 2004 until July 2005 would have thus contributed to an integrated analytical overview of the threat. Clearly, these warnings made absolutely clear that the threat was not only very real, it was escalating. July 2005 was the deadline for a terrorist attack on the London Underground emanating from the very same terrorist network revolving around al-Qaeda's Finsbury division, under the tutelage of a far-reaching international network with connections as diverse as Europe, North Africa and Pakistan, and which had already been subject to previous counter-terrorist operations and on-going surveillance activities.

As far as we know, the British security services made no response to this credible and urgent threat – except for the disputed warning given to Netanyahu. JTAC did not acknowledge the gravity of the threat that was unfolding before its eyes. On the contrary, a little less than a month before the London bombings, JTAC circulated a threat-assessment memo stating, 'At present there is not a group with both the current intent and the capability to attack the UK' – in other words, that there was no imminent threat of attack against the UK, and that there was no UK group capable of carrying out an attack. The JTAC assessment precipitated the government's lowering of the threat level from 'severe general' to 'substantial', the fourth most serious threat level.[268] Thus, three weeks prior to the looming July deadline, when the threat level should have been elevated, intelligence operations intensified, police presence in London consolidated, and other precautionary procedures implemented, JTAC did the very opposite. Although Home Secretary Clark quickly justified the lowering of the threat level by noting that it did not directly affect the alert level – which determines mitigating or protective action locally – intelligence expert Crispin Black rightly points out, 'it is almost impossible to defend that "there was no significant diminution to specific protective measures". This is why London was left virtually undefended as police officers were extracted out of London to Gleneagles for the G-8 Summit'.[269]

What can explain this inexplicable lowering of the threat level at a time when urgent warnings of an imminent terrorist attack on the London public transport system by July 2005, were being received by British security services, to be conducted by an entrenched UK-based al-Qaeda network already connected to previous terrorist plots and well-known to the security services? Black suggests a potential answer, that of 'undue political influence on the intelligence apparatus.' Noting the 'widely accepted' fact that intelligence analysts and collectors 'came under intense pressure to produce intelligence' justifying Anglo-American military invasion of Iraq – to the extent that some of it was even 'made up', he cautions that, 'The Joint Intelligence Committee, supposedly independent of government (like JTAC), appeared to have actually been run by Downing Street officials.' Thus, at such a time of crisis, 'the most senior (and illustrious) intelligence analytical body in the country buckled under political pressure' to produce patently false intelligence. 'What kind of pressure', asks Black, 'was at work on the JTAC when it lowered, for example, its threat level on 2 June?'[270] That critical question, which Black unfortunately fails to answer, provides the primary subject matter of the next chapters.

## 4.2 Intelligence Assets

### The Mastermind – Now You See Him; Now You Don't

The bombers, clearly, did not work alone, but were part of a wider terrorist network in the UK. For several weeks after the terrorist attacks, police confirmed that they had obtained evidence that the bomber cell operated under the jurisdiction of at least one other person, a mastermind.

A fortnight prior to the London bombings, Special Branch noticed a Pakistani on a terrorist 'watch list' suspected of being connected to al-Qaeda 'entering the country through a sea port'. When MI5 was quickly informed, they 'decided not to track the suspect', apparently on the grounds that 'he was low risk'. Just before the attacks, the man flew out from a UK airport.[271] By mid-July, British investigators had revealed startling new details about this individual. Police told *The Times* that they had 'identified the British-born man who masterminded the suicide bomb attacks on London.' Described as 'the leader of the terrorist cell... in his thirties and of Pakistani origin', sources confirmed earlier reports that he had arrived at a British port in June 2005 and left the country one day before the attacks. Security sources also confirmed that the man was not simply a run-of-the-mill low risk suspect. He had reportedly 'been involved in previous terrorist operations and has links with al-Qaeda followers in the United States.' Police claimed to have obtained evidence that he had visited the bombers in Leeds, identified the Tube targets and trained his recruits in triggering their bombs.[272]

While a number of candidates were proffered, police and security officials were focusing the investigation on the most compelling evidence available that seemed to link the bombers directly to a known British al-Qaeda operative. Immediately after the London bombings, British investigators were attempting to locate 'a man they believed had entered the country two weeks before the bombings, contacted [alleged chief bomber Mohammed Siddique] Khan by phone, then left the country hours before the attacks'. The man was identified by US counter-terrorism officials as Haroon Rashid Aswat, a 30-year-old British national 'wanted in the United States for allegedly seeking to establish a terrorist training camp in Oregon in 1999'.[273] ITN News, elaborating on the evidence, reported that Aswat 'had telephone links with two of the suicide bombers.' British security sources confirmed that the alleged al-Qaeda planner 'had up to 20 conversations with Khan and another of the bombers, Shehzad Tanweer, one just hours before the blasts.' One senior Pakistani security official argued that 'this man had a crucial part to play in what happened in London.'[274]

On 20 July 2005, according to *The Times*, Aswat – described as the 'British al-Qaeda leader linked to the London terrorist attacks' – was being investigated by British police in Pakistan 'after the discovery of mobile phone records detailing his calls with the suicide bombers.' Intelligence sources confirmed that he had 'visited the home towns of all four bombers as well as selecting targets in London'. He also 'spoke to the suicide team on his mobile phone a few hours' prior to explosions. Intelligence sources also confirmed there had been 'up to twenty calls between Aswat and two of the bombers in the days leading up to the bombing', including a call from chief bomber Khan on the morning of 7 July 2005. Pakistani sources reported that Aswat had also stayed in a Pakistani madrassah in Sargodha with two of the bombers. He was apparently very well known to Western intelligence services. Not only was he on a British terrorist watch list, he was also far more than a 'low risk' operative. Security sources concede they believe that Aswat has had a 10-year association with radical Islamist groups, and also had direct contact with Osama bin Laden at an al-Qaeda training camp in Khalden, Afghanistan. FBI documents show that Aswat was sent to the US by 'a London-based cleric' in 1999, where he reportedly established terrorist training camps in Oregon, engaging in firearms and poisons training.[275] That London cleric is Abu Hamza al-Masri, Imam of the infamous Finsbury Park mosque. Aswat's activities at the mosque alongside al-Masri were closely monitored by British intelligence. MI5 informant Reda Hassaine, an Algerian journalist recruited to spy on radical Islamist networks in the UK and who was specifically tasked to track Abu Hamza's activities, describes how he witnessed Aswat's efforts to recruit young men at the mosque to al-Qaeda's cause:

> Inside the mosque he would sit with the new recruits telling them about life after death and the obligation of every Muslim to do the jihad against the unbelievers. All the talk was about killing in order to go to paradise and get the 72 virgins… He used to tell them look at your brothers, the mujaheddin [in Bosnia and Chechnya]… He was always wearing Afghan or combat clothes. In the evening he offered some tea to the people who would sit with him to listen to the heroic action of the mujaheddin before joining the cleric for the finishing touch of brainwashing.[276]

It was during his Finsbury Park stint that Abu Hamza sent him to establish an al-Qaeda camp in Oregon with Earnest Ujaama.[277]

It soon emerged, however, that Aswat, now 31 years old, although arrested in Pakistan was released within 24 hours, after which he travelled to South Africa and eventually Zambia – police had, it seems, only gone to Pakistan to track his movements. Aswat was later arrested in Zambia, where a British intelligence team subsequently travelled to question him. While in custody there, he had already confessed to Zambian investigators that he had previously been Osama bin Laden's bodyguard. Indeed, American authorities revealed that they had been hunting the al-Qaeda operative for years. In their view, he was the undoubted mastermind of the London bombings. Curiously, however, Scotland Yard had suddenly grown rather reticent about Aswat, refusing to confirm the conclusions of US intelligence officials. A British police spokesman commented, 'The Americans are obviously very interested in this arrest in Zambia and we are happy for them to take precedence. The man in custody there is not our priority at the moment.'[278] How could the central suspected mastermind of the London bombings not be a priority for British investigators?

Zambian authorities had already questioned Aswat over the 20 odd phone calls made on his South African mobile phone with some of the London bombers. But as *The Times* notes, Scotland Yard 'played down Mr Aswat's significance to the London bombings inquiry.'[279] Aswat was deported from Zambia on 7 August 2005 and arrested by British police on a US warrant. By mid-August, he was in court to challenge his prospective extradition to the US on charges of setting up a terrorist training camp in Oregon. Although, as the Associated

Press noted, Aswat's connection to the 7 July London bombers was apparent from their prolific telephone calls, 'Scotland Yard police headquarters said... that detectives were not interested in speaking to Aswat about the London attacks.'[280] Furthermore, British investigators distanced Aswat from the evidence, claiming that 'the calls *may have been* made to a phone *linked* [my emphasis] to Aswat, rather than the man himself'.[281] May have been? Linked? This is a decidedly incoherent caveat. On the one hand it confirms that the phone was certainly 'linked' to Aswat – i.e. he used it. On the other, it conjectures an unconfirmed possibility that perhaps someone other than Aswat was speaking to the bombers on his phone. This is a strange reason to suddenly lose all interest in the evidence of Aswat's connection to the London bomb attacks. The phone calls certainly indicate that the London bombers were in contact with either Aswat himself, or if not him directly then to someone who had access to his phone. (This is normal procedure for senior al-Qaeda operatives. Abu Faraj al-Libbi, for example, reportedly often had phone contact with London terrorist networks through an intermediary, rather than directly.)

Such backtracking is odd. Weeks earlier police and security sources had confirmed to the press that they had not only uncovered over a dozen calls between Aswat's South African mobile phone and several London bombers, but had seemingly perused their content to obtain more precise evidence of his direct role in schooling them in terrorist activity. Even now the police did not deny the *existence* of the phone calls between Aswat's phone and the bombers.

The response of British investigators to their own conjecture was to block any further investigation of Aswat's connection to the London bombings, as if his non-involvement was a foregone conclusion. They ignored compelling evidence of links between the bombers and a wider al-Qaeda terrorist network clearly under Aswat's jurisdiction. Why would they do this? As *The Times* noted in August 2005, 'several calls from Aswat's mobile telephone were made to the bombers in the days before the attacks.' The National Security Agency (NSA) of the United States most likely 'was monitoring the calls.' No wonder US intelligence officials are convinced that 'he assisted or mastermind the London attacks'. But the newspaper further hints at an explanation of the British reluctance to investigate Aswat's London terror connection:

> [Q]uestions are also being asked about whether the British did not wish to have Aswat arrested because he was seen as a useful source of information. To some, British intelligence is too willing to let terrorist suspects run in the hope of gathering useful leads and other information… Senior Whitehall officials also deny 'any knowledge' that he might be an agent for either MI5 or MI6.[282]

Whitehall sources deny 'any knowledge' that he might be a British intelligence agent, they do not deny that he is an agent. Such distinctions matter. The Whitehall sources consulted might well not need to know. Perhaps not surprisingly, authoritative confirmation of Aswat's firm links to British intelligence came not from Whitehall, but from the United States. In startling revelations, US terrorism expert John Loftus – a former Justice Department federal prosecutor assigned to the Nazi war crimes unit who held some of the highest security clearances in the US – gave a lengthy interview on America's conservative FOX News channel at the end of July 2005, exposing Aswat's longstanding intelligence connections.

He told FOX News host Mike Jerrick that although British

police have ostensibly been chasing after Aswat, in reality another 'wing of the British government, MI6 or the British Secret Service, has been hiding him'. Aswat is, in other words, 'a double agent', working for MI6 as an informant on al-Qaeda operations, while still being an active al-Qaeda operative. According to Loftus, however, the CIA and Mossad believe that the MI6 strategy goes beyond a case of merely securing information, and instead amounts to 'letting all these terrorists live in London not because they're getting Al-Qaeda information, but for appeasement. It was one of those you leave us alone, we leave you alone kind of things.' But British security services have not been alone in such dubious activity. Lofus reports that when the Justice Department wanted to indict Aswat and Earnest Ujaama for attempting to set up an al-Qaeda camp in Oregon, although Ujaama was successfully prosecuted for conspiracy to provide goods and services to the Taliban, they failed to indict Aswat. 'Well it comes out, we've just learned that the headquarters of the US Justice Department ordered the Seattle prosecutors not to touch Aswat', observed Loftus. In other words, senior elements of both the US and British governments are responsible for Aswat's long-term immunity. Citing US intelligence sources, Loftus confirms that British intelligence subsequently lied to its American counterpart, claiming that Aswat was dead and prompting the cessation of US investigations into him. Aswat then disappeared. Suddenly, in June 2005, he re-emerged on the radar screens of the South African secret services. CIA officials immediately began preparations to arrest him, but in Loftus' words, 'The Brits say no.' And the CIA leadership reined in its own investigators as a consequence of the British decision. The result, however, was catastrophic. By deliberately failing to apprehend Aswat, in Loftus' view, he was effectively granted a free hand to finalise the operational planning and execution of the 7 July terrorist attacks in London:

> Now at this point, two weeks ago, the Brits know that the CIA wants to get a hold of Haroon. So what happens? He takes off again, goes right to London. He isn't arrested when he lands, he isn't arrested when he leaves… He's on the watch list. The only reason he could get away with that was if he was working for British intelligence. He was a wanted man.[283]

Loftus' account should be taken seriously. He rose to fame primarily for uncovering CIA collusion with Nazi war criminals, and as president of the International Intelligence Summit – a prestigious forum for international consultation between Western intelligence agencies – continues to maintain close ties to active and former American intelligence officials.

Moreover, his account is corroborated by other intelligence officials. The *New Criminologist* cites one anonymous US official who was a long-term colleague of former FBI Counter Terrorism Special Agent and al-Qaeda hunter, the late John O'Neill, as supporting Loftus' accusations against both the Justice Department and MI6. The official notes that despite British attempts to distance Aswat from the evidence, both American and British intelligence officials still believe 'that British born Haroon Rashid Aswat was the brains behind the London attacks on July 7', on the basis of the 'score of calls' between Aswat and the London bombers. The *New Criminologist* further reports that Loftus' account 'is supported by many FBI agents'.[284] By late September 2005, the journal's chief editor, former Royal Marine Commander Christopher Berry-Dee, reported that 'Haroon Aswat – the man British Police believe was behind the London bombings – was working for MI6, it has been confirmed by leading US and French intelligence agents.' Despite the public backtracking of British authorities, Aswat remains 'the primary suspect as the mastermind' of the bombings.[285]

But that is not the case as far as the official investigation, and the official narrative, is concerned. By January 2006, District Judge Timothy Workman at Bow Street Magistrates Court ruled that Aswat could be extradited to the United States. Despite assurances from the US embassy in London that Aswat would be tried normally in a US federal court, the Magistrates Court had previously heard compelling evidence from a US legal expert that if extradited, there was an 'overwhelming risk' of being subjected to special measures such as solitary confinement, and even a possibility of being sent to Guantanamo Bay.[286] The US embassy's written promises were, said US attorney Thomas Loughlin, not binding on President Bush, and therefore effectively worthless. As such the 'risk remained' he would be 'designated as an enemy combatant... He could be held indefinitely in military custody without charge or trial of any kind – possibly until the war on terror is over.'[287]

There is no longer any interest, or even any mention, of Aswat's connection to the London bombings by British authorities.

To the contrary, in the wake of Loftus' revelations, British security officials inexplicably began denying that there was any mastermind at all involved in the London bombings. Around the time that Aswat was brought to Britain from Zambia, the *Independent* announced the results of an inquiry by MI5, MI6, GCHQ and the police, which decided that there is 'no evidence of any al-Qa'ida 'mastermind' or senior organiser'. The 7 July team worked in total isolation, and were radicalised solely by Mohammed Sidique Khan. One police source is cited:

> All the talk about 'Mr Bigs' and al-Qa'ida masterminds looks like something from a film script at the moment. Of course, things could change if new intelligence comes through, but it looks increasingly as if these people were largely working on their own.[288]

By rejecting the idea of a 'mastermind', the authorities can avoid discussion of the wider network within which the bombers operated. The need for a public inquiry could hardly be more clear.

## The Recruiter

Aswat was closely associated with Abu Hamza, having worked with him as his right-hand man in the late 1990s at the Finsbury Park mosque. Through Hamza, he was also connected to Omar Bakri. In the same FOX interview, Loftus reveals that al-Muhajiroun had itself been hired by British intelligence services for recruitment operations in the Balkans:

> What ties all these cells together was, back in the late 1990s, the leaders all worked for British intelligence in Kosovo. Believe it or not, British intelligence actually hired some Al-Qaeda guys to help defend the Muslim rights in Albania and in Kosovo... The CIA was funding the operation to defend the Muslims, British intelligence was doing the hiring and recruiting.

Loftus cites a detailed interview with Bakri in the London-based Arabic daily, *al-Sharq al-Aswat* in 2001, 'describing the relationship between British intelligence and the operations in Kosovo and al-Muhajiroun. So that's how we get all these guys connected.' Aswat was apparently already involved, having joined the operation in 'about 1995.'[289] In that interview, Bakri 'boasted that al-Muhajiroun sent Muslim youths on jihad training courses in Virginia, Michigan and the Missouri desert where they learned various techniques for guerrilla warfare, for making explosives and using shoulder-mounted missiles.' Between 300 and 400 people were sent on such courses each year, 'travelling as Europeans on British, French and German passports so that they did not need entry visas for the United States although most were of Asian or Arab origin. The training was organised by a British security firm that is managed by a Muhajiroun member.' Among the countries that the youths went to after completing military training, 'some went to Kashmir, and others to Chechnya and to Kosovo before that. Some remained in Britain because they were not fully trained ideologically.'[290]

In other words, Bakri and his al-Muhajiroun organisation have not merely been tolerated by British authorities despite involvement in al-Qaeda recruitment, terrorist training, and incitement to violence, murder and terrorism; they were actively protected by British security services in the late 1990s, operating as recruiting agents for British covert operations in the Balkans, especially in Kosovo.

Given Aswat's close association with Abu Hamza – having been his right-hand man at the Finsbury Park mosque – it comes as no surprise that Hamza too was apparently involved in the British security services operation. Videotapes shown to the jury at the Old Bailey where Hamza was tried and convicted in 2006 depict Hamza telling:

[H]is followers that he was a veteran of the Balkan wars of the 1990s, in which Arab Mujahidin went to Bosnia to fight the Serbs… he urged his listeners to travel to Albania and Kosovo to support the Islamic cause, the Egyptian-born cleric recalled his own jihad experiences. He said he had advised Algerian fighters in Bosnia.[291]

Rather than officially investigating or interrogating him, when Bakri left the UK to visit Lebanon, he was summarily debarred from returning to the country where he had operated with impunity for so many years on state benefits. While the press cheered his permanent exile, the government had removed yet another potential 7/7 conspirator from the scope of the criminal investigation.

## The Spiritual Leader

Other radical leaders and associates in the Finsbury division also have long-term connections to British intelligence. Abu Qatada's track record for the security services is perhaps most well documented. A month after 9/11, Qatada himself told the *Observer* that:

British security services offered him a chance to escape to Afghanistan. Abu Qatada, whose Bolton bank account was frozen last week when he was named on a US list of suspected terrorists, told the *Observer* that MI5 approached intermediaries to offer him a passport and an Iranian visa so he could leave the country.… The Home Office refused to comment on Abu Qatada's claim.[292]

Subsequently, amidst mounting international pressure from

Europe and the United States demanding his arrest and interrogation, Abu Qatada disappeared, and British authorities claimed that they had no idea where he was hiding. Meanwhile, investigators were perplexed as to why British authorities had not arrested him sooner.[293] 'But why hasn't he been caught?' asked the *Observer*. 'The French secret service believe they know: he is a spy. That is also the view of many in Britain's Islamic community. In prayer halls and private houses, the opinions are the same: "Qatada is an MI5 agent." '[294]

Citing European intelligence sources, *Time* magazine elaborated on the evidence that Qatada was, in fact, being protected by British security services:

> [S]enior 'European intelligence officials tell TIME that Abu Qatada is tucked away in a safe house in the north of England, where he and his family are being lodged, fed and clothed by British intelligence services. The deal is that Abu Qatada is deprived of contact with extremists in London and Europe but can't be arrested or expelled because no one officially knows where he is, says the source, whose claims were corroborated by French authorities. 'The British win because the last thing they want is a hot potato they can't extradite for fear of al-Qaeda reprisals but whose presence contradicts London's support of the war on terror.'[295]

*Time* magazine's findings were corroborated, but with more damaging detail, by revelations in *The Times* that Qatada was 'a double agent working for MI5, raising criticism from European governments, which repeatedly called for his arrest.' According to *The Times*, the British authorities:

[I]gnored warnings – which began before the September 11 attacks – from half a dozen friendly governments about Abu Qatada's links with terrorist groups and refused to arrest him… Abu Qatada boasted to MI5 that he could prevent terrorist attacks and offered to expose dangerous extremists, while all along he was setting up a haven for his terror organisation in Britain…. Indignant French officials accused MI5 of helping the cleric to abscond. While he remained on the run, one intelligence chief in Paris was quoted as saying: 'British intelligence is saying they have no idea where he is, but we know where he is and, if we know, I'm quite sure they do.'

Almost a year later Abu Qatada was found hiding in a flat not far from Scotland Yard.[296]

A leaked judgement from the Special Immigration Appeals Commission (SIAC) on Qatada's case demonstrates that British security services had contacted him at least three times, in June and December 1996 and February 1997. The judgement records that in his conversations with one British intelligence official, Qatada:

[C]laimed to 'wield powerful, spiritual influence over the Algerian community in London and was confident that he could use this influence to prevent any terrorist repercussions…' He maintained that a decision had been taken in Algeria not to mount operations against the United Kingdom… The appellant said he did not want London to become a centre for settling Islamic scores… and apparently said that he would 'report anyone damaging the interests of this country.'

The unnamed British intelligence officer is cited in the judgement as confirming that Qatada 'wielded considerable "spiritual, if not operational influence on an extensive number of Islamists of various nationalities and that, as a resident of the United Kingdom, I fully expected him to use that influence, wherever he could, to control the hotheads and ensure terrorism remained off the streets of London." ' The judgement continues to note that Qatada's interviews with British security services 'show that he accepted and indeed asserted that he did have influence over some of the extremists who might be expected to become involved in violence and terrorism.'[297]

These reports reveal a good deal. Firstly, British intelligence was fully aware of Abu Qatada's prominent connections to al-Qaeda and involvement in incitement to and support of terrorism. Indeed, they believed that his control over al-Qaeda affiliated terrorists in the UK was sufficiently strong so as to prevent future terrorist attacks against British targets. Thus, despite his heavy involvement in the support of international terrorism, British officials saw fit to recruit him to MI5, allow him to continue his involvement in terrorism abroad, and grant him protection from anti-terrorism laws.

As Qatada's legal representative, leading British lawyer Ben Emmerson QC, submitted in the preliminary SIAC hearing according to the *Guardian*, 'Mr. Emmerson said his client had been monitored by security services since the mid-1990s and "his actions had a large degree of tacit approval." '[298] Indeed, their detention in the UK appears to be only yet another bizarre strategy to keep them away from the scrutiny of the international intelligence community – and perhaps thereby to prevent further embarrassing or scandalous revelations about British intelligence and security policies. *The Times* noted, for instance, that:

[F]oreign governments are also criticizing the Government…Their complaint is that they have been given no access to the detainees. Investigators from Spain, Germany and Italy are desperate to question Abu Qatada, who they claim is a pivotal figure in cells they have under arrest in their own countries. Their requests to question him and some of the other suspects directly have been rejected by the Government. Investigators in Spain who named Abu Qatada as 'the spiritual leader of al-Qaeda in Europe,' say their own terror trials are hindered by Britain's refusal to let them interrogate the cleric… In spite of holding most of the terror suspects for many months, the men are providing the security services and police with little intelligence on terrorist activity in the United Kingdom.[299]

## The Preacher

What about the case of Aswat's spiritual mentor, Abu Hamza, the radical preacher at Finsbury Park mosque? Given the record so far, it would not be surprising to find that he too had connections to British intelligence. Like Qatada, Hamza had operated with impunity on UK soil despite his terrorist activities being monitored extensively by MI5, including the use of informants such as Reda Hassnaine, who warned the services repeatedly in no uncertain terms that Hamza posed a terrorist threat.

The extent of British official approval for Hamza's activities can be discerned from the only terrorism charge British authorities are prosecuting him for. The prosecution 'accuses al-Masri of possessing a book called the Encyclopedia of the Afghani Jihad, a document allegedly produced by Osama bin

Laden's al-Qaida network that provides the "basic rules of sabotage and terror" in highly technical detail.'[300] However, it quickly emerged during his trial that all 16 offences for which he had been charged had occurred with the tacit consent of British police, who were not only fully aware of his activities, but made no effort to shut him down.

The encyclopedia in Hamza's possession detailed a list of targets for terrorist attacks including Big Ben and the Statue of Liberty, as well as instructions on organising terrorist cells and the production and storage of explosives. David Perry, for the prosecution, confirmed that the Encyclopedia 'was taken by police from Abu Hamza al-Masri's home seven years ago but returned to him without question or warning.' It was impounded again by police in 2004 to form the basis of the terror charge. In addition to the terrorism manual, the Crown Prosecution Service furnished three videotapes to the court in which Hamza reportedly encouraged his followers to commit murder and attempted to incite racial hatred, particularly against Jews. They were among 600 tapes that had been confiscated by police in March 1999. But again, 'The videos… were returned with the encyclopaedia without the police taking any action.' The tapes included one in which Hamza advocated 'bleeding the enemies of Islam', which was also 'examined by detectives but… not referred to the Crown Prosecution Service.' Moreover, police had failed to interview Hamza about his sermons in 1999 when under investigation for incidents in Yemen in 1998. 'It was not until August 2004 that Abu Hamza was questioned at Paddington Green police station about the encyclopaedia and nine videotapes taken from his home.' Yet throughout this period, he reportedly 'had 'numerous discussions' with the police and MI5.'[301]

Spokesmen for Scotland Yard and the CPS justified the

failure to take action against Abu Hamza for so long – seven years in total – on the basis that the evidence available was 'clearly insufficient' to support a successful prosecution. This is, however, simply untrue. The files sent by Scotland Yard to the CPS in March 1999 and June 2003 were concerned solely with Hamza's reported connection to the kidnapping of 16 Western tourists in Yemen in 1998.[302] They excluded the mass of evidence in the form of hundreds of tape and video recordings, a terrorist training manual, implicating him unambiguously in incitement to violence and terrorist activity. The evidence used to successfully prosecute Hamza in February 2006 had almost all been found by the police seven years previously. Six of Hamza's convictions were soliciting to murder under the 1861 Offences Against the Person Act, three of threatening behaviour under the 1986 Public Order Act and only one of possessing a terrorism manual under the Terrorism Act 2000. Not only had authorities decided not to use the evidence at that time to prosecute Hamza, after reviewing the evidence, they simply handed it back to Hamza without a word of caution. Indeed, anti-terrorist sources now admit that the question of evidence was not the problem – taking action against Hamza's 'hate-filled rants' in which he incited violence and terrorism 'was not high among police priorities in 1999.'[303]

Why wasn't Hamza a priority? Much of the debate in the media after Hamza's conviction in February 2006 revolved around the inadmissibility of phone-tap intercept evidence in British courts. This was supposed to be the prime obstacle preventing detailed proof of Hamza's involvement in 'operational terrorist activity' being used to prosecute him on directly terrorist-related charges. But in reality irrespective of phone intercept evidence, the police have access to a wealth of additional evidence on Hamza's terrorist activitiy, which was not used in his trial, and which it seems authorities are in no hurry to make public. This evidence was retrieved by Reda Hassaine. As a Special Branch agent, he monitored Abu Hamza, infiltrated the Finsbury Park mosque, and on a daily basis gave his handlers detailed information about 'Abu Hamza's associates, his speeches and the attitudes of those around him.' After becoming an MI5 informant, he obtained 'scores of documents' containing 'communications from GIA [the al-Qaeda affiliated Armed Islamic Group] activists in Algeria' and information on 'cells planning terrorist attacks in Britain.'[304] He also gleaned other first-hand evidence about Hamza's involvement in terrorist activity, particularly as an al-Qaeda recruiter for multiple terrorist operations. Describing Hamza as 'the first spiritual leader of GIA' before Abu Qatada, he confirms that he witnessed their recruitment of al-Qaeda shoe-bomber Richard Reid.[305]

He also confirmed that 'two Egyptian-born men' who according to US security sources visited an Oregon ranch to help set up 'a possible terror-training camp' with convicted al-Qaeda terrorist Earnest Ujaama, were 'direct subordinates' of Abu Hamza. 'The two men came to Hamza's mosque in 1998 directly from terror-training camps in Afghanistan, he said... They wore Afghan combat clothes to the mosque, calling themselves mujahedeen.' As an informant for MI5 as well as the French General Directorate for External Security between 1997 and 2000, he was told that 'the two men were at the top of his watch list.' He told the American press that, '... it is sure that they belong to a terrorist network. There is no doubt... they were completely linked to al-Qaida and what was going on in Afghanistan.' One performed as a military specialist and the other as an intelligence adviser for al-Qaeda. 'Both are living in London. Neither has been arrested or formally accused of any wrongdoing.'[306]

Why have police, security services and the CPS refused to use the abundant evidence of al-Qaeda terrorist activity obtained by Hassaine for the prosecution case against Hamza? Why did Scotland Yard insist that there was 'no evidence' of that the London bombers had been inspired by Hamza despite confirmation from numerous credible reports that three of the London bombers – Khan, Tanweer and Lindsey – were attendees of the Finsbury Park mosque and heard his inflammatory speeches?[307]

In his court testimony in early 2006 when on trial for terrorism and race hate charges, Hamza confirmed that British security services had sought to recruit him to monitor radical groups and individuals and to deter terrorist attacks before his 2004 arrest. He referred to several meetings 'with officers from Britain's internal security services who told him they were asking Islamic clerics to "control hot-headed people and make sure everything is under control and there is no risk to anyone." ' In 1997, Hamza recalls, he asked MI5 officers about whether his sermons were considered a problem. One officer, he says, responded, 'You have freedom of speech. You don't have anything to worry about as long as we don't see blood on the streets.' By 2000, however, Hamza admitted that MI5 officers were unhappy, claiming that he was told, 'We think you are walking on a tightrope' and that 'there were some things that they don't like.' But despite such mild reservations, there was no apparent desire to sanction him legally.[308] Why did authorities fail to take action for so many years in spite of being fully aware of his activities? It is plausible that security services considered Hamza useful for intelligence purposes?

This is consistent with Reda Hassaine's description of how he was used by MI5, in the midst of his monitoring of Hamza, to facilitate the arrival and settlement in the UK of a known GIA terrorist from Algeria. In the summer of 1999, he was told by his MI5 handler 'Kevin' that a 'key associate of the chief of the GIA had recently arrived in the UK'. Hassaine was tasked 'to get close to him, to sort out his accommodation and welfare benefits and to teach him English. MI5 wanted to recruit him as an agent, Kevin said'. For the next 15 months Hassaine associated with militants 'who were deeply involved with the terrorists in Algeria', including people connected to Hamza and the Finsbury Park mosque. 'They told him of planned bombing campaigns in Paris, of assassinations, of attacks on Europeans in the country. All the information was relayed back to his handler. Assignment after assignment was completed successfully.' To get the information MI5 wanted on the GIA Hassnaine even had to burgle Hamza's and other militants' offices at the Finsbury Park mosque and elsewhere.[309]

But despite this wealth of information, neither the police nor MI5 moved to shut down the entrenched terrorist network around Hamza, connected to Algerian terrorists, that Hassaine was uncovering. Neither the al-Qaeda documentary evidence obtained by Hassaine, nor the extensive eyewitness reports he wrote up for Special Branch and MI5, were used by authorities to charge and prosecute Hamza for terrorist activity in relation to Algerian and wider al-Qaeda networks. Hassaine's expert testimony was not sought by the court which convicted Hamza. It is no surprise then that in his assessment, 'terrorist recruitment and fundraising by Islamic militants' under Hamza's tutelage 'were ignored for years by the British security services'.[310]

Hassaine's evidence is merely the tip of the iceberg. Four years before Hamza's belated conviction, intelligence sources confirmed that he had hosted 'British Islamic extremists' involved in 'weapons training with assault rifles.' They had regularly 'practised with Kalashnikov AK-47s at the Finsbury Park mosque' in special training sessions. Most disturbingly, MI5 was fully aware of the terrorist training programme, yet did nothing to shut it down despite knowing that Hamza was sending dozens of people to al-Qaeda terrorist training camps in Afghanistan, and despite compelling evidence that active mujahideen in various theatres of conflict had received training at the mosque. 'MI5 recruited worshippers at Finsbury Park who opposed' Hamza's hardline stance 'to help monitor the activities of extremists.' In early 2001, 'the agents told their handlers that several groups had been taught to strip and reassemble Kalashnikovs in the mosque's basement.' MI5 also knew that 'scores of young men were being sent from the mosque for training at camps in Afghanistan.' Agents reported that 'consignments of supplies' from the mosque included 'radio and telecommunications equipment' dispatched to Pakistan 'for eventual distribution in the Afghan training camps allied to or run by al-Qaeda.' The agents also confirmed 'a complex operation run by some men attending the mosque to provide volunteers with false documents.' MI5 also knew that volunteers who had 'fought in Afghanistan for the Taliban or for Islamic militants in Chechnya and Algeria boasted at the mosque of battles they had taken part in.'[311]

Such activity had continued at the Finsbury Park mosque for years. As early as 1995, foreign governments and intelligence services had warned British security services about the threat posed by Hamza. US intelligence investigations confirm that some of Hamza's terrorist training programmes were assisted by former British soldiers. The latter 'taught Abu Hamza's followers to use guns at a camp in Wales as part of an ad hoc terror training network.' By 1997, Hamza had established terror camps in the Brecon Beacons, at an old monastery in Tunbridge Wells, Kent, and in Scotland. Transcripts of interviews with suspected al-Qaeda terrorists held in Guantánamo Bay 'reveal that the British ex-soldiers, some of whom fought in Bosnia, were recruited to train about 10 of Hamza's followers at the Brecon Beacons camp for three weeks in 1998. The former troops taught them to strip and clean weapons and gave them endurance training and lessons in surveillance techniques.' At other camps, individuals 'were trained to use AK47 rifles, hand guns and a mock rocket launcher.' Although the legal value of the testimonies is questionable, the details have been independently corroborated by other witnesses. Indeed, Hamza made no effort to conceal the extensive training sessions, which were openly advertised at Finsbury Park mosque. 'But the British security services were either unconcerned or ignorant about Hamza's activities,' according to the *Observer*.[312] We know, however, that MI5 was certainly not ignorant, and had a wide network of informants inside the mosque providing detailed information on Hamza's terrorist activity.

Based on the ample evidence available of Hamza's illegal incitement to violence and terrorism, as well as his direct operational connections to al-Qaeda terrorism obtained by MI5 informant Hassaine, it is clear that the authorities' failure to act on this evidence was not for lack of evidence, nor due to disbelief in the seriousness and reality of Hamza's terrorist involvement. According to former Home Secretary David Blunkett, the government for example was fully aware of the threat posed by Hamza, but security services were reluctant to act:

So much for those in the security services who told me when I was Home Secretary that I was exaggerating the threat and the closure of the Finsbury Park mosque where he preached his evil message would be a 'massive overreaction'. There was a deep reluctance to act on the information coming out of Abu Hamza's own mouth. And some in the police and security services did not want to believe how serious it all was.[313]

Blunkett also claimed the police and Crown Prosecution Service did not want to take action against Hamza for fear of sparking a race crisis. His comments are useful in underlining the real and inexplicable desire of police and security services to simply leave Hamza alone to continue his illegal activities unhindered – evidence was not the issue. However, Blunkett's claim that authorities did not take Hamza seriously is clearly wrong. Authorities were fully aware of his involvement in terrorist activities and incitement to violence. They knew that Hamza had connections with dangerous terrorist networks in Algeria and elsewhere, and was involved in recruiting for al-Qaeda operations. They knew of his extensive terrorist training programmes across the UK, his regular recruitment of British Muslims to al-Qaeda, and his supply of equipment to mujahideen operations abroad. In this context, the idea that police were worried about a race crisis is also difficult to take seriously. Hamza was always a potential threat to national security not only in the UK, but outside the UK. Hamza never enjoyed widespread support among British Muslims, who overwhelmingly rejected his politics. As it was, his eventual arrest in 2005 caused no widespread increase in tension in the Muslim community. In fact, Blunkett's admission of official reluctance to move against Hamza is damning. As Home Secretary, Blunkett had the statutory authority to order police and security services into action on the basis of the compelling evidence available, under the extensive powers granted by anti-terrorism legislation. If he had done so, Hamza could have been easily charged and prosecuted seven years ago on the same grounds used to secure his 2006 conviction. But British authorities collectively failed to act. Either they refrained from moving against Hamza because they thought that doing so would prevent violence in Britain, or for some other reason.

## The Financier?

According to Saudi intelligence, the London Underground bomb plot was financed by a Libyan businessman linked to Islamic extremists in the UK. Moreover, he is not an unknown figure – already the subject of an 'international intelligence operation', the unidentified Libyan terrorist financier was reportedly in the UK prior to the bombings, after which he disappeared. The Saudi account alone raises some pertinent questions. If this figure has been investigated for some time by intelligence services in relation to his involvement in terrorist activity, how was he, as a known associate of Islamist terrorists, able to enter and leave the UK unmolested? Only a full inquiry can hope to establish the identity of this man.

## The Trainer

Investigators established that a number of the London bombers had travelled to Pakistan months before the attacks where they underwent terrorist training in al-Qaeda camps. Shehzad Tanweer, for example, reportedly contacted members of two outlawed local groups and trained at two camps in Karachi and near Lahore. These camps are run largely by two al-Qaeda affiliated groups, Laksha-e-Taiba and Jaish-e-Mohammed, both of which are closely linked to senior al-Qaeda operative Ahmed Omar Sheikh Saeed (Saeed is also the latter's leader), who has a long history of involvement in terrorist operations. He orchestrated the 1994 hijacking in India in which he kidnapped and threatened to murder three British citizens. He quickly moved up al-Qaeda's ranks, until he became notorious as a terrorist 'with many names but one purpose: waging a war of terror against Indian and American targets.' His other aliases include, 'Sheikh Syed, Mustafa Muhammad Ahmed, Chaudhry Bashir Ahmed Shabir and Imtiaz Siddique.'[314] Osama bin Laden's relationship to Sheikh is so close that within a few years of joining al-Qaeda, bin Laden described him as his 'favoured son.'[315]

He eventually became al-Qaeda's financial chief. According to Magnus Ranstorp – Deputy Director of the Center for Study of Terrorism and Political Violence at the University of St Andrews – Sheikh 'is also linked to the financial network feeding bin Laden's assets, so therefore he's quite an important person... because he transfers money between various operatives, and he's a node between al Qaeda and foot soldiers on the ground.'[316] British police officials believe that Sheikh 'trained the [9/11] terrorists in hijacking techniques.'[317] Intelligence officials from India, Pakistan and the United States also independently confirm that Sheikh was deeply involved in the financing of the 9/11 terrorist attacks, sending $100,000 to chief 9/11 hijacker Mohamed Atta on the instructions of former ISI chief General Mahmoud Ahmad. Reports from US intelligence sources, however, indicate that he sent far more than that, between $250,000 and $325,000.[318]

Top US government sources confirmed that 'US investigators now believe Sheik Syed, using the alias Mustafa Muhammad Ahmad, sent more than $100,000 from Pakistan to Mohammed Atta, the suspected hijacking ringleader who piloted one of the jetliners into the World Trade Center.'[319] Indeed, his name had previously surfaced in relation to the financing of the 1998 US embassy bombings. In the New York court hearings to prosecute the conspirators in those attacks, it was revealed that 'an al Qaeda operative known as "Sheik Sayid"... controlled the group's finances... Sheik Sayid is now reported to be the finance chairman of al Qaeda and the man suspected of wiring money from Pakistan to Mohamed Atta.'[320]

Sheikh Saeed is currently in a Pakistani prison under a death sentence, convicted for the murder of *Wall Street Journal* correspondent Daniel Pearl. Despite that, as former Labour Cabinet Minister Michael Meacher MP pointed out in the *Guardian*, it is possible that Saeed could have orchestrated the London bombings from his jail cell.[321] Former Pakistani government officials report that he continues to be active from jail, maintaining contact with colleagues and followers in Britain.

Credible reports, however, establish that Sheikh Saeed is a triple agent, working for Pakistan's ISI, America's CIA, and Britain's MI6. According to the *Pittsburgh Tribune Review*, 'Saeed Sheikh has acted as a 'go between' for the 'tall man' — as bin-Laden is known — and the Inter Services Intelligence (ISI).' Sheikh's entrenched ISI-al-Qaeda connections have always been known to Washington, 'Many and varied sources have told Washington officials that in all these attacks, Saeed Sheikh had logistical and operational support from the ISI in Karachi and Islamabad. ISI also helped him form and operate the Jaish-e-Muhammed — Muhammed's Army — for his terrorist campaigns in Kashmir.'[322] Citing US intelligence sources,

*Newsweek* observes that Sheikh 'did little to hide his connections to terrorist organizations, and even attended swanky parties attended by senior Pakistani government officials.' US law enforcement and intelligence officials believe that 'Sheikh has been a 'protected asset,' of Pakistan's shadowy spy service, the Inter-Services Intelligence, or ISI.'[323]

However, the British and American governments have demonstrated consistent reluctance to investigate Sheikh for his involvement in both the 1994 kidnapping, the 1998 US embassy bombings and the 9/11 terrorist attacks. As observed by India's *Frontline* magazine, in September 2001, after 9/11, 'the UK served a letters rogatory on India, asking for information on Sheikh in relation to the 1994 kidnapping of its nationals. It is unclear why it has taken that country so long to initiate the legal proceedings, and why the US has chosen not to act so far.'[326] Similarly in the United States, Sheikh 'was secretly indicted by a grand jury in Washington last November [2001] for his role in the 1994 kidnapping.'[325] Noting the 'secret' nature of the indictment, CNN wondered why, 'Justice Department officials won't say what prompted that indictment, which came more than six years after the incident.'[326] In other words, both countries only chose to indict Sheikh for his role in the 1994 terrorist act after the 9/11 attacks.

Why did Pakistani, American and British law enforcement authorities do nothing for so long in relation to Sheikh, throughout the track record of his increasingly successful terrorist career – even until after 9/11? 'Despite face-to-face meetings between President Musharraf and President Bush, US Ambassador to Pakistan Wendy Chamberlain and FBI Director Robert Mueller, Saeed Sheik was neither arrested nor placed under surveillance' – this was even after his involvement in 9/11.[327]

This basic government negligence granted free rein to Osama's financial chief to fund the 9/11 hijackers, although Sheikh, who did little to conceal his terrorist connections, could easily have been apprehended by the Pakistani authorities at the request of the US and UK governments. Even now, despite having been sentenced to death in Pakistan for the murder of Daniel Pearl, the British and American governments have blocked all inquiries into his involvement in the 1994, 1998 and 9/11 terrorist attacks.

Apart from his status as a Pakistani intelligence asset, British press reports suggest his recruitment to MI6. According to *The Times*, 'British-born terrorist Ahmed Omar Saeed Sheikh was secretly offered an amnesty by British officials in 1999 if he would betray his links with al-Qaeda.' [328] The *Daily Mail* similarly confirmed that, 'Britain offered Sheikh a deal that would allow him to live in London a free man if he told them all he knew.'[329] Both reports claim that Sheikh refused the offer. However, by the beginning of the next year, as if by magic the British Foreign Office decided 'to allow him to enter Britain,' without even being investigated. The three Britons who had been kidnapped, held hostage, and threatened with death by Sheikh in 1994 – Rhys Partridge, Miles Croston, and Paul Rideout – were 'appalled to learn that Sheikh, a British passport holder, would be allowed to return to Britain without fear of charge.'[330] Sheikh subsequently 'proceeded to London, where he reunited with family' in 'early January 2000.'[331] He again visited his London home in 'early 2001' where he was spotted by a neighbour.[332]

Amazingly, a Foreign Office spokesman justified the decision to allow him into the country without charge and lacking even a police investigation, 'He has not been convicted of any offences. He has not even been brought to trial.'[333] But this explanation was misleading. The British government had ample evidence – including the first-hand testimonials of the three kidnapped British citizens that Sheikh had been involved. They had ample evidence to make a case yet chose not to do so. After 9/11 the US government secretly indicted him, and the British government quietly requested investigative assistance from India, for his role in the 1994 kidnapping. Why were these measures postponed for so long? And why the huge secrecy even now?

As noted above, in 1999, the British security services – despite being fully cognisant of his involvement in al-Qaeda including the 1994 and 1998 terrorist operations (in fact, the offer of a deal implies that they had enough to charge him for his role in the 1994 or 1998 attacks) – offered Sheikh free rein inside the UK on condition that he act as an informant on al-Qaeda. The offer indicates firstly that the government had sufficient intelligence on Sheikh's activities to know of his terrorist activities as an al-Qaeda operative; secondly that his track record would normally necessitate his immediate arrest upon entry into the UK; and thirdly that MI6 was willing to bypass the normal requirements of law if he merely provided information. In this context, the claim that Sheikh refused the MI6 offer of amnesty is false, since Sheikh was only to be permitted amnesty in the UK if he became an MI6 informant. In other words, British security services granted free reign to Osama bin Laden's actual financial chief to do as he pleased on British soil, having recruited him to MI6 at least as late as 1999 (and perhaps even earlier). This means that after his release in 1999, Sheikh was used and tracked by British intelligence as an MI6 asset.

But Sheikh's connections do not end there. According to the *Pittsburgh Tribune-Review*, high-level Pakistani government officials believe that Ahmed Omar Sheikh is not only an ISI agent but also an active CIA operative:

> There are many in Musharraf's government who believe that Saeed Sheikh's power comes not from the ISI, but from his connections with our own CIA. The theory is that with such intense pressure to locate bin Laden, Saeed Sheikh was bought and paid for.... It would be logical for the CIA to recruit an intelligent, young political criminal with contacts in both India and Pakistan.[334]

Pakistani government officials would obviously only hold this opinion about Sheikh on the basis of actual evidence available to them. Notably, this report does not refer to one, but rather 'many' informed insiders within the Pakistani administration confirming that Sheikh is a CIA informant, as well as an ISI operative.

Together these reports indicate that the consistent pattern of Anglo-American inaction toward Ahmed Omar Sheikh Saeed and terrorists connected to him was not merely the product of random indifference occurring without rhyme or reason. Rather, this systemic inaction was the product of a long-standing Anglo-American policy rooted in Sheikh's connections to the ISI – and more pertinently his apparent connections to MI6 and the CIA.

There seems little chance that Sheikh's possible role in orchestrating the London bombings, let alone his confirmed role in the 1994, 1998 and 9/11 terrorist operations, is to be investigated. Indeed, authorities seem happy to allow him to reside in prison away from the public eye where he can reportedly plot further terrorist attacks without much hindrance, protected by Pakistani security. As Michael

Meacher noted one day after the fourth anniversary of 9/11, 'Astonishingly his appeal to a higher court against the [death] sentence was adjourned in July for the 32nd time and has since been adjourned indefinitely.' The MP describes this as 'remarkable', but perhaps a more appropriate term is 'criminal', as it amounts to obstruction of justice.[335]

# 5. Blowback:
## Covert Operations, Secret Ties

Every leading member of al-Qaeda's Finsbury division – Omar Bakri, Abu Hamza, Abu Qatada – has according to credible reports, a close relationship to Britain's security services. It is plausible that the use of these individuals by MI5 and MI6 as intelligence assets, in some capacity, fundamentally compromised the services' ability to investigate impartially the terrorist networks surrounding them on the one hand; and on the other, seriously impeded Scotland Yard's ability to follow up independent police investigations into their terrorist activities in a manner fully consistent with the law.

1. Did the relationship hinder investigations into the groups behind 7/7?
2. Has it hindered subsequent investigations? If so, what could be more important than disrupting Islamist terrorist networks in Britain?

This means that political pressure on police and intelligence investigations is inextricably conjoined to a vast apparatus of British intelligence policies established by senior intelligence and Downing Street policymakers, which seriously compromises the actual functioning of intelligence gathering and investigation. As a result of these policies, intelligence services have become virtually wedded to the very activities, groups and individuals they are statutorily obliged to investigate.[336]

An entrenched and growing network of al-Qaeda-affiliated terrorists of more than a hundred in number – and consisting of possibly up to several thousand – has operated in the UK, with immunity from the law, despite being implicated in numerous instances of international terrorism. What is most perturbing about this phenomenon is that it has occurred under the leadership of a handful of unscrupulous extremist clerics with links to British security services.

To some extent, this phenomenon can be explained by the Covenant of Security, which amounts to an intelligence doctrine of terrorist appeasement. The Covenant means that British authorities allow radical Islamists to use the UK as a base of operations for international terrorist activity, as long as they do not target British interests at home. However, the Covenant is not sufficient to explain the full extent of the problem. When Omar Bakri, for example, had announced the annulment of the Covenant in January 2005, this annulment meant two things: firstly, that UK-based terror networks would be willing to target the British mainland; secondly, that those networks would no longer benefit from an official, if tacit, agreement of toleration and protection. But even in the aftermath of the London bombings, authorities have actively attempted to avoid prosecuting some of the same individuals implicated in the 7 July attacks. Bakri provides a prominent example of this.

Not only was Bakri *not* interrogated as a suspect in relation to the terrorist attacks, he was permitted to leave the country for Lebanon, and then debarred from returning to UK soil – thus removing him from UK jurisdiction. But while Bakri is now enjoying a life of freedom in Lebanon, the terrorist network he nurtured in the UK continues to function under the nose of

British security services. Bakri apparently retains the same directive influence over this network despite being outside the UK. On the same internet chat forum Bakri used in January 2005 to declare war on Britain, the forum's administrator 'Mizaan' in October 2005 was promulgating Bakri's terrorist message with equal ferocity. 'I still study with Sheikh Omar Bakri Muhammad', he said proudly. 'He used to be in the UK with us, we used to study with him as much as we could. And inshalla (with God's help) he's my only sheikh.' He added, 'He is doing very well in Lebanon':

And today there is the camp of Islam behind Sheikh Osama Bin Laden, the emir [leader] of jihad today, and we have the camp of kuffar led by George Bush with his cross. So yes we are two distinct groups, and we should never stand with the kuffar....

We should, all of us, glorify the terrorism. And we should incite religious hatred. Don't worry... it's not illegal for us to say that mujahadin [jihad fighters] on 9/11, were the magnificent 19, and it's not illegal for us to say that Mohammad Sidique Khan [the suicide bomber who blew himself up in London] and the four on 7/7 [London attacks], that they were the fantastic four – now we can say so without any worry.

We will always glorify killing the kuffar in the name of Allah. To raid the kuffar in the name of Allah. Even if some women and children are caught in the raid by accident. They are part of them, it is not your fault...

The kuffar wants to force their own homosexuality on the Muslims. The mujahadin have every right to hit back. So don't be surprised if the mujahadin do another 7/7, and another 9/11...

177

In fact, we should give them another magnificent day in history. Another fantastic four [the four London suicide bombers]. We should hit them time after time, day after day, every single week, every single month, every single year, we should hit them from every side, from the left and the right. From the planes above them, and the trains below them, we should hit them every way we can.

Even if it's just a man kuffar, if your target kills him, even if 20 women among them are killed by accident on the way, it is no problem. And that is what happened with the shahada [martyrs] when they went to raid.

So don't think what happened on 7/7 or 9/11 was something new, no, that's the Sunnah [sayings and actions of Muhammad]. There's never been jihad without casualties.[337]

The British state shows no interest in using its existing legal powers to neutralise terrorist networks in Britain, despite open threats of a new wave of terrorist attacks. This cannot be explained by the Covenant of Security, which ceased to function after 7 July 2005. What then can explain the ongoing British government reluctance to shut down this network?

A glimpse of an answer has already been seen in the role of Bakri and al-Muhajiroun supporting British covert operations in Kosovo. This covert relationship between the British intelligence establishment and the Islamist groups has no mandate from the British people and greatly increases the danger from terrorist networks in the UK. It is at least possible that it has also obstructed criminal investigations into a serious terrorist atrocity.

The international terrorist network implicated in the London bombings extends to a number of regions, including the

Balkans, Asia, and Africa (mainly North and West). In all these areas militant Islamist networks have operated in collaboration with the military and intelligence institutions of Britain, the US and European countries. These policies and operations, many of which continue to exist today, can be linked to concerted attempts by American, British and European states to secure a variety of regional strategic and economic interests, largely related to energy concerns. This long history of collaboration is the starting point for any serious analysis of the 'war on terror' and the deep ambiguities in British state policy.

Much of this has occurred in partnership with the USA. The British state, more than any other European Union member, has integrated its foreign policy with that of the United States. This takes the form of what some observers describe as a 'special relationship' which has existed since the Second World War and which has origins going back much further. As a result, British foreign policies cannot be understood without their relationship to those of its leading American ally.[338] For this reason, I will be focusing in the following discussion not merely on British or European policy, but on the relationship between these and overarching American grand-strategies.

## 5.1 The Balkans

### Scope of the Police Inquiry

Although the British press has remained largely silent on the subject, British investigators began investigating the Balkan connection immediately after forensic tests indicated that the bombs used contained C-4. According to British military and defence analyst Paul Beaver, the new CIA chief Porter Goss quietly visited Sarajevo and Tirana in the wake of the London bombings 'to express grave concerns of Washington because of [these governments'] cooperation with radical Islamic groups.' According to Beaver, 'a part of the investigation dealing with the London blasts is aimed at links between radical Islamists in Bosnia and Kosovo with international terrorist groups.'[339]

According to senior Bosnian government sources, British anti-terror investigators arrived in the Bosnian capital, Sarajevo, in late January 2006 to investigate the Bosnian link to the London bombings. British investigators were interested in 'four British citizens of Afro-Asian origin who had been under surveillance in Bosnia, one of which is believed to be the brother of one of the London suicide bombers.' The four reportedly arrived in the western Bosnian city of Bihac in late October 2005, and 'were under surveillance for suspected radical Islamic activities in Britain.' They were traced to Sarajevo in December, where they remained for about a month before leaving the country. An official from the Bosnian Federation police service revealed that the four British citizens spent most of their time in Sarajevo at the Saudi-funded King Fahd Mosque, 'which is frequented by naturalized Bosnians from Arab countries and fundamentalist Bosnian Muslims who have joined the Wahhabi movement of strict Islam.' While in Sarajevo, the four also reportedly visited the suburb of Hadzici several times, which 'appeared to be the base for a Bosnian, or even European, "terror cell".'[340]

But the Balkans connection has received little coverage in mainstream Western media. Just under a week after the 7 July attacks, the GIS/Defense & Foreign Affairs intelligence service for governments reported that 'despite firm linkages to 9/11, Madrid, and London attacks, Bosnian Jihadist networks remain "out of bounds".'[341] There is a simple reason for this:

British and American governments have actively fostered these terrorist networks to this day. Detailed investigation in the region would not only reveal deep ambiguities in Anglo-American policy in the Yugoslav wars. It would also reveal the extent to which the British and Americans promoted the very network that planned the London bombings.

## Anglo-American Sponsorship of al-Qaeda in Bosnia

Although the West's role in financing and arming the mujahideen in Afghanistan to repel Soviet invasion is well known, ongoing ties between al-Qaeda and the Anglo-American alliance in the post-Cold War period are rarely acknowledged. However, it is now well documented that between 1992 and 1995, the Pentagon 'assisted with the movement of thousands of Mujahideen and other Islamic elements from Central Asia into Europe, to fight alongside Bosnian Muslims against the Serbs.' Having thus created the mujahideen as an active militant force in Afghanistan, 'Western intervention in Bosnia appears to have globalised' the scope of mujahideen activities.[342] Indeed, it is fair to say that despite the demise of the Cold War, the Western strategic alliance with al-Qaeda never ceased. Rather, it merely shifted to a new theatre of military operations – from Afghanistan to Eastern Europe, Central Asia, and the Balkans.

Much of the details of the alliance have been authoritatively documented in the official Dutch inquiry into the 1995 Srebrenica massacre, which contains an in-depth report on Western intelligence in the Bosnian conflict by Professor Cees Wiebes of Amsterdam University. In a review of the Wiebes report for the *Guardian*, British political scientist Professor Richard Aldrich of the University of Nottingham described

the Dutch inquiry's most salient findings, based on five years
of unrestricted access to Dutch intelligence files and interviews
with key officials:

> Now we have the full story of the secret alliance between
> the Pentagon and radical Islamist groups from the Middle
> East designed to assist the Bosnian Muslims – some of
> the same groups that the Pentagon is now fighting in 'the
> war against terrorism.' Pentagon operations in Bosnia
> have delivered their own 'blowback'.

The policy created a 'vast secret conduit of weapons smuggling
though Croatia' and was 'in flagrant violation of the UN
security council arms embargo against all combatants in the
former Yugoslavia.' The conduit was arranged by the intelligence agencies of 'the US, Turkey and Iran, together with a
range of radical Islamist groups, including Afghan mojahedin.'

British intelligence services obtained documents on the
secret alliance early on in the Bosnian war. But rather than
taking the United States to task for allowing these activities,
the UK instead turned a blind eye. Aldrich continues:

> Arms purchased by Iran and Turkey with the financial
> backing of Saudi Arabia made their way by night from
> the Middle East. Initially aircraft from Iran Air were
> used, but as the volume increased they were joined by a
> mysterious fleet of black C-130 Hercules aircraft. The
> report stresses that the US was 'very closely involved' in
> the airlift. Mojahedin fighters were also flown in, but
> they were reserved as shock troops for especially hazard-
> ous operations.... Rather than the CIA, the Pentagon's
> own secret service was the hidden force behind these

operations... American Awacs aircraft covered crucial areas and were able to turn a blind eye to the frequent nightime comings and goings at Tuzla.[343]

The secret arms shipments from Iran began in 1992, and were first discovered by the CIA on 4 September 1992. An Iran Air Boeing 747 was found at Zagreb airport in Croatia containing arms, ammunition, anti-tank rockets, communication equipment, uniforms, and helmets for the Bosnian Muslim Army. Around 30,000 soldiers were armed and equipped by Iran and Turkey in one three to five-month period in late 1993 in this manner.[344] US military intelligence at first tacitly consented to the conduit, but then later actively supported it. On April 27, 1994, President Clinton 'decided to give a green light to the arms supplies.'[345]

This secret US-backed conduit between Iran, Turkey, Saudi Arabia, and the Bosnian Muslims was also used to fly in al-Qaeda mujihadeen forces connected to Osama bin Laden from Afghanistan, Algeria, Chechnya, Yemen, Sudan, and elsewhere. The Pentagon directly facilitated the influx. According to the Defense & Foreign Affairs: Strategic Policy report published by Washington DC's International Strategic Studies Association, 'The Mujahedin landing at Ploce are reported to have been accompanied by US Special Forces equipped with high-tech communications equipment.' Intelligence sources indicated that 'the mission of the US troops was to establish a command, control, communications and intelligence network to coordinate and support Bosnian Muslim offensives – in concert with Mujahideen and Bosnian Croat forces.' The US military, in other words, was actively coordinating on the ground with several thousand members of bin Laden's al-Qaeda network in Bosnia.[346]

Consequently, as estimated by US Lt Col. John Sray who worked as an intelligence officer in Sarajevo in 1994, 'Approximately 4,000 Mujihadeen, supported by Iranian special operations forces, have been continually intensifying their activities in central Bosnian for more than two years.'[347] According to Yossef Bodansky, former Director of the Congressional Task Force on Terrorism and Unconventional Warfare, most reliable intelligence estimates indicate that the number of al-Qaeda affiliated mujahideen operating in Bosnia at this time was more than 10,000.[348]

In a succinct overview of this policy, Director of the Centre for Research on Globalisation (CRG) Professor Michel Chossudovsky of the University of Ottawa finds that, 'The evidence amply confirms that the CIA never severed its ties to the "Islamic Militant Network." Since the end of the Cold War, these covert intelligence links have not only been maintained, they have in fact become increasingly sophisticated.'[349]

But what was the role of other NATO allies in the Pentagon– al-Qaeda alliance? The extensive Dutch intelligence files on the operation show how much European governments involved in the Bosnian conflict must have known about it. None of them questioned the wisdom or intent of the policy, which has clearly contributed to heightened ethnic tensions in the region, rather than reversing them, by escalating inter-ethnic violence which quickly led to horrific crimes.

And what of the British role? The Dutch files confirm that British intelligence was fully aware of the US covert operation, but chose not to protest it. According to Professor Wiebes, 'The UK Defence Intelligence Staff (DIS) was also aware of the American secret arms supplies to the ABiH [the Bosnian Muslim Army].' A British intelligence official explained that the DIS 'never made an issue of them, so as not to further damage the sensitive relationship with the US services.' While an internal DIS analysis concluded that the US arms deliveries were 'probably led by the NSC [National Security Council]... the DIS received a direct order from the British government not to investigate this affair.'[350]

However, the British role went far beyond merely acquiescing in an exclusively American strategy. According to Michael Meacher MP, former Labour Environment Minister, as part of the operation the American and British governments also turned to 'Pakistanis in Britain' to support the influx of radical Islamists into Bosnia. The Pakistani government, then led by Benazir Bhutto, sent a contingent 'formed from the Harkat-ul-Ansar (HUA) terrorist group' trained by Pakistan's Inter-Services Intelligence (ISI) at the request of the Clinton administration. Approximately 200 'Pakistani Muslims living in the UK went to Pakistan, trained in HUA camps and joined the HUA's contingent in Bosnia'. The operation was conducted 'with the full knowledge and complicity of the British and American intelligence agencies.'[351]

## Manipulating Bosnia

The influx of the mujahideen, the secret delivery of arms shipments, were components of a wider Anglo-American strategy of manipulating the Bosnian Muslims in a manner which made war inevitable.

On 18 March 1992 the EU had successfully brokered an agreement in Lisbon among the Bosnian Muslim, Croatian and Serb communities. Following the agreement, the Bosnian Republic would have been partitioned 'into three ethnically based cantons, which were to have been loosely joined in a confederation that would function as a sovereign state.'[352] It was, admittedly, an imperfect agreement – but it could have prevented the war, saving the lives of hundreds of thousands of refugees.

The agreement was largely sabotaged by Washington, which urged Bosnian President Alija Izetbegovic to declare Bosnian statehood, 'saying that this was justified by the referendum on March 1 on independence.'[353] 'The problem with that referendum', observed the *New York Times*, 'was that although the Bosnian Muslims and Croats overwhelmingly endorsed it, the Bosnian Serbs boycotted it, warning that it was a prelude to civil war.' Rejecting the validity of the referendum, the Serbs made clear that they found its terms unacceptable.[354] Washington knew that pushing Bosnia into declaring statehood would mean the eruption of ethnic conflict, primarily between Muslims and Serbs. Jose Cutileiro, Secretary-General of the Western European Union, observes that 'the Muslims reneged on the agreement' signed at Lisbon which was to be the basis for future negotiations. 'Had they not done so, the Bosnian question might have been settled earlier, with less loss of (mainly Muslim) life and land.' But Cutileiro notes that the decision was not Izetbegovic's, 'To be fair, President Izetbegovic and his aides were encouraged to scupper that deal and to fight for a unitary Bosnian state [by Western mediators]'.[355] Predictably then, the Bosnian Serbs attacked as soon as the Izetbegovic government was recognised in April 1992.[356]

A number of Muslim groups in two separate areas of Bosnia challenged the legitimacy of the US-backed government of Alija Izetbegovic. They supported 'a policy of cooperation and trade with the other nationalities of the region', and 'condemned Izetbegovic for right-wing nationalist policies and reliance on US military aid.' According to General Charles G. Boyd, former Deputy Commander-in-Chief of the US European Command, the alternative government of Bosnian Muslim leader Fikret Adbic was 'one of the few examples of successful multi-ethnic cooperation' in the region. Adbic, a powerful local business-man, 'was a member of the Bosnian collective presidency. He outpolled Izetbegovic in national elections', but was 'expelled from the government' by Izetbegovic.[357]

When Adbic self-declared autonomy in the northwest Bihac area, Izetbegovic's forces, utilizing mujahideen shock troops and with US assistance, crushed his Muslim movement. Adbic's regime, opposed to US intervention and keen to explore peaceful cooperation with its Serbian and Croatian neighbours, had to be eliminated.[358] Six US generals participated in planning the August 1994 offensive against Adbic, violating a UN-declared safe area.[359]

The Bosnian Serbs, in alliance with Croatian Serbs and Adbic's Bosnian Muslim forces, reorganised to initiate a counter-offensive. In response, 'US bombers under NATO command came to Izetbegovic's defense.'[360] Balkans expert Joan Hoey records the catastrophic results, '[The Fifth Corps' offensive] out of the UN-designated 'safe area' of Bihac...[led] to the expulsion of about 10,000 Serbs, who escaped to neighboring Serb-held Croatia, following the tens of thousands of Bosnian Muslims who had fled the earlier Bosnian Fifth Corps offensive.'[361]

Much of the violence from the Bosnian Muslim side was due to the brutality of al-Qaeda's mujahideen. One Bosnian army chief, Nasir Oric, even had the audacity to boast of his army's bloody raids on Serb villages where he presided over ruthless and repeated massacres of hundreds of civilians.[362]

As the violence escalated, plans for a campaign of mass murder in Srebrenica were brought to fruition by the Serbs. But although the US and UK powers had already actively interfered in the region, both overtly and covertly, they were not willing to protect Srebrenica. 'American intelligence agencies began observing a Bosnian Serb military build-up around Srebrenica in late June', reported the *Washington Post*. 'There were reports that Bosnian Serb Gen. Ratko Mladic was furious about a series of raids by Srebrenica-based Muslim troops on neighboring Serb villages, and that he wanted to teach the Bosnian government a lesson. US intelligence analysts concluded... that the Serb aim was to 'neutralize' the enclave.'[363] The United Nations had also anticipated the Serb attack. A three-month investigation by *Newsday* found that 'some top UN military aides had predicted the Serb attack on Srebrenica months before it occurred and advised that the only defense was NATO air power.'[364] But NATO air power was ruled out from the start. As Balkans expert Tim Judah concludes, the US and Britain gave a green light to the Serb assault on Srebrenica. They did 'nothing to prevent' the oncoming massacre, but made sure to exploit it 'to distract attention from the exodus of Krajina's entire population which was then taking place' in Croatia.[365]

According to Professor Francis Boyle – whose expertise is certified by the Prosecutor's Office of the International Criminal Tribunal of Yugoslavia (ICTY), which called him to testify as the Expert Witness on the evolution of the Bosnian 'peace plans' – all these events were 'part of a long-standing common criminal purpose and plan' by a number of Western powers 'to carve-up and destroy the Republic of Bosnia and Herzegovina'. Boyle, who also instituted legal proceedings on behalf of the Republic of Bosnia and Herzegovina before the International Court of Justice in The Hague against the rump Yugoslavia for violating the 1948 Genocide Convention, argues that the Srebrenica genocide occurred 'with the full knowledge and approval of several UN and Western officials. The fragmentation of Yugoslavia, in other words, had been what some Western powers had hoped for, as revealed by then US Ambassador to Yugoslavia Warren Zimmerman in January 1992 before the outbreak of hostilities, 'We are aiming for a dissolution of Yugoslavia into independent states.'[366]

## The KLA–NLA Connection

The Anglo-American strategy of sponsoring al-Qaeda networks in the Balkans continued after the Bosnian conflict. As early as 1996 – and possibly years earlier – Kosovan Liberation Army (KLA) representatives had met with American, British and Swiss intelligence services.[367] As Ralf Mutschke, Assistant Director of Interpol's Criminal Intelligence Directorate, testified before Congress in December 2000, 'In 1998, the US State Department listed the KLA as a terrorist organization, indicating that it was financing its operations with money from the international heroin trade and loans from Islamic countries and individuals, among them allegedly Osama bin Laden.' Mutschke also confirmed that Osama bin Laden sent one of his top military commanders to Kosovo to lead 'an elite KLA unit during the Kosovo conflict.'[368]

But in that very year both Britain and the United States were deeply involved in the training and arming of the same group. We already know from the confirmation of former US federal prosecutor John Loftus that British security services used al-Muhajiroun to facilitate the recruitment of British Muslims to join KLA operations in Kosovo. Former and serving members of the British 22nd Special Air Services Regiment (SAS) had teamed up with three British and American private security companies under the strategic directive of the US Defence Intelligence

Agency (DIA) and MI6. Senior British military sources confirmed that the KLA training programme was conducted by MI6 on the DIA's request. 'MI6 then sub-contracted the operation to two British security companies, who in turn approached a number of former members of the (22 SAS) regiment. Lists were then drawn up of weapons and equipment needed by the KLA.' The programme was launched before NATO's bombing campaign in March 1999.[369]

The existence of the covert assistance to the KLA was corroborated by several other investigations. The *Sunday Times* for instance quoted 'American intelligence agents' who had 'admitted they helped to train the Kosovo Liberation Army before NATO's bombing of Yugoslavia.' CIA officers were 'developing ties with the KLA and giving American military training manuals and field advice on fighting the Yugoslav army and Serbian police' under the cover of cease-fire monitors. The US military gave KLA commanders 'satellite telephones and global positioning systems.' KLA commanders also 'had the mobile phone number of General Wesley Clark, the NATO commander.'[370] There is no longer any doubt that both the UK and the US had 'clandestine camps inside Albania to teach the KLA effective guerilla tactics.' British SAS and US Delta Force instructors were training KLA members in 'weapons handling, demolition and ambush techniques, and basic organisation.'[371]

But in 1999, a Congressional report by the US Senate Republican Party Committee confirmed the KLA's involvement with:

- The extensive Albanian crime network that extends throughout Europe and into North America, including allegations that a major portion of the KLA finances are derived from that network, mainly proceeds from drug trafficking; and

- Terrorist organizations motivated by the ideology of radical Islam, including assets of Iran and of the notorious Osama bin-Ladin – who has vowed a global terrorist war against Americans and American interests.[372]

US intelligence reports from that year similarly proved not only the KLA's al-Qaeda funding, but also that numerous KLA fighters trained in al-Qaeda camps in Afghanistan and Albania, and numerous al-Qaeda mujahideen joined the ranks of the KLA. The reports substantiated a 'link' between bin Laden and the KLA, 'including a common staging area in Tropoje, Albania, a center for Islamic terrorists.' KLA-sponsored border crossings into Kosovo from Albania of hundreds of foreign fighters include 'veterans of the militant group Islamic Jihad from Bosnia, Chechnya and Afghanistan,' carrying forged Macedonian Albanian passports.[373]

The Anglo-American allies used KLA operations as a lever of destabilisation that would, as in Bosnia, escalate ethnic hostilities. KLA leaders explained that 'any armed action we undertook would bring retaliation against civilians'; 'the more civilians were killed, the chances of intervention became bigger'. Attacks were designed to generate a climate that might justify Western intervention.[374]

In response to the escalating tit-for-tat, the UN Security Council demanded a ceasefire and negotiations in September 1998. US envoy Richard Holbrooke brokered an agreement between Serbia and the KLA, granting the KLA 'a reprieve, time to reorganise and rearm, and, as they told anyone who cared to listen, time to prepare for their spring [1999] offensive.'[375]

After the October ceasefire, the KLA predictably violated the terms of the agreement, initiating a new wave of attacks 'leading to statements [by Serb authorities] that if the [Western Kosovo Verificaton Mission (KVM) monitors] cannot control these units the government would.'[376]

Although Serb retaliations were certainly brutal, the notion that they amounted to a policy of genocide is contradicted by internal German government reports. Documents produced by the German Foreign Office in response to court requests concerning the status of Kosovan Albanian refugees in Germany, state repeatedly that neither ethnic cleansing nor genocide were committed by either party in Kosovo. Citing the German intelligence reports, in late February 1999 a German court observed:

> There is no sufficient actual proof of a secret program, or an unspoken consensus on the Serbian side, to liquidate the Albanian people, to drive it out or otherwise to persecute it in the extreme manner presently described... Events since February and March 1998 do not evidence a persecution program based on Albanian ethnicity. The measures taken by the armed Serbian forces are in the first instance directed toward combatting the KLA and its supposed adherents and supporters.

On 11 March 1999, only two weeks before the commencement of NATO bombing, the Upper Adminstrative Court at Munster further concluded, 'Ethnic Albanians in Kosovo have neither been nor are now exposed to regional or countrywide group persecution in the Federal Republic of Yugoslavia.'[377]

Around the same time, the Serbian Parliament issued a little-noted resolution supporting 'the idea of UN forces to monitor a political settlement there.'[378] The Serbian National Assembly had called loud and clear for the continuation of peaceful negotiations with the objective of:

[R[eaching a political agreement on a wide-ranging autonomy for Kosovo and Metohija, with the securing of a full equality of all citizens and ethnic communities and with respect for the sovereignty and territorial integrity of the Republic of Serbia and the Federal Republic of Yugoslavia.[379]

The Anglo-American strategy in Kosovo, however, was to make war inevitable, not to avoid war – so instead of pursuing the opportunity for peace presented by the Serb Parliamentary decision, NATO officials had imposed last-minute terms in Rambouillet's 'Interim Agreement for Peace and Self Govern-ment in Kosovo' which sabotaged any possibility of a peaceful resolution. The terms were contained in 'Appendix B', which provided for NATO's de facto colonisation of Yugoslavia in the form of the occupation of Kosovo, 'unrestricted passage and unimpeded access' for NATO aircraft, tanks and troops throughout Yugoslavia, immunity 'from all legal process, whether civil, administrative, or criminal', among other items.[380] In July 2000, to the resounding silence of the British press, former Defence Minister Lord Gilbert 'told the House of Commons that the Rambouillet terms offered to the Yugoslav delegation had been "absolutely intolerable" and expressly designed to provoke war.'[381]

NATO intervention, it seems, produced the humanitarian catastrophe, rather than the catastrophe having been averted by NATO's war. But the Allies had anticipated this anyway. According to the *Sunday Times* reporting well before NATO air strikes, President Clinton knew that 'air strikes might provoke Serb soldiers into greater acts of butchery.' Clinton and his cabinet members, including Defence Secretary William Cohen and National Security Adviser Sandy Berger were briefed by Gen. Hugh Shelton, Chairman of the Joint Chiefs of Staff.[382] A month after the bombing, Gen. Wesley Clark, Supreme Commander of NATO during the campaign, had further important revelations. The NATO air war against Serbia 'was not designed as a means of blocking Serb ethnic cleansing. It was not designed as a means of waging war against the Serb and MUP forces in Kosovo. Not in any way... That was not the idea.'[383]

So what was the idea? When KLA forces began transferring their operations to Macedonia under the banner of the National Liberation Army (NLA), their Anglo-American sponsorship did not cease. Long after the end of the Kosovo conflict and the demise of the Milosovic regime in Yugoslavia, in late January 2001, Western Special Forces were still training KLA guerrillas. According to foreign diplomatic sources, the former KLA had:

[S]everal hundred fighters in the 5km-deep military exclusion zone on the boundary between Kosovo and the rest of Serbia...

- Certain Nato-led K-For forces were not preventing the guerrillas taking mortars and other weapons into the exclusion zone;
- The guerrilla units had been able to hold exercises there, including live-firing of weapons, despite the fact that K-For patrols the zone;
- Western special forces were still training the guerrillas, as a result of decisions taken before the change of government in Yugoslavia.[384]

A *Sunday Times* investigation found that two of the Kosovo-based commanders leading the Albanian push into Tetovo, Macedonia, 'were trained by former British SAS and Parachute Regiment officers.' They included one who called himself 'Bilal', who was 'organising the flow of arms and men into Macedonia', and a veteran KLA commander 'Adem Bajrami' who helped coordinate the Tetovo assault. 'Both were taught by British soldiers in the secretive training camps that operated above Bajram Curri in northern Albania during 1998 and 1999.'[385]

In May 2001, US diplomat Robert Fenwick – head of the Organization for Security and Cooperation in Europe – held a secret meeting in Prizren, Kosovo, with Albanian and former KLA (now NLA) leaders, to which Macedonian officials were not invited. According to James Bisset, former Canadian Ambassador to Yugoslavia, Bulgaria, and Albania (1990–1992), the meeting made clear that 'the United States was backing the Albanian terrorist cause.' One month later, 400 former NLA fighters were surrounded by Macedonian security forces in the town of Aracinovo near the capital, Skopje. Just as they began moving in, NATO ordered them to pull back. US Army buses from Camp Bondsteel, Kosovo, swept in to escort the NLA fighters to safety.[386]

By August 2001, Scott Taylor – Canada's top war reporter, former soldier and editor of *Esprit de Corps Military Magazine* – reported in detail on how he witnessed first-hand in Tetovo the clandestine American and British support for the ethnic Albanian guerrillas at the height of their anti-Macedonia insurgency. Noting that such support is vehemently denied by Western governments, Taylor pointed out that:

[T]here is no denying the massive amount of materiel

and expertise supplied by NATO to the guerrillas… The UCK [NLA] commanders welcomed me with a shout of, 'God bless America and Canada too for all that they have provided to us!' In the well constructed UCK bunkers overlooking the besieged city of Tetovo, there is ample evidence of US military hardware. Everything from sidearms and sniper rifles to menacing-looking grenade launchers are emblazoned with a 'Made in the USA' logo.

An abundant stock of sophisticated night vision goggles provides the UCK with a tremendous tactical advantage over the Macedonian security forces. By nightfall, the Macedonians are compelled to hole-up in their bunkers while the UCK roam with impunity throughout the Tetovo streets.

'Snake' Arifaj, a 22-year-old platoon commander with the UCK, proudly displayed his unit's impressive arsenal and said, 'Thanks to Uncle Sam, the Macedonians are no match for us.'

The extent of US support to the guerrillas was highlighted in early August 2001 when the Macedonian government loudly protested the delivery of supplies by two US helicopters to an Albanian village in the mountains above Tetovo. US spokesmen said the helicopters were only providing much needed humanitarian assistance. The reality of the matter, however, was revealed by a local NLA commander known only as 'Commandant Mouse,' who confirmed that the supplies had consisted of 'heavy mortars and ammunition' to the NLA. As if to vindicate his claim, on 16 August the NLA began firing 120mm and 82mm mortars at Tetovo. Taylor, who witnessed the mortar attacks, argues that their duration and intensity proved that the NLA was receiving a continuous and abundant supply of ammunition. US military assistance to the ethnic Albanian guerrillas was also more direct. According to Taylor, 'The US also frequently used their tactical helicopters to gather intelligence inside Macedonia, without authorization from the Macedonian government. The sight of the US choppers prompted the ethnic Albanian villagers to cheer wildly, waving their arms to encourage 'their' airforce.'[387]

In what appeared to be a welcome turnaround to this policy, in summer 2001 President George W. Bush signed two decrees purportedly depriving 'Albanian extremists who were threatening the stability of Macedonia' of all financial or material support, and barring them from entry into the United States. But as George Szamuely reported, 'The US decrees were more rhetoric than reality.' One KLA–NLA fighter, Commander Rrustem, had 'earned fame during the Kosovo war as one of the most successful guerrilla commanders.' Since then, he has become 'a favourite with NATO commanders, whose glowing commendations line the walls of his office. Certainly if the Americans have reservations about him they have yet to show it: on Tuesday two separate US army teams came to his base to train his men.'[388]

On 22 June 2002, a secret European intelligence report leaked through the respected military analysis firm, the Clingendael Institute, to Dutch National Radio documented ongoing US arms and training to the NLA. The report confirmed the German *Hamburger Abendblatt's* story that 17 military advisers from the Virginian-based private US defense contractor Military Professionals Resources Inc. (MPRI) accompanied the NLA fighters evacuated from Aracinovo. The Dutch report also reveals that high-level US officials maintained constant telephone connection with the NLA rebels. The conversations were recorded by European intelligence.

Although the conversations ceased when US intelligence uncovered the tapping, the communications were restored after special computers with phone technology were supplied by the US to the NLA.[389]

### KLA–NLA: Al-Qaeda's Balkans Nexus

The KLA–NLA nexus is al-Qaeda's most prominent operational network in the Balkans. According to Yossef Bodansky, former Director of Congress's Task Force on Terrorism, the Albanian network is headed by Muhammad al-Zawahiri, the engineer brother of Ayman al-Zawahiri who is bin Laden's right-hand man and mentor. According to Fatos Klosi – head of Shik, the Albanian intelligence service – a major al-Qaeda network was established in Albania in 1998 under the cover of various Muslim charities serving as a springboard for European operations. The network, Klosi noted, had 'already infiltrated other parts of Europe from bases in Albania through traffic in illegal immigrants, who have been smuggled by speedboat across the Mediterranean to Italy in large numbers.'[390]

The Macedonian Interior Ministry has provided the US National Security Council with a detailed report on al-Qaeda activity in the Kumanovo-Lipkovo region of Macedonia, including lists of operatives' names and in particular the role of two units, one consisting of 120 al-Qaeda connected fighters, the other of 250. Members of the KLA–NLA units are not only Macedonian and Kosovan Albanians, but also mujahideen from Turkey, Saudi Arabia, Pakistan, Jordan, and Chechnya, some trained in al-Qaeda camps in Afghanistan. The US has done little in response. 'Officials at the NSC and CIA were polite and received the information with thanks, but little else has happened,' noted one Macedonian official.[391]

Yugoslav intelligence, working on behalf of Interpol, has corroborated these findings, noting that, 'The American CIA has also been made aware that last year the mujahedeen had a training camp in the village of Tropoja in northern Albania.' On 23 October 2001, Interpol released a report personally linking Osama bin Laden to the Albanian mafia. Interpol also documented that one of bin Laden's senior lieutenants was commander of an elite Albanian unit operating in Kosovo in 1999. Macedonian intelligence, however, complains that NATO political pressure and direct US interference constitutes the biggest obstacle to investigating the al-Qaeda presence in the region.[392]

So powerful is the al-Qaeda presence in the Balkans that Osama bin Laden himself was issued a Bosnia-Herzegovina passport in 1993 – the same time that American and British intelligence services were actively organizing the influx of al-Qaeda mujahideen to fight with the Bosnian Muslim Army – by the Bosnian embassy in Vienna, according to the Bosnian Muslim weekly *Dani* reporting on September 24, 1999. In the summer of 1998, a joint CIA–Albanian intelligence operation discovered that mujahadeen units from at least half a dozen Middle East countries were streaming across the border into Kosovo from bases in Albania. According to Albanian intelligence chief Fatos Klosi, bin Laden had actually visited Albania himself to oversee al-Qaeda's consolidation. The Yugoslav news agency Tanjug confirmed the same in April 2000, noting that he had landed in Kosovo from Albania, 'Until recently, bin Laden was training a group of almost 500 mujahadeen from Arab countries around the Albanian towns of Podgrade and Korce for terrorist actions in Kosovo.' Tanjug added that a contingent of 2000 'extremists' planned 'to set off a new wave of violence.'[393]

These reports are considered credible by Interpol. As

reported by the Swiss financial daily *Neue Zürcher Zeitung*, Gwen McClure of Interpol's Criminal Subdivision officially informed a group of parliamentarians from NATO countries on 23 October 2001, of bin Laden's longstanding infiltration of the region, including his meeting in Albania during which he established 'many structures and networks… for propaganda and fundraising activities and for providing the Algerian armed groups with logistical support.'[394]

Corroborating Bodansky's report, Albanian intelligence sources cited by Toronto's Centre for Peace in the Balkans (CPB) confirm that, 'One of the leaders of an elite KLA unit was Muhammed al-Zawahiri, the brother of Dr Ayman al-Zawahiri, a leader in an Egyptian Jihad organisation and a military commander of Osama bin Laden.' Kosovo, the CPB observes, is 'a paradox where several mortal enemies… Osama bin Laden and the CIA – are standing shoulder to shoulder training the KLA.'[395] Elaborating on the al-Zawahiri connection, the Macedonian daily *Dnevnik* cited intelligence sources reporting that a group of '50 mujahideen' had entered Macedonia via Kosovo and 'taken up positions in the mountains of Skopaska Crna Gora nearby Skopje…. An Egyptian national, the younger brother of Ayman al-Zawahiri – the commander of al-Qaeda responsible for the Balkan operations – is in charge of the terrorist groups that recently entered Macedonia.' Intelligence sources noted that the plan to expand al-Qaeda operations in the Balkans was being supervised by Ayman, while his younger brother Muhammed was charged with recruiting mujahdeen. Dnevnik noted that the KLA–NLA's 113 Brigade named Ismet Jashar along with the rapid intervention unit Baruti were 'stationed at a Kosovo training camp near the village of Ropotovo in the US-run sector. Zawahiri was in charge of the terrorist training camp.'[396]

On 16 October 2001, Macedonia's Novosti cited sources in the Russian peacekeeping force in Kosovo who corroborated the above:

> A training camp of Albanian militants functions near the village of Ropotovo, close to Kosovska Kamenica, in the Yugoslav province of Kosovo, which is controlled by the American force, sources from the Russian peacekeeping force in Kosovo reported…. According to [the sources], the camp is now training 50 Afghan and Algerian mujahideen, led by Zaiman Zawahiri. He is reportedly the brother of one of the closest associates of international terrorist Osama bin Laden. This camp prepares militants for terrorist formations in Kosovo and Macedonia.[397]

According to the Arabic daily *al-Sharq al-Awsat* (16 April 1999), sources linked to bin Laden in London revealed that Ayman al-Zawahiri himself, leader of the Egyptian Islamic Jihad, was 'currently' in Albania. 'Al-Zawahiri and Abu-al-Faraj travelled to Albania some weeks ago, heading a company of Arab mujahideen,' even though Albania 'is now in the grip of US intelligence.'[398]

## Ayman al-Zawahiri: Anglo-American Intelligence Asset

Ayman al-Zawahiri, bin Laden's notorious right-hand man and al-Qaeda's operations chief, claimed responsibility on behalf of the terrorist network for the 7 July terrorist attacks in London on the infamous videotape, in which chief bomber Mohammed Siddique Khan also appeared. Al-Zawahiri worked closely with Abu Faraj al-Libbi, who was directly involved in the planning and coordination of the London bombings, and who had contact with UK terror networks planning the attacks.

Ayman al-Zawahri is on the FBI's 'Most Wanted Terrorist' list, which refers to him as having 'been indicted for his alleged role in the August 7, 1998, bombings of the US Embassies in Dar es Salaam, Tanzania, and Nairobi, Kenya…. The Rewards For Justice Program, United States Department of State, is offering a reward of up to $25 million for information leading directly to the apprehension or conviction of Ayman Al-Zawahiri.'[399] Al-Zawahiri is described as bin Laden's top deputy, but even that, according to the *Guardian*, perhaps understates his significance in al-Qaeda. 9/11 hijackers Atta and Khalid al-Midhar were reportedly members of al-Zawahiri's Islamic Jihad. He was also implicated in the 1981 assassination of Anwar Sadat. Intelligence analysts believe that he now controls much of bin Laden's terrorist finances, operations, plans, and resources. In Afghanistan, al-Zawahiri has reportedly acted as bin Laden's spokesman. His main terrorist vehicle Egyptian Islamic Jihad has been linked with the Islamic Group of Egypt, who perpetrated the 1993 World Trade Center bombing. Indeed, he appeared in a video alongside bin Laden in which they threatened retaliation against the US for imprisoning the Blind Sheik. According to the State Department's 1997 *Patterns of Global Terrorism*, al-Zawahiri is leader of the Vanguards of Conquest, believed to have perpetrated the 1997 Luxor massacre and a 1995 assassination attempt against Egyptian President Mubarak.[400]

Despite this well-documented and notorious record of terror, al-Zawahiri was granted asylum in the 1990s by a variety of European countries, including Denmark and Switzerland. But most shockingly, he was even granted residence in the United States, according to an expert testifying before the House of

Representatives Judiciary Subcommittee on Immigration in January 2000, who said 'that he was one of a number of Islamist activists who had been granted green card status by the US immigration service.'[401]

Indeed, as the *New York Times* reported, he travelled to and around the US in 1995 to raise funds for al-Qaeda, gathering thereby approximately half a million dollars. Although he reportedly used a false name, there is no doubt that his receipt of a right of residency from the US State Department directly facilitated his entry and tour of the US. His travels to the US were facilitated by al-Qaeda operative Ali Mohamed – a naturalised American born in Egypt – then US Army Special Forces officer and FBI informant.[402] More than 10,000 pages of Egyptian state security documents obtained by the *Sunday Times* demonstrate that 'Islamic fundamentalists under the command of Ayman Al-Zawahiri… established sleeper cells across the western world and were plotting sophisticated attacks.' Among al-Zawahiri's operatives in the US 'in the early 1990s were a communications specialist, a special forces officer, two wealthy doctors and a chain of fundraisers…. A base in Santa Clara, California, was used from 1990 to co-ordinate communications with terrorists' cells around the world, including Bin Laden's Sudanese base. Other operatives were based in New York.'[403]

An extraordinary report by US Congress's former terrorist expert Yossef Bodansky, currently Director of Research at Washington DC's International Strategic Studies Association, pointed to al-Zawahiri's recruitment by the CIA in 1997. According to Bodansky writing in February 1998, intelligence sources revealed:

[D]iscussions between the Egyptian terrorist leader Dr Ayman al-Zawahiri and an Arab-American known to have been both an emissary of the CIA and the US Government in the 1980s. Egypt's President Husni Mubarak is convinced this information is accurate and has already undertaken major steps to address the challenge. Moreover, to-date, the independent sources that provided this information have proven highly reliable and forthcoming....

In the first half of November 1997, Ayman al-Zawahiri, the leader of the Jihad Organization and the Vanguard of Conquest terrorist organizations, met a man called Abu-Umar al-Amriki [al-Amriki means the American] at a camp near Peshawar on the Pakistan-Afghanistan border. High-level Islamist leaders insist that in this meeting Abu-Umar al-Amriki made al-Zawahiri an offer: The US will not interfere with nor intervene to prevent the Islamists' rise to power in Egypt if the Islamist Mujahedin currently in Bosnia-Herzegovina [B-H] refrain from attacking the US forces. Moreover, Abu-Umar al-Amriki promised a donation of $50 million (from undefined sources) to Islamist charities in Egypt and elsewhere.

This was not the first meeting between Abu-Umar al-Amriki and al-Zawahiri. Back in the 1980s, Abu-Umar al-Amriki was openly acting as an emissary for the CIA with various Arab Islamist militant/terrorist movements then operating under the wings of the Afghan Jihad. In the late 1980s, in one of his meetings with al-Zawahiri, Abu-Umar al-Amriki suggested that al-Zawahiri would 'need $50 million to rule Egypt.' At the time, al-Zawahiri interpreted this assertion as a hint that Washington would tolerate his rise to power if he could raise this money.

Thus, the mention of the magic figure – $50 million – by Abu-Umar al-Amriki in the November 1997 meeting has been interpreted by al-Zawahiri and the entire Islamist leadership, including Shaykh Usamah bin Ladin, as a reaffirmation of the discussions with the CIA in the late 1980s. The Islamist leaders are convinced that in November 1997, Abu-Umar al-Amriki was speaking for the CIA – that is the uppermost echelons of the Clinton Administration…. [T]here is no doubt that the November 1997 meeting between Abu-Umar al-Amriki and al-Zawahiri took place.[404]

Shockingly, through 'al-Amriki' the CIA had offered first to fund al-Qaeda to the tune of $50 million through the vehicle of bin Laden's right-hand man al-Zawahiri and second to allow al-Qaeda to target the secular regime of Hosni Mubarak. The condition for this deal was simply that al-Qaeda mujahideen 'refrain from attacking the US forces' in the Balkans.

Was the deal struck? Al-Zawahiri's subsequent activities in the Balkans on behalf of Anglo-American interests, suggests it was. But at first glance, this seems tenous. In December 1997, for example, al-Zawahiri's Jihad Group issued a special bulletin threatening an apocalyptic war on American and Israeli targets on a global scale. As Bodansky noted, at first sight the Jihad bulletin 'seems to suggest that the US request for al-Zawahiri not to strike out is not being heeded to.' But on further reflection, 'al-Amriki was talking only about al-Zawahiri's not striking out against the US forces in B-H [Bosnia-Herzegovina]. *Nothing was said about transferring the Islamist Jihad to other 'fronts': Egypt, Israel, or the heart of America, for that matter.*[my emphasis]'[405]

Although the CIA displayed a clear red light to al-Zawahiri

for anti-US operations in the Balkans, it did not display a red light for anti-US operations anywhere else. In other words, the CIA's offer to al-Qaeda was explicitly an arrangement for al-Qaeda to cease targeting US interests in the Balkans. But by not signaling a clear red light for anti-US operations outside the Balkans, the CIA–al-Zawahiri agreement suggests the existence of an implicit decision to tolerate al-Qaeda's targeting of US interests everywhere else – including, for that matter, in Africa, New York, and Washington DC. It is plausible to conclude that effectively, the CIA–al-Zawahiri agreement amounted to a green light to al-Qaeda to launch attacks in Egypt and, indeed, anywhere except the Balkans, as well as a promise to not interfere in such attacks.

In hindsight, mujahideen operations in the Balkans support the conclusion that al-Qaeda accepted the offer, and the US government assented to it. Thus, on 17 November 1997, Ayman al-Zawahiri's forces conducted the terrorist attack in Luxor killing 62 innocent Western tourists, including Britons, which undermined the very economic foundations of the Mubarak regime by damaging Egypt's tourist industry.[406] According to Bodansky, 'The virtually deafening silence of the Clinton administration' in response to the Luxor massacre 'had to reassure Zawahiri and bin Laden that Abu-Umar al-Amriki had spoken with its backing, and a rejuvenated call to arms followed.'[407]

Britain plays a direct role in providing a safe haven for al-Qaeda terrorists working under al-Zawahiri's jurisdiction. According to the Egyptian government, at least seven men linked to terrorism – including leaders of al-Zawahiri's group which perpetrated the Luxor massacre – 'were, or still are, living in Britain, some as political refugees.' The UK government's failure to investigate the individuals prompted the Egyptian

President Hosni Mubarak to denounce Britain for 'protecting killers'. The extremist groups trying to overthrow his government, he complained, were operating out of London.[408]

Ayman al-Zawahiri along with his brother have been deeply active in the Balkans, recruiting and training mujahideen to join the ranks of the KLA–NLA nexus sponsored by American and British military intelligence services. Not only is al-Qaeda refraining from targeting Anglo-American interests in the Balkans, they are actively collaborating with Anglo-American military intelligence and NATO military assistance to secure the alliance's covert interests.

At face value, this revelation represents perhaps one of the most fatal holes in the official narrative. 'Al-Amriki' appears to have been a CIA/al-Qaeda go-between facilitating at least one strategic policy agreement between the two blocs. His meeting with al-Zawahri illustrates that al-Qaeda's utility as an asset for covert operations can outweigh Western interest in genuinely eliminating the terrorist network. US intelligence clearly was fully aware of al-Zawahiri's whereabouts and movements. Rather than making any attempt to arrest him or to at least alert Egyptian security to his location so that they could do so, no effort at all was made to apprehend him. Instead, the CIA sent its emissary to forge a mutually convenient post-Cold War pact with the devil. The British government has merely followed its American ally subserviently in this affair, participating actively in the sponsorship of al-Zawahiri's al-Qaeda–KLA–NLA networks, without any apparent concern for the ramifications of such a dangerous policy. This of course begs the question: What is the end-goal of Anglo-American strategy in the Balkans?

*Keeping the Peace (Guarding the Oil)*

As of 2003, NATO had 12,000 troops stationed in Bosnia,[409] although by 2005, NATO this had reduced slightly to 11,000 troops in Bosnia, Kosovo and Macedonia – still no small figure.[410] This purported exercise in peacekeeping has, however, focused less on peacekeeping and more on securing powerful Anglo-American corporate interests. As former US Congressman Lee Hamilton commented in the *New York Times*, 'We have completely taken over the control of the Balkans. US officials exercise managing functions in all states of the former Yugoslavia. We are virtually the pro consul.'[411] The essence of the US agenda in Kosovo was candidly revealed by President Clinton himself during the NATO intervention, 'If we're going to have a strong economic relationship that includes our ability to sell around the world, Europe has got to be a key... That's what this Kosovo thing was all about.'[412]

Unfortunately, Clinton's candid slip of the tongue about the 'Kosovo thing' was not given the press attention it deserved. In a single phrase, the American President had revealed that NATO intervention in Kosovo was not partially, but entirely, about permanently opening up European markets to a US-dominated regional privatisation programme.

One had to look elsewhere, however, for more detailed admissions. Over a month before the bombing campaign, Michael Lelyveld, chief correspondent for the Journal of Commerce, predicted the inevitability of a US military intervention in the Balkans due to strategic and economic interests in the Caspian region:

As important as the Caspian region is... there are temptations that may make US military involvement only a matter of time… Having said yes to Eastern Europe, the US and NATO may not be able to close the door on a region that is seen as a strategic prize. Eastern Europe has no resources to compare with the Caspian's oil.[413]

There were 'many reasons,' Lelyveld continued, why a prospective US military presence in the region 'appears inevitable, if policies continue on their current course'. They all revolve around the issue of protecting the planned pipeline routes to Caspian oil, 'Security for the planned Baku-Ceyhan oil pipeline and the trans-Caspian gas line may be impossible without some US role or credible support… Washington has also worked tirelessly to promote its interests in the region, bending pipelines away from Russia and Iran.'[414] Kosovo is particularly favourable for this project since its position, coupled with the NATO military presence, potentially allows the US to control the flow of Caspian oil to the European market. Lelyveld's prescient analysis was echoed here in London by the British Helsinki Human Rights Group, which observed that Anglo-American policy in Kosovo has been 'tied to economic considerations including the ambition to control oil and gas pipelines from Central Asia and the Caucasus region via the Black Sea.'[415]

Macedonia also plays a key role in regional Anglo-American interests. At the heart of traditional trade routes, north–south and east–west, Macedonia is the key to stability in the southern Balkans.[416] In particular, Macedonia is crucially located in relation to energy transit routes, and NATO intervention from the beginning was concerned to protect these routes allowing access to regional energy resources. As General Michael Jackson, then commander of NATO (KFOR) troops in the region, commented in 1999, 'Today, it is absolutely necessary to guarantee the stability of Macedonia and its entry into NATO. But we will certainly remain here a long time so that we can also guarantee the security of the energy corridors which traverse this country.'[417] Reference to the energy corridors, according to the *Guardian*, pertains to 'the Trans-Balkan pipeline', and will run 'from the Black sea port of Burgas to the Adriatic at Vlore, passing through Bulgaria, Macedonia and Albania. It is likely to become the main route to the west for the oil and gas now being extracted in central Asia. It will carry 750,000 barrels a day.'[418]

Britain is heavily involved. The Trans-Balkan pipeline project is controlled by an Anglo-American consortium known as AMBO, which largely excludes the participation of the competing European oil company Total-Fina-Elf. The signing of various 'Memoranda of understanding' (MOU) with the governments of Albania, Bulgaria and Macedonia lend the Anglo-American consortium exclusive rights over the pipeline project, '[The] MOU states that AMBO will be the only party allowed to build the planned Burgas-Vlore oil pipeline. More specifically, it gives AMBO the exclusive right to negotiate with investors in and creditors of the project. It also obligates [Bulgaria, Macedonia and Albania] not to disclose certain confidential information on the pipeline project.'[419] According to the US Trade and Development Agency, the project is necessary because it will 'provide a consistent source of crude oil to American refineries', 'provide American companies with a key role in developing the vital east-west corridor', and 'advance the privatisation aspirations of the US government in the region'.[420]

## 5.2 Central Asia

*Fuelling Terror: The New Anglo-American Drugs Trade*

Throughout the 1990s, British and American governments actively sponsored the emergence of al-Qaeda terrorist networks throughout the Balkans in order to assist al-Qaeda operations in Bosnia, Kosovo and Macedonia. This process granted the mujahideen a new ability to operate globally across multiple borders. They were able to move from the Balkans to other areas in Central Asia, as well as to Europe.

Indeed, in testimony before the House of Representatives Judiciary Committee, Frank Ciluffo of the Globalized Organised Crime Program, confirmed that 'the KLA raise part of their funds from the sale of narcotics. Albania and Kosovo lie at the heart of the "Balkan Route" that links the "Golden Crescent" of Afghanistan and Pakistan to the drug markets of Europe.' He confirmed that 80 per cent of heroin destined for Europe, worth about $400 billion a year, passes through this route.[421]

British forces have led US, European and local forces purportedly involved in the attempts to eradicate Afghanistan's burgeoning drug trade after the removal of the Taliban regime. 'But to British officials' embarrassment,' reported the *Sunday Telegraph*, 'the level of opium cultivation during their stint at the helm has reached an all-time high of nearly half a million acres.'[422] The Taliban had in fact banned the cultivation of opium poppies during its last year of rule in Afghanistan before post-9/11 American intervention. By 2003, under the reign of US-sponsored Northern Alliance warlords, Afghanistan 'retook its place as the world's leading producer of heroin.'[423] This is hardly the big surprise that American and British officials claim it to be. Indeed, they had carefully selected veteran drug-traffickers to return to power in the new post-Taliban Afghanistan.

According to former senior Indian intelligence official Bahukutumbi Raman, who has testified several times as an expert witness to the Committee on International Relations and Armed Service Committee of the US House of Representatives, Haji Ayub Afridi, was released from a Pakistani jail 'reportedly at the request of the CIA', returning to Afghanistan on behalf of US designs. Raman names another major figure in the drug-trade, Haji Abdul Qadeer, who 'was the CIA's choice as the Governor of the Nangarhar province [in 2001] in which Jalalabad is located.' During the 1980s Afghan war against Soviet occupation, Qadeer 'played an active role under the control of the CIA and the Directorate-General For External Security (DGES), the French external intelligence agency, in organising the heroin trail to the Soviet troops from the heroin refineries of Pakistan owned by Haji Ayub Afridi, the Pakistani narcotics baron, who was a prized operative of the CIA in the 1980s.' At that time, Qadeer and Afridi were 'close associates in running this drug trade with the blessings of the CIA.' In other words, the post-Taliban re-narcotisation of Afghanistan occurred under the auspices of the Anglo-American intervention.

Raman cites 'reliable sources in Afghanistan' for his claim that the Anglo-American 'war on drugs' in Afghanistan is a sham:

> The marked lack of success in the heroin front is due to the fact that the Central Intelligence Agency (CIA) of the USA, which encouraged these heroin barons during the Afghan war of the 1980s in order to spread heroin-addiction amongst the Soviet troops, is now using them in its search for bin Laden and other surviving leaders of

the Al Qaeda, by taking advantage of their local knowledge and contacts. These Pakistani heroin barons and their Afghan lieutenants are reported to have played an important role in facilitating the induction of Hamid Karzai into the Pashtun areas to counter the Taliban in November, 2001. It is alleged that in return for the services rendered by them, the USA has turned a blind eye to their heroin refineries and reserves.[424]

Although the post-9/11 drug-traffickers in Afghanistan are distinct from the Taliban and not directly affiliated to al-Qaeda, their drug-trafficking system remains inextricably linked to the 'Balkan Route' used by al-Qaeda affiliated narcotics networks which provide Afghan heroin to European drugs markets. Tacit Anglo-American consent to the massive escalation in opium poppy cultivation in the Afgho-Pakistani 'Golden Crescent' contributes directly to the criminal financing of al-Qaeda terrorist networks in the Balkans.

Al-Qaeda activity in the Balkans, then, is inextricably connected to criminal networks operating throughout Central Asia. Here, too, British and American policy systematically supported al-Qaeda not merely during the Cold War, but certainly all the way up to 9/11. In some cases, elements of this support continue today in significant ways. It is for this reason that no meaningful mention can be made of terror networks in the Balkans without acknowledging their connections to the wider Central Asian region.

### Azerbaijan: BP, al-Qaeda, and the Oil Coup

No sooner had the Soviet-backed Najibullah regime collapsed in April 1992, the Tajik and Pashtun factions, led by Ahmed

Shah Massoud and Gulbuddin Hekmatyar respectively, began competing for power. As Professor Peter Dale Scott reports, a number of Uzbek and Tajik mujahideen began launching cross-border raids against Tajikistan and later Uzbekistan. Even in the years up to 1992, the Tajik rebels were 'actively supported' by Massoud and Hekmatyar 'when both continued to receive aid and assistance from the United States,' through Saudi Arabia and Pakistani military intelligence services. These raids 'contributed materially to the destabilization of the Muslim Republics in the Soviet Union (and after 1992 of its successor, the Commonwealth of Independent States)'. As in Yugoslavia, the Americans wanted to see the break up of the formerly socialist multinational state.

In 1991, the first Bush administration had expressed support for a proposed oil pipeline from Azerbaijan, across the Caucasus, to Turkey. In the same year – during a Congressional ban on US arms sales to the country – three veteran US covert operations experts Richard Secord, Heinie Aderholt, and Ed Dearborn, all formerly active in Laos and later with Oliver North's Contra operations, landed in Baku through the auspices of a company called 'MEGA Oil.' The three were career US Air Force officers, but had in the past been seconded to the CIA. In Azerbaijan, they 'engaged in military training', and established an air transport network 'which soon was picking up hundreds of mujahedin mercenaries in Afghanistan.'[425] Hekmatyar – who was still in receipt of US aid and an ally of Osama bin Laden – was recruiting Afghan mujahideen 'to fight in Azerbaijan against Armenia and its Russian allies.'[426]

By 1993, at least two thousand Afghan mujahideen had arrived in Azerbaijan, and been armed with thousands of dollars of weapons.[427]

The Azeri mujahideen presence was funded and supported

by Osama bin Laden. According to the 9/11 Commission, bin Laden had established an NGO in Baku which became a launching base for terrorist operations across the region, including in Dagestan and Chechnya in Russia.[428]

The mercenaries played a crucial role in the eventual coup that toppled elected president Abulfaz Elchibey, and brought to power former KGB agent Heidar Aliyev in 1993. But it did so within the parameters of a primarily British strategy connected to the interests of British Petroleum. As Professor Scott observes, the mujahideen 'contributed to the ouster of Azerbaijan's elected president, Abulfaz Elchibey'. The Islamists 'helped supply [the] muscle' required to support a strong 'Azeri leader willing to stand up to the former Soviet Union.' Such a leader was necessary, given what was at stake:

> [A]n $8 billion oil contract with a consortium of western oil companies headed by BP [British Petroleum]. Part of the contract would be a pipeline which would, for the first time, not pass through Russian-controlled territory when exporting oil from the Caspian basin to Turkey. Thus the contract was bitterly opposed by Russia. [429]

The mujahideen operations had seriously weakened Elchibey's government. The tipping-point came in June 1993. Azerbaijan was already on the verge of civil war, and the government attempted unsuccessfully to disarm mutinous paramilitary forces led by former troop commander Suret Huseynov. Elchibey was discredited and forced to flee.

Months later, BP presided over the victorious western consortium of companies dominating the regional oil trade in a £5 billion deal described as the 'contract of the century', dutifully signed by Heidar Aliyev. In 1998, Prime Minister Blair gave

Aliyev 'red-carpet treatment when he visited London' in the words of the *Sunday Times*, 'to sign a friendship treaty and $13 billion (£9.5 billion) in contracts with BP and other British firms.'[430]

The other firms that participated in BP's oil consortium included America's UNOCAL, and Saudi firms Delta Oil and Nimir Petroleum. UNOCOL has a long history of involvement in Central Asia. The current President of Afghanistan is a former consultant to the company. A May 1999 report by the US Embassy in Saudi Arabia records that Delta Oil was created by 50 prominent Saudi investors in the early 1990s, the prime force behind which 'appears to be Mohammed Hussein Al-Amoudi, who is based in Ethiopia and oversees a vast network of companies involved in construction, mining, banking and oil.' Nimir Petroeum is controlled by Khalid bin Mahfouz, the head of Saudi Arabia's National Commercial Bank. The US Treasury Department has expressed concerns about the movement of funds from the bank to charities suspected of links to al-Qaeda. Khalid bin Mahfouz himself as well as the bank have denied any involvement in the financing of al-Qaeda and have publicly condemned terrorism in all its forms.

Britain's man in Azerbaijan, President Aliyev, went on to make good use of the same mujahideen mercenaries that aided his rise to power. No sooner had he taken the reins of government, in the summer of 1993 Aliyev hired over 1,000 Islamist fighters, flown in from Afghanistan, for the war against Armenians in Nagorno Karabakh. According to an associate of bin Laden, bin Laden himself led at least two of the battles.[431] Four years later, the radical Islamist groups affiliated to al-Qaeda in Azerbaijan pledged to support President Aliyev against the Armenians, on condition that they could use Azerbaijan as a base of operations without hindrance.[432] The

August 1998 bombings of US embassies in Kenya and Tanzania – which had been facilitated by operatives associated with bin Laden's London office – were reportedly perpetrated by al-Qaeda cells not only in East Africa, but also in Baku. The FBI found that about 60 of the more than 100 phone calls made from bin Laden's satellite phone were to al-Qaeda operatives in Baku, who in turn made calls to the East African cell.

Rather than taking action against Azerbaijan for harbouring terrorists, both the British and American governments applauded the allegedly fraudulent electoral victory of Heidar Aliyev's successor, President Ilham Aliyev, in October 2003 'which even the State Department has said was tarnished by fraud.' While US Secretary of Defence Rumsfeld congratulated the new President,[433] British Foreign Secretary Jack Straw met him in London in December 2004, about which he told the press that discussions had 'focused on energy issues', namely Azerbaijan's role as 'an important energy partner for the UK.' He noted that 'UK companies are playing a leading role in the development of Azerbaijan's oil and gas industry including the Baku Tbilisi Ceyhan pipeline project – which will provide a major export route for oil from the Caspian region to world markets.'[434]

## Anglo-American Jihad in the Caucasus

Al-Qaeda operatives in Azerbaijan routinely use the country as a base for launching operations throughout the region, moving their activities to nearby regions of Dagestan and even Chechnya. Strong British and American ties to Azerbaijan throughout this process raise questions about the wisdom and integrity of maintaining relations with a regime that appears to harbour al-Qaeda. Moreover, there is concrete evidence that the Anglo-American allies have deliberately used Azerbaijan as a principal vehicle to secure the covert sponsorship of al-Qaeda terrorist networks in Chechnya and elsewhere within the Caucasus.

Former Congressional terrorism expert Bodansky reported one year before 9/11 that the US government was actively involved in 'yet another anti-Russian jihad' in the summer of 2000:

> As if reliving the 'good ol' days' of Afghanistan of the 1980s, Washington is once again seeking to support and empower the most virulent anti-Western Islamist forces. The US crossed the line in mid-December 1999, when US officials participated in a formal meeting in Azerbaijan in which specific programs for the training and equipping of mujahedin from the Caucasus, Central/South Asia and the Arab world were discussed and agreed upon.

The Azerbaijan meeting precipitated 'Washington's tacit encouragement' of Muslim allies, 'mainly Turkey, Jordan and Saudi Arabia', and US private security companies 'to assist the Chechens and their Islamist allies to surge in the Spring of 2000 and sustain the ensuing jihad for a long time.' The US sees the Chechen jihad as an opportunity to 'deprive Russia of a viable pipeline route through spiraling violence and terrorism', thus facilitating the establishment of the Baku-Tbilisi-Ceyhan pipeline route across the region. 'US-assisted escalation and expansion of the war in Chechnya should deliver the desired debilitation of Russia.' Thus, the US was 'fanning the flames of the Islamist jihad in the Caucasus through covert assistance [and] tacit encouragement of allies to actively support the mujahedin.'[435]

Pakistan is another Muslim ally that has facilitated

al-Qaeda's hijacking of the Chechen resistance on behalf of American regional geostrategic ambitions. As early as 1994, Chechen warlord Shamil Basayev was spotted by Pakistani intelligence officers in Azerbaijan in command of about 1,500 Afghan mujaheddin fighting in Nagorno Karabakh. In April, the Pakistani Inter Services Intelligence 'arranged for Basayev and his trusted lieutenants to undergo intensive Islamic indoctrination and training in guerrilla warfare in the Khost province of Afghanistan' at a camp run by bin Laden's then associate Gulbuddin Hekmatyar. In July, Basayev graduated to a camp in Pakistan to get trained 'in advanced guerrilla tactics', where he met the highest ranking Pakistani military and intelligence officers, including 'Minister of Defence General Aftab Shahban Mirani, Minister of Interior General Naserullah Babar, and the head of the ISI branch in charge of supporting Islamic causes, General Javed Ashraf, (all now retired).' Pakistan's involvement in Chechnya therefore goes far beyond the mere supply of weapons and expertise – 'the ISI and its radical Islamic proxies are actually calling the shots in this war.'[436]

Britain's role in this is unambiguous. As the leading strategic ally of the United States, the UK has always maintained close ties to Azerbaijan – from which the plan to activate the regional covert sponsorship of al-Qaeda mujahideen was formally commenced in 1999 by the United States – and continues to provide extensive military and financial assistance to Pakistan, Turkey, Jordan and Saudi Arabia, all of whom are integrally involved, like the Azeris, in this programme. Anglo-American relations with Azerbaijan have focused on promoting the Baku-Tbilisi-Ceyhan (BTC) pipeline as a part of the East-West energy corridor, allowing landlocked Azerbaijan to deliver its oil to the west through Georgia and

Turkey. BP is the designated operator of the Azeri, Chirag, and Guneshli (ACG) oil field and the Shah Deniz natural gas field. Along with American oil companies, BP has invested billions of pounds in the BTC pipeline project. Azerbaijan has also provided an air corridor for Anglo-American military operations in Afghanistan and Iraq, joining coalition forces in the latter.[437]

## 5.3 North and West Africa

The role of a number of North and West African nations as theatres of operation for al-Qaeda networks involved in the London bombings was clear from a secret meeting between the intelligence chiefs of the United States, Britain, Algeria, Mali, Mauritania and Niger shortly after the 7 July attacks. At this meeting, which occurred in the capital of Mauritania, the London bombings were at the top of the agenda. In particular, British and American security chiefs were investigating the role of several senior al-Qaeda terrorists suspected of having masterminded the attacks from North and West Africa. Indeed, credible sources confirm that the military-grade explosives used in the bombings, although originating in the Balkans, was shipped to the UK via established al-Qaeda trafficking routes passing through North and West Africa.

Algeria in particular plays a prominent role in hosting terrorist networks implicated in operations within Europe. The Finsbury division led at various times by Qatada, Hamza and Bakri has strong material and ideological connections to Algerian Islamist militants. Both Qatada and Hamza in particular reportedly have had direct association with Algerian terrorist networks.

## The Algerian Connection

The Algerian terror crisis began in 1991 with the complicity of the western powers. In December, a legitimate opposition political party, the Islamic Salvation Front (FIS), won a landslide victory in Algeria's national democratic elections which all observers agreed had been free and fair. Before parliamentary seats could be taken, in January 1992 the Algerian military moved to cancel the election results, and rounded up tens of thousands of Algerian FIS voters into concentration camps in the the Sahara.[438] Forcing the FIS to disband, the army officially took power.[439]

The military coup was supported by the United States, Britain and France 'in an effort to prevent Islamic fundamentalists coming to power through the ballot box.'[440] A democratically elected Islamist government in Algeria was viewed by US policymakers as 'hostile to American hegemonic aspirations in the region' and therefore 'unacceptable in Washington.' The new military regime, in contrast, displayed welcome 'willingness to collaborate with American regional ambitions,' which included 'collaborating with Israel in establishing a Pax Americana in the Middle East and North Africa.'[441]

Not long after the coup, hundreds of civilians were mysteriously massacred by an unknown terrorist group shortly identified as a radical offshoot of the FIS calling itself the 'Armed Islamic Group' (GIA). So far the total civilian death toll from the GIA massacres in Algeria is nearly 150,000.[442] The GIA is also implicated in terrorist atrocities outside Algeria and has been 'linked to terrorist attacks in Europe.'[443] According to Stephen Cook, an expert on Algeria at the Brookings Institute, 'there are Algerian [terrorist] cells spread all over Europe, Canada, and the United States.'[444] According to the new Algerian military regime, the GIA was composed of bitter former FIS members retaliating against the junta by murdering civilians. In reality, the GIA had never cooperated with the FIS – the two groups were politically and ideologically distinct.[445]

In fact, the GIA's origins were in 'the house of the Muhajirin in 1989 in Peshawar.' From here, on the border of Pakistan and Afghanistan, 'the first hard core of 'Algerian Afghans' launched their terrorist campaign against Algeria.' The al-Qaeda veterans of the Afghan war against the Soviets, 'trained in the Afghan militias, returned to Algeria with the help of international networks, via Bosnia, Albania, Italy, France, Morocco or Sudan.'[446] According to Jane's *Defense Weekly*, in the late 1980s between 400 and 1,000 Algerians who trained as bin Laden's mujahideen in Afghanistan joined various armed groups in Algeria. By January 1993, most of these groups united under the banner of the GIA.[447] The latter forged close links to al-Qaeda 'in the early 1990s,' when the UK-based Abu Qatada 'was designated by bin Laden as the spiritual adviser for Algerian groups including the GIA.'[448]

The GIA had quickly developed an affiliated splinter sub-faction, the Salafist Group for Preaching and Combat (GSPC). Both groups, despite a degree of autonomy, operated in close association, and had 'developed ties with Al-Qaeda early on.' From 1997 to 1998, al-Qaeda achieved further 'large-scale penetration of Algerian groups.'[449]

In November 1997, Secretary-General of Amnesty International, Pierre Sane, observed that in that year alone 'Algerians have been slain in their thousands with unspeakable brutality… decapitated, mutilated and burned alive in their homes,' with torture, 'disappearances' and extrajudicial executions becoming 'part of the daily reality of Algerian life.' He also noted, importantly, that 'many of the massacres have been within shouting distance of army barracks, yet cries for help have gone unanswered, the killers allowed to walk away unscathed.' Surprisingly, the majority of the massacres had 'taken place in areas around the capital Algiers, in the most militarised region of the country.'

Over the years, credible evidence has emerged pointing inescapably to the conclusion that the al-Qaeda-affiliated GIA is a creature of the Algerian secret services. Dr Hamoue Amirouche, a former fellow of the Institut National d'Etudes de Strategie Globale (Algiers), noted at the beginning of 1998 that:

> [T]he military regime is perpetuating itself by fabricating and nourishing a mysterious monster to fight, but it is demonstrating daily its failure to perform its most elementary duty: providing security for the population. In October 1997, troubling reports suggested that a faction of the army, dubbed the 'land mafia,' might actually be responsible for some of last summer's massacres, which... continued even after the Islamic Salvation Army, the armed wing of the FIS, called for a truce, in effect as of October 1, 1997.[450]

The French magazine *Paris Match* reported that this 'land mafia' consisted of Algerian military-intelligence officers who wanted to cleanse premium lands of peasant occupants in anticipation of the privatisation of all the land in 1998.[451]

Other reports cast doubt on Algeria's role in the violence. Robert Fisk refers to 'evidence that the massacred villagers were themselves Islamists, and increasing proof that the Algerian security forces remained – at best – incapable of coming to their rescue.' This has 'cast grave doubt on the government's role in Algeria's dirty war.'[452] The *Sunday Times* similarly noted that the genocidal massacre of over 1,000 villagers in the first three weeks of 1998 occurred 'within 500 yards of an army base that did not deploy a single soldier, despite the fact that the gunfire and screams would have been clearly audible. Villagers said that some of the attackers wore army uniforms.'[453] Further questions were raised in light of the testimony of a 23-year-old Algerian army conscript who spoke of 'watching officers torture suspected "Islamist" prisoners by boring holes in their legs—and in one case, stomach—with electric drills in a dungeon called the "killing room".' Most pertinently, however, 'he claimed that he found a false beard amid the clothing of soldiers who had returned from a raid on a village where 28 civilians were later found beheaded; the soldier suspects that his comrades had dressed up as Muslim rebels to carry out the atrocity.'[454]

But these doubts were finally confirmed in multiple critical confessions from Algerian insiders defecting from positions in the regime's military intelligence agencies. In a detailed report, British journalists John Sweeney and Leonard Doyle interviewed ' "Yussuf-Joseph" a career secret agent in Algeria's securite militaire until he defected to Britain.' Joseph, who spent 14 years as an Algerian secret agent, told Sweeney and Doyle that, 'The bombs that outraged Paris in 1995 – blamed on Muslim fanatics – were the handiwork of the Algerian secret service. They were part of a propaganda war aimed at galvanising French public opinion against the Islamists.'

As for the massacres in Algeria, blamed on the GIA, they are in fact 'the work of secret police and army death squads.... The killing of many foreigners was organised by the secret police, not Islamic extremists.' In "Joseph's" own words:

I used to read all the secret telexes. I know that the GIA has been infiltrated and manipulated by the government. The GIA has been completely turned by the government... The death squads organise the massacres. If anyone inside the killing machine hesitates to torture or kill, they are automatically killed.... The FIS aren't doing the massacres.

Another former Algerian secret service officer known as Captain 'Haroune' –who was authenticated by the British Foreign Office – defected and sought asylum in London. He informed a British House of Commons All-Party Committee that his ex-colleagues carried out 'dirty jobs, including killing of journalists, officers and children.' The murder of seven Italians in Jenjen in July 1994 was, he disclosed, perpetrated by state military security death squads to blacken the name of 'Islamic fundamentalists.' Arrested suspects for the murder were merely scapegoats forced to sign confessions under torture.[455] In 1998, the former Algerian agent told Swiss TV that:

It's the army which is responsible for the massacres; it's the army which executes the massacres; not the regular soldiers, but a special unit under the orders of the generals. It should be remembered the lands are being privatized, and land is very important. One has first to chase people from their land so that land can be acquired cheaply. And then there must be a certain dose of terror in order to govern the Algerian people and remain in power.[456]

In November 1997, a serving officer with the Algerian military known as 'Hakim' contacted the French newspaper *Le Monde* to express the feelings of a group of officers who were sickened by their work. In an interview with John Sweeney, Hakim corroborated the separate testimonials of 'Joseph', confirming that the 'two bombs that killed eight and wounded 143 in Paris in 1995 were planted at the instigation of the Algerian junta.' In his own words, Hakim stated, 'We have become assassins, working for a caste of crooks who infest the military. They want everything: oil, control of imports, property.'

The objective of the operation had been to 'win over public opinion in discrediting the Islamists.' He also disclosed that the GIA's terrorist leader Djamel Zitouni, although presented as 'public enemy number one' was in fact an agent of the Algerian regime. 'He was recruited in 1991 in an internment camp in the south of Algeria, where thousands of Islamists had been imprisoned.' According to Hakim, the junta had used Djamel to win control over the GIA in 1994, but he was 'liquidated' when for reasons unknown 'he did not respect the contract.' Hakim's courageous revelations soon led to his own liquidation. *The Observer* reports that:

> Hakim was tracked down by the Algerian secret police shortly after he contacted *Le Monde*. They took away his diplomatic passport and sent him to the south – to the Sahara. His family were placed under close watch and were very frightened. (At no time have Hakim's family been in touch with *The Observer*.) Then they heard he had been killed in a helicopter accident.[457]

The orchestration of the 1995 Paris metro bombings by Algerian security services using militant Islamists on the ground is no longer disputable. The whole process has been documented in the most comprehensive studies including that of the respected French journalists Lounis Aggoun and Jean-

Baptiste Rivoire, in their *France-Algeria: Crimes and Lies of the State*.[458] The defector Joseph has alleged that 'at least' two of the bombs were planted by the Algerians working for the state.

The detailed testimony of former Algerian Army Special Forces officer, Second Lieutenant Habib Souaidia, further confirms the GIA's function as an instrument of Algerian intelligence. In his landmark book, *The Dirty War*, Souaidia exposes how the GIA has been used to liquidate opposition to the regime. One example of his first-hand knowledge of army atrocities against civilians is particularly pertinent and is cited here in detail:

It happened one night in March, 1993. After I finished my shift I was summoned to my commanding officer, Major Daoud. He ordered me to take my people to guard a truck on its way to one of the villages. I went outside and I saw the truck. I peeked inside and saw the silhouettes of dozens of commando fighters from one of the special units. They were carrying knives and grenades. I was told that they were on their way to a 'special mission.'

I drove behind the truck until it stopped in the village of Dawar Azatariya where the inhabitants were suspected of supporting the FIS movement. I was asked to remain with my men outside the village. Two hours later the truck came back. One of the officers took a blood-stained knife that he held near his throat, making a sweeping side to side motion. I didn't need any additional signs to understand what had happened in the village. Two days later there were headlines in the Algerian press: 'Islamic attack in Dawar Azatariya. Dozens killed in the massacre.' I couldn't believe my eyes. I felt that I had been an accomplice to a terrible crime… I wanted to write about the dirty war that was directed against innocent civilians, whose only crime was that they were well-disposed toward Islam. This war is still going on. Thus far more than 150,000 people have been killed, and those responsible for this crime are the generals who head the army. They are fighting to defend their rule and the enormous amount of property they have accumulated…. France has given me political asylum, but this cannot prevent me from declaring that it has abetted the murderous generals to protect its interests.[459]

Souaidia has further noted that Algerian government penetration of domestic Muslim terrorist networks was extremely thorough. Not merely the GIA, but numerous affiliated and autonomous Islamist militant factions were sponsored and manipulated at their inception. 'Several armed islamist groups… were created in the weeks that followed the stopping of the electoral process [in 1992],' he confirms. These groups were in addition to already extant radical groups such as Takfir wal-Hijra. Although 'these groups were autonomous compared to the FIS… it was already being said at the time that they had been infiltrated or manipulated by the Securite Militaire (SM).'[460]

Another senior former Algerian intelligence officer has described the Algerian junta's cooptation of Algerian Islamist networks. Col. Mohammed Samraoui – a member of the post-coup Algerian junta, deputy director of Algerian counter-intelligence (DRS), and later top counter-intelligence officer in Europe based at the Algerian Embassy in Bonn – notes that all 'the terror groups in the underground' including the GIA, the GSPC, and others, 'were bred and manipulated by the secret service of Algeria.' In July 1991, the secret services established the first artificial Islamist terror base 50 kilometres from Algiers. After their arrest, Islamists from opposition groups were 'turned' and used to run operations by the secret services. These operations were behind the endless series of GIA terror attacks in Algeria. Indeed, all key GIA emirs were operatives of the secret services.[461] In spring 1995, one French-based Algerian secret agent, Ali Touchent, was actively infiltrating Islamist networks as an agent provocateur, inciting disaffected men of North African background to commit terrorist attacks in France. Although Touchent was publicly identified by Algerian authorities as 'the European ringleader of the GIA and by French investigators as the key organiser' of the 1995 Paris attacks, he miraculously evaded capture, instead returning to Algeria to settle 'in a secure police quarter of Algiers.' In fact, Samraoui confirms that, 'French intelligence knew that Ali Touchent was a DRS operative charged with infiltrating pro-Islamist cells in foreign countries.' Despite that, he was protected.[462]

Algerian terror networks connected to the GIA and GSPC – which in turn is interlinked with al-Qaeda – are in fact a product of the Algerian intelligence agencies which are manipulated and coopted in the service of elite interests. The precise structure of this relationship is unclear. What is certain, however, is that while on a personnel-level the GIA and GSPC interpenetrate with al-Qaeda, on an organisational level the Islamist networks are manipulated by Algerian intelligence services which, both interpenetrate the groups and manipulate them through cooptation of key group members.

The most disturbing implications of these reports is that, despite their avid denials, Western governments and intelligence agencies are fully cognisant – if not deeply complicit – in the

Algerian state's manipulation of the Algerian terror networks. For example, after the publication of the confessions of Algerian defector 'Joseph' in several European newspapers:

> The Algerian ambassador to Italy was called in 'for consultations.' The next day, the Italian ambassador to Algeria was, in his turn, called in, 'for consultations.' The office of the Italian Prime Minister quoted British intelligence sources dismissing Joseph's story. The office of the French Interior Ministry dismissed the story. The Algerian ambassador to London, His Excellency Ahmed Benyamina, dismissed the story as 'fanciful.' All these dismissals had one thing in common: they were delivered at one remove.[463]

The coordinated chorus of denial being sung by the West was a collective act of conscious deception. According to lawyer and Algeria expert Richard McLeod, 'When France withdrew from Algeria, it retained very close links with an elite group within Algerian society, namely the generals.'[464] An account by the *Observer* about the French response to evidence of the Algerian role in the 1995 Paris bombings is particularly instructive:

> After the [summer 1995 Paris] bombings, the then French Interior Minister, Jean-Louis Debre, was asked at an off-the-record lunch whether it was possible the Algerian secret police had been behind the bombings. He said: 'The Algerian securite militaire would like *us* to go up the wrong trail so that *we* [i.e. the French] can eliminate people who annoy them [the Algerian secret services].'[465]

The French government, has maintained close military intelligence ties with the Algerian state. Friendly relations continue despite the deep ambiguity that surrounds the struggle between the Algerian state and Islamists.

Indeed, Western intelligence agencies know far more about the crisis then they have publicly conceded. A remarkable *Guardian* report recorded the collapse of a three-year terrorist case 'when an MI5 informant refused to appear in court after evidence which senior ministers tried to suppress revealed that Algerian government forces were involved in atrocities against innocent civilians.' The report refers to 'secret documents showing British intelligence believed the Algerian government was involved in atrocities, contradicting the view the government was claiming in public'.

The Foreign Office documents 'were produced on the orders of the trial judge' 18 months late, and disproved 'the government's publicly-stated view... that there was 'no credible, substantive evidence to confirm' allegations implicating Algerian government forces in atrocities.' The documents showed that according to Whitehall's Joint Intelligence Committee, 'There is no firm evidence to rule out government manipulation or involvement in terrorist violence'. One document stated, 'Sources had privately said some of the killings of civilians were the responsibility of the Algerian security services'. A January 1997 document concludes, '[Algerian] military security would have... no scruples about killing innocent people.... My instincts remain that parts of the Algerian government would stop at nothing.' Multiple documents 'referred to the 'manipulation' of the GIA being used as a cover to carry out their own operations'. A US intelligence report confirmed that 'there was no evidence to link 1995 Paris bombings to Algerian militants'. On the contrary, 'one killing at the time could have been ordered by the Algerian government'. Crucially, a Whitehall document cites the danger to British government interests if this information becomes public – 'if revealed,' it warns, it 'could open us to detailed questioning by NGOs and journalists.' [466]

Why would the British government fear public scrutiny of its Algerian policy? Perhaps a glimpse of an answer is provided by two French reports on the Algerian intelligence-backed GIA masterminds of the 1995 Paris bombings. According to the French daily *Le Figaro*, 'The track of Boualem Bensaid, GIA leader in Paris, leads to Great Britain. The British capital has served as logistical and financial base for the terrorists.'[467] *Le Parisien* further reported that one of the Algerian-backed organisers of the 1995 Paris attacks was Abou Farres*, a former leader of the Afghan mujahideen. Although he was already wanted for involvement in the Algiers Airport bombing, Farres was granted a residence visa in London in 1992, from where he recruited impoverished Muslim youngsters from Paris suburbs and sent them to al-Qaeda training camps in Afghanistan.[468]

In the year 2000, the *Sunday Times* reported that the British government sold through the government of Qatar 'almost £5m in military equipment to the Algerian army, despite a record of atrocities committed by its soldiers that contravenes the ethical foreign policy espoused by Robin Cook, the foreign secretary.' The purchase was negotiated by BAe Systems, formerly British Aerospace, with the Qatar armed forces. The purchase order formally sent to BAe stated that Qatar was 'to gift, free of charge, all of the items (as per the attached list) to the armed services of the state of Algeria.' The order went on to offer 'an end-user certificate for Algeria, a document that details where the arms will end up. Last week BAe confirmed

* Abou Farres is a pseudonym. The man's real identity is unknown.

the May 31 order, which followed extensive consultations, and said it expected government approval.' The order, worth £4.6 million, included, '20 Land Rover Defender 110 rapid deployment vehicles with hot climate specifications (at a total cost of £596,666); 50 Land Rover Defender 110 pickup trucks with hot climate specifications (£618,333), down to 500 Pilkington Optronics Kite night vision sights (£1.75m).'[469] Reuters subsequently confirmed the sale on July 19, 2000.[470] Such sales are routine. Foreign Office figures show that in 2000, Britain sold goods worth a total of £2 million directly to Algeria. In 1999, Britain had sold goods worth £5.5 million directly.[471]

The US government is also deeply connected. On 8 November 2002, US Undersecretary of State for Political Affairs Marc Grossman went to Algiers and described joint 'US-Algerian goals' as, 'simultaneous work in anti-terrorism... and economic cooperation.'[472] According to US historian James Ciment at the City College of New York, author of *Algeria: The Fundamentalist Challenge*, there is reason to suspect 'secret connections between the United States and the Islamists' in Algeria:

> A 1996 Rand study commissioned by the US Army, which was recently made public, added fuel to the fire. The report downplayed GIA atrocities and advised Washington to work with the Islamists, arguing that they were inevitably going to play a major role in Algerian affairs. It also noted that the Islamists were not necessarily enemies of the United States, since they have openly called for US investment to replace that of the hated French. In the hothouse atmosphere of Algerian politics, that sort of analysis constitutes tacit, if not direct, support.[473]

The US Army-Rand report is disquieting evidence of the pro-GIA sentiments of the US military policy establishment. Former ABC News correspondent John Cooley, reports the presence of '500 to 600 American engineers and technicians living and working behind barbed wire' in a collection of 'protected gas and oil enclaves in Algeria.' US commercial involvement 'began in earnest… in 1991.' At the end of that year, the regime 'opened the energy sector on liberal terms to foreign investors and operators.' The main US firms include 'Arco, Exxon, Oryx, Anadarko, Mobil and Sun Oil.'[474] According to European intelligence sources, CIA meetings with Algerian Islamist leaders from 1993 to 1995 are responsible for the lack of terrorist attacks on US oil and agribusiness installations in Algeria.[475]

But according to former Algerian secret service operative 'Joseph,' Western culpability in the subversion of the GIA and the consequent domestic and international terror threat extends far wider than London and Washington:

> Algerian intelligence agents routinely bribe European police, journalists and MPs. Joseph said he paid one French MP, who cannot be named for legal reasons, more than 500,000 francs (about $90,000) in bribes… Joseph said: 'I personally delivered a suitcase containing 500,000 francs to one French MP with strong links to the French intelligence services.'

'All the intelligence services in Europe know the government is doing it,' Joseph continues, 'but they are keeping quiet because they want to protect their supplies of oil.'[476] The extent of this secret network of corruption extending throughout Europe is unknown. But as the *Observer* notes, Algeria 'squats on huge oil and gas deposits worth billions. It supplies the gas that warms Madrid and Rome. It has a 31.8 billion pounds contract with British Petroleum. No Western government wants to make trouble with the state of Algeria. Its wealth buys silence, buys complicity.'[477] Indeed, Algeria has the fifth largest reserves of natural gas in the world, and is the second largest gas exporter, with 130 trillion proven natural gas reserves. It ranks fourteenth for oil reserves, with official estimates at 9.2 billion barrels. Approximately 90 per cent of Algeria's crude oil exports go to western Europe, including Britain, France, Italy, Germany, the Netherlands, and Spain. Algeria's major trading partners are Italy, France, the United States, Germany, and Spain.[478]

In other words, the Algerian Islamist terror network under the wing of the GIA and GSPC is a major player in the North African branch of al-Qaeda, implicated in not merely domestic massacres but international terrorist attacks, particularly in Europe. The GIA/GSPC-al-Qaeda network, however, is a product and tool of the Algerian military intelligence services. Britain, France and the United States are fully cognisant of this, yet maintain a close alliance with the Algerian generals, providing the junta-GIA/GSPC–al-Qaeda nexus with extensive financial and military support, and even intelligence and counter-terrorist coordination. Yet the same powers publicly lament the problem of terrorism emanating from the same North African nexus implicated in the London bombings, and actively propagate a false narrative of the Algerian conflict.

## The GSPC: Instrument of Covert Destabilisation

In the post-9/11 period, the al-Qaeda affiliated GIA sub-faction – the GSPC (Salafist Group for Preaching and Combat)

– has gained increasing prominence not only within Algeria itself, but within the wider North and West African region. Al-Qaeda-affiliated GSPC mujahideen have been active in Chad, Niger, Nigeria, Mali and Mauritania since 2003. As Agence France-Presse reported, masterminds of the Madrid attacks – who were also involved in the planning for the 7 July attacks in London – operated from a 'rear base' of al-Qaeda in North/West Africa, where Morocco borders Mali, Mauritania and Algeria. The GSPC reportedly plays a prominent role in this base.[479] By 2006, the group was actively involved in recruitment and training programmes dispersing fighters to Syria, Iraq, Morocco, Algeria and Nigeria for potential terrorist operations.[480]

The GSPC rose to particular prominence in separate incidents in February and March 2003, when 32 European tourists were taken hostage in southern Algeria. The hostages were taken to northern Mali, where they were held for six months until being released in Gao, Mali. The perpetrators fled with relative ease through Niger to Chad, where GSPC leader Ammar Saifi (also known as Abderazzak El Para) was captured by a Chadian rebel group and eventually extradited back to Algeria.[481]

Apart from the testimonials of multiple Algerian intelligence defectors to the effect that all Algerian Islamist terror networks including the GSPC have been penetrated by Algerian security services, French journalists have uncovered specific evidence of Algerian intelligence subversion of the GSPC. El Para has been identified on the GSPC website since 2004 as a key leader of the terrorist organisation. He was reportedly chief of personal security for Algerian Defence Minister Gen. Khaled Nezzar from 1990 to 1993. In 1992, he began to mingle among Algerian Islamist terror networks, eventually becoming the

GSPC's number two leader. According to the French magazine *Paris Match*, El Para was 'in charge of establishing al-Qaida in the Sahara', that is, throughout north-west Africa. GSPC units under El Para's leadership originating in northern Algeria 'made forays into the Sahara and were then pushed by Algerian security forces into the southern desert, and from there into northern Mali.'[482] Salima Mellah and Jean-Baptiste Rivoire writing in *Le Monde Diplomatique* confirmed that according to several hostages in the Spring 2003 incidents, 'their kidnappers regularly communicated by radio and that Algerian army helicopters quickly appeared over the places in which they were being held, even though they were moved frequently. If El Para had been spotted by the army, why wasn't he put out of action?' When the first group of hostages was freed by an Algerian army operation on 12 May 2003, the suspicious circumstances were plain to see. *Le Monde* reported:

> According to the official account, the military carried out a 'brief attack during which precautions were taken to protect the lives of the hostages'. On closer examination, however, the operation looks like a put-up job. Instead of using the hostages as human shields, El Para's men ordered them to take cover in caves. When they emerged after the attack, the tourists were surprised to see no dead or wounded, nor any sign of bloodshed, although the military were reported to have killed four kidnappers.

One of the hostages openly suspects that the entire episode was orchestrated by Algerian military-intelligence, commenting that:

> The Salafists were well aware of what was about to

237

happen. They marched us 20km through the desert to a predetermined location, a geographically suitable venue for our 'liberation'. It occurred to me much later that the whole thing might have been staged by the Algerian military... I still wonder whether there are links between the Salafists and the army.

Indeed, *Le Monde* continues to note that although the GSPC kidnappers 'were surrounded by government troops and had no motor vehicles', some of them 'miraculously escaped, only to reappear soon after with the second group of hostages, over 1,000km away.' That group of hostages was 'freed in Mali on 18 August, in even stranger circumstances, after Germany, Austria and Switzerland had reportedly paid a ransom of $5m'. Subsequently, it became increasingly clear that El Para, 'the ex-army officer whose terrorist operations were so helpful to the Algerian regime in its quest for international support *was still secretly in the pay of his former employers* [my emphasis].' *Le Monde* goes on to describe Algeria's inexplicable reluctance to capture and arrest El Para despite repeated opportunities to do so. When he was finally 'back in the hands of the DRS' by November 2004 under the pressure of bad publicity, the Algerian junta played down his terrorist significance within the GSPC. The regime moved swiftly to rehabilitate his public image, encouraging him to express support of 'President Abdelaziz Bouteflika's plan for a general amnesty covering both terrorists and military leaders implicated in crimes against humanity during the "dirty war".'[483] In the meantime, however, the actual status of El Para is unclear – with some reports stating that he has been freed, and others that he is in the custody of Algerian security services.

There is little doubt then that GSPC leader El Para, who has been integrally involved in escalating al-Qaeda activity in north-west Africa, had continued to work on behalf of Algerian military-intelligence. In late June 2005, he was sentenced by a court in Algiers in absentia to life inprisonment under conviction of setting up a terrorist group. Algerian authorities refused to allow his participation in the trial proceedings, claiming that he remained in custody at a secret location to prevent the disclosure of 'national security-sensitive information he is believed to hold.' What conceivable information could El Para, a former Algerian army paratrooper, have that Algerian security services consider 'sensitive'? Even the presiding judge who convicted him observed, 'For us there are no indications that he is under arrest.' More likely, El Para was being protected – not for his own sake, but for the sake of keeping his dubious Algerian intelligence connections under wraps from legal and public scrutiny.[484]

Indeed, according to renowned social anthropologist Jeremy Keenan – Senior Research Fellow and Director of Sahara Studies at the University of East Anglia – the unresolved 'questions about intelligence extend to the actions and very existence of at-large Salafist second-in-command Abderrazek Lamari, alias "El Para,"' who masterminded the 2003 hostage kidnapping. Keenan notes that 'contradictory Algerian intelligence reports and eyewitness testimonies suggest collusion between agents of Algeria's military intelligence services and the Salafist Group.' Not surprisingly, the State Department has 'declined to comment on the matter.' The United States needs the GSPC terrorist threat to justify the extension of US hegemony to north-west Africa. 'Without the GSPC,' observes Keenan, 'the US has no legitimacy for its presence in the region.'[485]

In several extraordinary analyses published in the peer-reviewed academic journal *Review of African Political Economy*, Keenan documents 'an increasing amount of evidence to suggest that the alleged spread of terrorist activities across much of the Sahelian Sahara, has indeed been an elaborate deception on the part of US and Algerian military intelligence services.' He discusses extensive evidence that the 2003 El Para 'hostage-taking was initiated and orchestrated by elements within the Algerian military establishment', an operation most likely 'condoned by the US.' Other suggestive evidence indicates that 'El Para was "turned" by the Algerian security forces in January 2003.' He had earlier been 'held responsible for an attack on an Algerian army convoy at Teniet El-Abed in the Aures mountains on 4 January 2003,' purportedly carried out by the GSPC. El Para was reportedly 'captured on the mountain and "turned". His first mission for his new masters was... to organise the abduction of the German-speaking tourists.' Keenan thus finds that the expansion of the GSPC presence in the Sahara under El Para was jointly facilitated by US and Algerian security services.[486]

Thus, for example, in oil-rich Niger, US military involvement is supposed to be containing 'the al Qaeda-linked Salafist Group for Preaching and Combat (GSPC), Algeria's last powerful rebel force, which it fears is recruiting and regrouping further south after being largely chased from its homeland.' US Major Sulaoua Barmou Moussa told Reuters, '[E]xperience has shown us that if we do not act in time, various armed groups could be called into working with elements of the GSPC.'[487]

*Frontline of the War: Securing Anglo-American Supply*

As has been the case in the Balkans, it is no coincidence in this context that this al-Qaeda/GSPC activity has played directly into the hands of both Algerian and American mutual interests in the north-west African region. As informed observers in Algeria previously noted, 'the sole justification for an American presence in the region is the GSPC. If El Para is killed and officially identified, or is captured and handed over to a third country, many things may have to be reassessed.'[488] Al-Qaeda/GSPC activity in north-west Africa has focused on oil-rich nations, particularly the Niger Delta and Nigeria, the latter increasingly becoming a likely flashpoint for terrorist operations. Mohammed Naeem Noor Khan, the al-Qaeda computer engineer arrested in Pakistan in 2004 who provided extensive information on al-Qaeda terrorist planning for multiple plots including several targets in London (the London Tube network being a major target), reportedly told investigators that al-Qaeda uses websites and email addresses in Nigeria.[489] More than a year earlier in February 2003, Osama bin Laden himself in a taped message to his followers singled out Nigeria as a country ripe for al-Qaeda 'liberation' operations against American 'enslavement'.[490]

Al-Qaeda/GSPC destabilisation efforts in the region on behalf of Algerian military-intelligence, apparently at least tacitly supported by the United States, have been used to justify regional American expansionism. New US-sponsored joint military programmes with north-west African states facing increasing internal turmoil and instability fostered by Algeria's al-Qaeda networks have been launched consolidating American control over lucrative north-west African oil and gas reserves.

US and Algerian regional operations were directly involved in the construction of a 'terror zone' across southern Algeria, northern Nigeria, Mauritania, Northern Mali, Northern Niger and Chad. In July 2003, under US auspices, Algeria, Chad,

Niger and Nigeria 'signed a cooperation agreement on counter-terrorism that effectively joined the two oil-rich sides of the Sahara together in a complex of security arrangements whose architecture is American.'[491]

The agreement was quickly followed up with what has become the principal vehicle of American involvement, the Pan-Sahel Initiative, a $7.75 million military programme providing training and equipment to Algeria, Chad, Niger, Mali and Mauritania to 'improve their border security and deny the use of their sovereign territory to terrorists and criminals.'[492] One thousand US Special forces, marines and contractors were sent to these countries in January 2004 to supply extensive military counter-terrorist assistance and coordination. The US is expanding the programme to include Nigeria, Morocco and Tunisia, with a new budget of $500 million for the period until 2011, now with a new name, the 'Trans-Sahara Counter-Terrorism Initiative'.[493] The US has a contingent of 2,000 troops stationed at a US military base in Djibouti, described as being positioned on the frontline in the 'war on terror', and is actively coordinating the establishment of a further dozen bases across the region. Another major US military base operates from Tamanrasset in the south of Algeria, with 400 Special Forces. Algeria is viewed as pivotal to US plans for future military deployment in the region.[494]

A major consideration behind the consolidation of regional US military hegemony is access to Africa's strategic raw materials on which the US increasingly depends, namely 'manganese (for steel production), cobalt and chrome vital for alloys (particularly in aeronautics), vanadium, gold, antimony, fluorspar and germanium – and for industrial diamonds.' However, access to West African oil reserves remains the pre-eminent factor. Experts agree that by 2015,

'Africa will become the US's second-most important supplier of oil, and possibly natural gas, after the Middle East.' In particular, the US is exploring two strategic routes: in the west, the Chad-Cameroon pipeline and, in the east, the Higleig-Port Sudan pipeline.[495] Northwest African oil reserves currently meet 17 per cent of US needs. An Algerian company, Sonatrach, plays a major role in US oil exploration as the largest company in Africa, with an estimated turnover of $32 billion in 2004.[496]

According to the US National Intelligence Council, supplies of West African oil to the United States will rise to 25 per cent of US imports by 2015. In May 2001, the Bush administration's national energy policy released in May 2001 described West Africa as 'one of the fastest growing sources of oil and gas for the American market.'[497] Other officials have been even more candid, such as Acting Assistant Secretary of State for African Affairs Charles Snyder, who told a conference in Washington DC in April 2003 that, '... thanks to the oil deposits we're finding every day in and near Africa, I can say with a straight face 30 per cent of our oil will come from there, and I promise you it is a strategic interest.'[498] As of 2005, US and British energy companies (including BP-Amoco) had already invested an estimated $45 billion into extracting African oil reserves, with plans to invest a further $50 billion.[499]

Another major joint Anglo-American enterprise is the West African Gas Pipeline, one of the region's largest trans-boundary investments projected to cost $617 million, and slated to transport gas from Nigeria through Benin and Togo to Ghana. Apart from having the blessings of the World Bank, the two principal companies involved are the UK's Shell and the USA's Chevron.[500]

*Terrorists are Forever: Diamonds are for Keeps*

American and British duplicity prevails over another dimension of al-Qaeda's long-term activities in West Africa: the illicit diamond trade. Almost since its inception, al-Qaeda sought to exploit gemstones in West Africa, East Africa and Europe. Since the late 1990s, this activity began to focus on diamond smuggling as a way of both financing terrorist operations and assisting the movement of terrorist finances outside formal financial sectors. The first phase of al-Qaeda's diamond trading operations began in 1996 when bin Laden lived in the Sudan. It was boosted after the 1998 US embassy bombings in Africa when the Clinton administration froze $240 million in Taliban and bin Laden assets. In late 2000, a third phase began with the arrival of senior al-Qaeda leaders in Liberia, then under the Presidency of Charles Taylor. Al-Qaeda established a monopoly arrangement to purchase diamonds through Taylor with the Revolutionary United Front (RUF) in Sierra Leone, in order to transfer value from other assets. The fourth phase began around January 2001, when al-Qaeda diamond purchases escalated rapidly until just before 9/11. Indeed, in the 14 months prior to 9/11, Belgian police traced $20 million worth of Sierra Leone diamonds via the RUF bought up by al-Qaeda in what constituted 'a rapid, large-scale value transfer operation that allowed the terrorist group to move money out of traceable financial structures into untraceable commodities.'[501]

The diamonds, mined by RUF rebels, were taken by senior RUF commanders to Monrovia, Liberia, according to US and European intelligence sources, where they would be exchanged for cash at a safe house protected by the Liberian government. The diamond dealers were selected by Ibrahim Bah, the RUF's principal diamond dealer, who fought alongside the mujahideen in Afghanistan against Soviet forces. The then-Liberian President Charles Taylor would receive a commission on each transaction. In September 1998, Bah, on behalf of Taylor, arranged for senior bin Laden adviser and al-Qaeda terrorist planner Abdullah Ahmed to visit Monrovia, to arrange a permanent diamond purchasing agreement. Weeks later, two other senior al-Qaeda operatives met with Bah. Like Abdullah Ahmed, they – Ahmed Khalfan Ghailani and Fazul Abdullah Mohammed – are on the FBI's Most Wanted Terrorist list for involvement in the 1998 US embassy bombings, which were planned and orchestrated through bin Laden's London office, affiliates of which remain at large in the UK.[502]

A confidential dossier compiled by war crimes prosecutors from the UN Special Court for Sierra Leone, led by American David Crane, cites credible eyewitness testimony proving that as many as six senior al-Qaeda operatives were laundering millions of dollars of funds through Sierra Leone diamonds, by dealing directly with the then-Liberian President Taylor, 'It is clear that al-Qaeda has been in West Africa since September 1998 and maintained a continuous presence in the area through 2002.' Witnesses confirmed that Taylor personally gave the operatives entree to 'the shady West African world of guns, cash and diamonds.'[503]

The UN findings have been corroborated by the results of an aggressive year-long European law enforcement investigation into al-Qaeda financing, which concluded in 2002 that two West African governments – Taylor's Liberia and Burkino Faso – had hosted al-Qaeda operatives who oversaw the massive illicit diamond trading. For his services, Taylor had received $1 million. But senior European intelligence sources involved in the investigation 'said they have been baffled by the lack of

US interest, particularly by the CIA, in their recent findings. The CIA, which in the past has downplayed reports of al Qaeda's diamond connections, declined to comment.'[504]

This was not the first time the CIA had inexplicably ignored crucial information that could be used to take decisive action to track and shut down a significant dimension of the financial architecture of international terrorism. *Washington Post* journalist Douglas Farah relates that:

> The first time the CIA had ignored compelling information that would have shed light on the diamond trade between Liberia's Charles Taylor and those close to al Qaeda took place in February 2001. Allie Derwish [...] a Lebanese-American diamond dealer who had initiated the diamond deals that eventually led to al Qaeda, contacted the US embassy in Belgium. After waiting several days for a response, Derwish finally won a meeting with a political officer from the US embassy to whom he described the safe house in Liberia, diamonds for weapons deals and the roles of key players including Ibrahim Bah, whose satellite phone number he provided.[505]

There is no suggestion that Mr Derwish acted improperly. His indirect involvement with al-Qaeda was doubtless inadvertent and he was keen to cooperate. Yet, according to Farah, he 'was told to stop calling the US embassy.' In other words, the principal US intelligence and law enforcement agencies, despite receiving credible intelligence on Taylor's harbouring of al-Qaeda operatives in connection with extensive terrorist financing operations through the West African diamond trade, refused to act. They did not want to shut down this financing operation. Farah notes another missed opportunity when 'in the days immediately preceding the 9/11 al Qaeda strike against the US', a civilian known as Cindor Reeves:

> [C]alled the US embassy in Sierra Leone to warn of an impending attack against American interests...
>
> At a meeting with a political officer from the US embassy on September 10, Reeves recounted how he had been with Ibrahim Bah a few days previously when Bah received a phone call from an Arabic speaker. Hanging up the phone, Bah told Reeves to wait and see what would happen to the United States, which thought it was the world's policeman, in the next few days. 'The US,' asserts Farah, 'won't comment on that meeting.'[506]

The information might have contributed to the decision by senior Pentagon officials on 10 September 2001 to cancel their travel plans to New York for the next day, 9/11. Officials took measures to protect themselves, but not the general public.[507]

Despite the US government's avid denials, there is other compelling reason to believe that the government was intimately aware of Taylor's al-Qaeda financing activities. Shortly after 9/11, the US Defence Department 'approved a special forces raid to capture Al Qaeda leaders under Taylor's protection in 2001, but called it off and never reactivated the plan'. In the meantime, 'senior leaders of Al Qaeda continued to receive Taylor's protection.' Subsequent reports alleged that the plan was cancelled because the operatives could not be firmly identified; but this does not explain the ongoing failure to relaunch the plan, nor does it explain why the US government continues to officially deny the al-Qaeda diamond connection despite the fact that the Defence Department clearly had specific intelligence on the matter prompting a plan of action (that was aborted from on high). Additionally, after Taylor was deposed from the Liberian Presidency in 2003 under pressure from rebel and opposition factions, he was saved by the US government which brokered a deal with Nigeria permitting him to live there in exile. Despite being under 'increasing pressure to help persuade Nigeria to turn Taylor over to the UN tribunal in Sierra Leone, which has indicted him in connection with atrocities in various West African nations', the US government has consistently refused. What can explain this continued tacit protection of Taylor? According to a number of UN officials, US policy is related to the fact that the US 'used Taylor as a CIA informant and backed his Revolutionary United Front in the mid-1990s.'[508]

This is corroborated by Joseph Melrose, former US Ambassador to Sierra Leone until September 2001, who reports, 'I've heard that he was on the US payroll. It's very possible some of these other characters [in the Taylor regime] have been, too.' Melrose also noted the reluctance to admit the al-Qaeda/Taylor diamond connection, 'For some reason our intelligence people have been very anxious to disprove this as happening, something that can't be disproven.' Indeed, Taylor himself bragged that 'he worked for the CIA for years.'[509] Investigations by the London-based NGO Global Witness confirm that both the CIA and FBI for 'long had tried to publicly minimise links between conflict diamonds and Islamic militant groups, including al-Qaida', for fear of exposing 'their own longtime links with Charles Taylor.' Indeed, Taylor received CIA payments until at least January 2001, in the midst of his diamond trading activity with al-Qaeda.[510]

Taylor's principal diamond-trade representative, Ibrahim Bah, who facilitated the al-Qaeda meetings with Taylor, also has CIA ties. Doug Farah notes that instead of formally investigating or apprehending him, the CIA 'paid Ibrahim Bah for information and tried to recruit him as a permanent CIA asset.' Simultaneously, the CIA attempted to fraudulently discredit the key witness, Farah's source Cindor Reeves, about Bah's 9/11 warning, by deliberately setting him up 'to fail a polygraph exam, in order to say that he "was not trustworthy".' A senior US official with intelligence access subsequently confirmed to Farah that the CIA meeting with Reeves had been 'a set up. It was meant to show your source as being unreliable for two reasons: to be able to discredit him if his meetings with embassy personnel ever became public; and to clear the way for dealing with Bah, who can now be portrayed as reputable.'[511]

Another of Taylor's close associates and business partners linked to the al-Qaeda diamond trading is the notorious international criminal and former Russian military officer Victor Bout, one of the world's largest illicit arms dealers. Following numerous investigations by the UN and several countries, Bout became the subject of UN sanctions and an international arrest warrant. Taylor came to power in Liberia with the assistance of Bout's prolific arms supplies, and in return issued him aeroplane registrations. Bout also often received payment from Taylor in diamonds. Apart from supplying arms to both sides in African civil wars, before 9/11 Bout provided weapons to the Taliban. After 9/11, he 'furnished weapons to bin Laden.' According to Belgian security sources, this did not stop the United States 'from entrusting him [Bout] with arms shipments to the Northern Alliance' to fight the Taliban. Diplomatic sources confirm that under US pressure, Bout's name has been inexplicably removed from lists of individuals subject to sanctions submitted to the UN Security Council. His name, for instance, 'disappeared from the British list submitted in April [2004], although it was still at the head of that list in January's version.' Sources note that 'the initiative came from the United States, which put pressure on London to obtain this clemency.' More recently, Bout's criminal services have been contracted out to the US military. 'Viktor Bout seems to be back at work in Iraq', reported a shocked *Le Monde* citing multiple credible sources. His aircraft, which were 'flying under the name of an airline company, British Gulf, likely to disappear as fast as it was created, are assuring "transport of material" for the American army.' In return for services rendered, 'Viktor Bout is about to receive a kind of amnesty that will allow him to resume his large scale activities.'[512]

A suspected top associate of Bout, Sanjivan Ruprah, also appears to have been a long-term US intelligence informant. According to UN reports, he was tied to West Africa's illicit diamond trade, used by al-Qaeda, and 'arranged for Bout to be paid for his weapons deliveries with diamonds from Sierra Leone, Congo and Angola.' UN reports also identify Ruprah as 'a key intermediary between Bout and Taylor', and was issued a Liberian diplomatic passport in the name of Samir M. Nasr, describing him as 'Liberia's deputy commissioner for maritime affairs.' Bout also ran guns for Abu Sayyaf terrorists in the Philippines according to UN investigators. In early February 2002, Ruprah was arrested in Belgium, following which he began providing his interrogators with 'more information about Bout's suspected arms pipeline to the Taliban, which ruled Afghanistan until last November, and al Qaeda, which the Taliban had sheltered there.' But curiously, prior to his arrest by the Belgian authorities, Ruprah had already been in regular contact with US intelligence officials – who in contrast *displayed no interest at all in arresting him* for his criminal activities. 'Before the arrest, Ruprah, a Kenyan, had secretly been in contact with US officials in recent months, providing them with information about Bout,' US officials admitted. The Belgian arrest had taken US officials by surprise who insist that 'they had made no deal with Ruprah.' Why would a hardened criminal and top associate of Viktor Bout spontaneously, graciously, begin providing US intelligence agencies with information on the criminal activities of his own network? Why would US authorities receive secret information from a criminal of such stature, banned from international travel by the UN, while allowing him to continue his activities unhindered? The circumstances strongly suggest that Ruprah was, indeed, a US intelligence informant.[513]

It is difficult to avoid the conclusion in this context that al-Qaeda diamond financing operations facilitated through the criminal activities of Taylor and his associates, have been, and continue to be, at least tacitly protected by the US intelligence community. The US government continues to officially deny the existence of West Africa's longstanding al-Qaeda diamond connection, despite the conclusive findings of European and UN law enforcement investigations, and the private misgivings of countless anonymous senior US intelligence officers. Revelations in the international media did not prevent the US government and its agencies from actively shielding Taylor from prosecution, Bah from investigation, Bout from legal sanction, Ruprah from arrest, and senior al-Qaeda operatives facilitating multi-million dollar diamond transactions from capture by Special Forces.

US policy toward al-Qaeda's financial infrastructure in West Africa vis-à-vis illicit diamond trading is incommensurate with stated Anglo-American counter-terrorist initiatives in relation to key north-west African countries alleged to be hotspots of al-Qaeda/GSPC destabilisation operations. On the one hand, the United States is aggressively spearheading the wholesale militarisation of the Sahara-Sahel region on the pretext of rolling back al-Qaeda terrorist penetration. On the other, the US turns a blind eye to, tacitly condones, if not even actively protects, al-Qaeda profiteering through West African diamond smuggling centred on Liberia and Sierra Leone. The contradictory logic of these two policies cannot be reconciled within the conventional portrayal of the 'war on terror'. However, the picture becomes perfectly coherent in light of the duplicity of the GSPC/al-Qaeda phenomenon in northwest Africa as the product of an elaborate US-Algerian intelligence deception. In both cases, the overall trajectory of US security policies in the region has been to effectively facilitate regional Islamist activity, rather than curb it. In turn, the growth of this activity provides the principal pretext for the expansion of American military hegemony, and the consolidation of Anglo-American oil interests, in the region.

Indeed, US strategy in north-west Africa has since inception operated in tandem with Britain, whose role as usual appears largely obscured and is given little attention in the press. Nevertheless, secret government documents leaked to the *Guardian* in late 2003 confirm in no uncertain terms that what is happening in north-west Africa is being jointly coordinated by both the United States and the United Kingdom. A US report to both President Bush and Prime Minister Blair referred to a thoroughly Anglo-American strategy to 'secure African oil':

> We have identified a number of key oil and gas producers
> in the West Africa area on which our governments and
> major oil and gas companies could cooperate to improve
> investment conditions, good governance, social and

political stability, and thus underpin long term security of supply.

British officials were tasked to evaluate 'investment issues facing Africa that could be ripe for US–UK coordinated attention.' The same report noted the unification of Anglo-American interests in 'the huge energy potential of Russia, Central Asia and the Caspian', concluding that 'we have similar political, economic, social and energy objectives' in these regions.[514]

As for Britain, the government has played an even more direct role than the United States in the illicit al-Qaeda diamond smuggling operations in Sierra Leone and Liberia.

As noted above, phase three of al-Qaeda's diamond smuggling operations in Sierra Leone began in late 2000, whereby al-Qaeda bought diamonds via the RUF. After January 2001, al-Qaeda's diamond smuggling operations in Sierra Leone escalated until just before 9/11, and continued thereafter albeit at least through to 2002.

This period from 2000 to 2002 of al-Qaeda's intensifying diamond smuggling in Sierra Leone, is *precisely the same period in which the British government intervened in the country and restored the diamond trade to state control*. In 1999, the British conceived an Anglo-American strategy to forge an alliance with RUF rebels to consolidate control over rebel diamond mining and smuggling activities. The US and British allies pressured the Sierra Leone government to accept a settlement with the RUF in July 1999, the Lome Peace Agreement. Monitoring the settlement was a contingent of 5,000 UN peacekeeping troops in Freetown and other parts – but none in RUF strongholds, where diamond smuggling activities, including those of al-Qaeda were escalating. Worse still, under the Lome Agreement, the Anglo-American allies compelled the central government to accept the appointment of RUF leader Foday Sankoh as Chairman of a government Commission for the Management of Strategic Mineral Resources (CMRRD), a 'key post' overseeing the 'exploitation of Sierra Leone's diamond wealth'. Sankoh was also granted immunity from prosecution. Most Sierra Leoneans 'were outraged at the deal – they said the amnesty and Mr Sankoh's appointment as diamond overlord appeared to reward the rebels.'[515] 'That his men were then spreading terror by amputating the limbs of children was not a consideration', observed John Pilger.[516]

Delighted by his new-found legitimacy as official Anglo-American sponsored overlord of Sierra Leone's diamond wealth, Sankoh proceeded to pursue negotiations with individuals and companies on behalf of the RUF to mine, buy and sell the country's diamonds. He signed numerous agreements with international business firms in the name of the Commission, and the RUF. RUF diamond dealer Ibrahim Bah, Charles Taylor's al-Qaeda go-between, was involved in these negotiations. In the same period, Bah had established a permanent diamond smuggling agreement with senior al-Qaeda operatives.[517]

It was not long, however, before RUF impunity undermined the fragile peace agreement, resulting in the resumption of hostilities in May 2000, and the embarrassing collapse of the UN peacekeeping effort. In March, Washington had already realised that Sankoh was an unreliable ally. According to the *Wall Street Journal,* the US embassy in Freetown brokered a 'top-secret meeting' on 22 March between 'the multinational corporations that control Sierra Leone's diamond mines, the Freetown government and the RUF rebels... The RUF was told it had to surrender the mines or face an American-backed war.' The *Journal* reported in detail that:

What appears to lie behind the breakdown of the peace process in Sierra Leone was US and British determination to wrest control of Sierra Leone's rich diamond mining areas from the RUF rebels. For several months Washington and London have been leading efforts to break the financial power base of the RUF by trying to centralise the diamond trade. The key role of mining interests in the fighting is nothing new in Sierra Leone. Rival mining companies, security firms and mercenaries from South Africa, Britain, Belgium, Israel and the former Soviet Union have poured weapons, trainers, fighters and cash into the country. They have backed the government or the rebels in a bid to gain access to the country's high quality gems.[518]

During this period, Pilger notes, illicit diamond smuggling continued undiminished 'with many of Sierra Leone's diamonds sold for cash and smuggled through Liberia.'[519] British military intervention to prop up the failing UN mission and reconstruct the Sierra Leone government included the input of 800 troops, arms and training programmes designed to consolidate the Kabbah regime under British tutelage.[520]

The *Telegraph* remarked that 'administratively, Britons have been seconded to most major government ministries in an attempt to establish a functioning state... Key positions are held by the British under a bureaucratic form of re-colonisation'. Immediately, the intervention aimed at breaking RUF monopoly over the diamond mines and rehabilitating British-backed state control thereof.[521] Sierra Leone expert Ambrose Ganda noted that in the process, British intervention had shored up pervasive political corruption in the form of 'a select group of Sierra Leonean patrons in government and their clients.'[522] Informed sources in Freetown alleged that elements of the Sierra Leone state itself were involved in diamond smuggling and mining, both personally and through proxies.[523] In other words, by late 2000 – coinciding with the third major phase of al-Qaeda diamond smuggling in Sierra Leone – the illicit diamond trade had begun to move concertedly out of the RUF monopoly and into the clutches of the US-British-backed Kabbah regime. This process was more or less complete by early 2001, when local al-Qaeda diamond smuggling reached its fourth major phase of escalation. Al-Qaeda diamond smuggling in Sierra Leone peaked *during the period in which Britain and the United States had established control over the country's diamond mines via the Kabbah regime*.

The British government is intimately acquainted with the corrupt activities of its proxy regime in Sierra Leone. The UK Department for International Development approached the problem of political corruption by establishing and funding a new 'anti-corruption commission made up of Sierra Leonean officials and British specialists.' The commission, operating under the Anti-Corruption Act of 3 February 2000, at first seemed to offer a serious avenue for weeding out the high-level sources of illegal activity, having been granted 'extensive powers of search and arrest.' In the course of its inquiries, the commission 'collected clear evidence of deep corruption among civil servants and ministers. Working with British intelligence, it has tracked down bank accounts and secret correspondence, and gathered information that would otherwise have been well hidden.' But inexplicably, although the commission was powerful as an information-gathering mechanism for the British government, the latter had fatally limited its ability to enforce legal sanctions. 'The commission lacks the power to prosecute, and in late 2001 members of the commission expressed frustration with government interference in its investigations', reported Africa's Institute for Security Studies. Indeed, according to the International Crisis Group, not only is the anti-corruption commission impotent, it 'continues to be used as a political tool by the president's inner circle.'[524] It is difficult to avoid the implication that al-Qaeda's diamond smuggling operations occurred largely under the auspices of the Sierra Leone state, with British state knowledge and complicity.

Indeed, the post-intervention illicit diamond trade in Sierra Leone has not receded. As late as 2004, the country 'officially' exported $130 million worth of diamonds, UN special envoy Daudi Mwakawago confirmed that the 'diamond industry in Sierra Leone actually exported somewhere between $300 million and $500 million' that year. In other words, under British tutelage up to two-thirds of the diamond industry remains unregulated and subject to smuggling.[525] British strategy in Sierra Leone, pursued in tandem with its principal ally the United States, successfully transferred the illicit diamond trade away from the RUF into the hands of the state, a process coinciding directly with the escalation of al-Qaeda's Sierra Leone diamond smuggling operations.

# Conclusions and Recommendations

## 6. Domestic Policy Toward Islamist Terrorism

For more than a decade, the British state has tolerated and indeed promoted the establishment within the UK of a terrorist network connected to al-Qaeda. The network is presided over by a number of senior operatives who constitute a loosely affiliated de facto leadership. These operatives, in turn, are linked to international al-Qaeda-affiliated terrorist groups responsible for the orchestration of terrorist attacks in the United States, Western Europe, the Middle East and South Asia. The activities of this network are tightly monitored by MI5 and MI6 as a matter of routine.

British state policy of tolerating and facilitating terrorist activity within the UK consists of the following practices:

1. Granting asylum, and in some cases even citizenship, to individuals from abroad with strong suspected terrorist connections;
2. Permitting such individuals to continue to pursue their terrorist activities on British soil with impunity, including the establishment of extensive terrorist training and financing operations;
3. Refusing to charge or prosecute them despite what arguably amounts to compelling evidence of systematic violations of British law.

Despite token arrests of a small number of major suspected terrorists, arbitrary arrests (and subsequent release without charge) of thousands of innocent people under anti-terrorist powers, and fervent government rhetoric about the wonders of summarily deporting alleged terrorists, these practices do in fact remain in place in the post-7/7 period. The British-based al-Qaeda-affiliated terrorist network behind 7/7, although well known to authorities, continues to function intact, with its operational ability relatively unimpeded. This is largely because authorities have continued to suppress the real nature of this network and its frightening international dimensions. The role of key suspected terrorist leaders in the planning and execution of the London bombings is being consistently ignored and downplayed. Instead, authorities have generated an implausible and at times patently inconsistent narrative claiming that the London bombers were merely home-grown 'clean skins', in relation to which there is no decisive evidence of an al-Qaeda connection, or an international component.

However, any serious analysis cannot fail to conclude that an international network linked to al-Qaeda was involved in the London bombings. The type of explosives that appear to have been used, the unacknowledged sophistication of the attacks, the bombers' connection to an al-Qaeda-affiliated network, the role of multiple senior al-Qaeda operatives at different levels in the planning and execution stages, all converge on the conclusion that the London bombings were an al-Qaeda operation. Moreover, the intelligence services had the four bombers well in sight in the years prior to 7/7, categorised as suspected terrorists connected to previous UK terror plots masterminded by the same terrorist leadership that planned the Tube bombings. The apparent efforts of British authorities to systematically suppress this conclusion are most likely designed to conceal their abject failure to take action against this network, despite ample evidence of its existence and activities having been available, and despite extensive and reasonably precise advanced warning of an imminent domestic terrorist attack on the London Tube network to be executed by July 2005.

The failure can only partially be explained by the 'appeasement paradigm' that has dominated the intelligence services' approach to UK-based Islamist terrorism under the 'Covenant of Security'. Pre-7/7, the mounting tide of urgent warnings of an impending terrorist attack on British soil by Islamist extremists did not sway authorities into taking appropriate preventive action. Post-7/7, the ongoing silence on the role of key al-Qaeda officials in 7/7, amounting almost to a form of tacit protection – such as in the debarring of Omar Bakri from return to the UK, who now continues to oversee the operations of the same UK-based networks from Lebanon this time without fear of British legal jurisdiction – continues although the Covenant clearly is no longer in effect. Thus, the appalling paralysis of the British national security system (in the sense of the system purportedly established to protect the security of the British people) requires another explanation. For this, we need to look at the covert alliance between elements of the British state and Islamist terrorist networks on an international scale.

### 7. International Policy Toward Islamist Terrorism

The *raison d'etre* of the British state's munificent approach to the activities of Islamist terrorists within the UK, although at first sight obscure, becomes perfectly comprehensible when the international dimension of the activities of these domestic terrorists is closely examined. Doing so reveals that British state domestic policy is inextricably entwined with its international policy, since the subject of both is an al-Qaeda-affiliated Islamist terrorist network operating simultaneously within and outside the UK. From this perspective it is inevitable that the policy cannot be fully understood without fully grasping both the domestic and international dimensions of its subject.

Operating within an American strategic framework, British state foreign policy has for more than a decade systematically facilitated al-Qaeda's emergence, activities, proliferation and consolidation in key regions considered vital to Anglo-American strategic and economic interests. This has included the support of affiliated terrorist and criminal networks. Compelling evidence to this effect has been unearthed with respect to the Balkans, Central Asia and north-west Africa, including of course in Afghanistan where Osama bin Laden's network was at its inception nurtured to the tune of hundreds of millions of dollars.

In all cases, the central trajectory of British state policy has been defined by the overarching objective of securing control over strategic resources and raw materials, especially oil and natural gas. The activities of Islamist terrorist groups affiliated to al-Qaeda through the interpenetration of training, finances, arms and fighters have been sponsored by the Anglo-American alliance through the provision of direct assistance and indirectly via state intermediaries, invariably resulting in regional destabilisation. This in turn tends to precipitate intensive regional Anglo-American military interventionism, which is functionally and operationally designed to protect access to resources. The bulk of these transnational connections of effective sponsorship between the US, UK, some western European powers, and al-Qaeda, continue to exist today without significant diminution. This of course raises serious questions not only about 7/7, but about previous terrorist attacks against Western targets in the post-Cold War period.

British state foreign policy generates through its own geostrategic logic a framework of parameters within which domestic policy must operate. For policy abroad to succeed, it requires the cooperation of relevant policies at home. In order to effectively protect networks abroad that facilitate security for the state's perceived interests, individuals residing within the UK who operate within these international Islamist networks by the same logic must be left alone to continue their activities, many of which are often intrinsically bound up with facilitating the operations of their colleagues abroad. As such, British state foreign policy toward Islamist terrorist networks implies de facto protection for terrorists at home affiliated to those networks. In other words, the covert alliance between British state interests and Islamist terrorist networks abroad fatally undermines the ability of the state to guarantee domestic national security. The mechanisms by which this occurs can be specified as follows:

1. Numerous Islamist terrorist networks outside the UK have extensive connections to operatives inside the UK, who use Britain as a logistical base to organise the recruitment, planning, training and financial elements of terrorist activity. Many of their activities involve repeated violations of British law.

2. Many of these individuals with international terrorist connections preside as leaders over UK-based radical organisations that function primarily as centres for the recruitment and indoctrination of British Muslims.

3. Although closely monitored and well known to authorities, they have been permitted to continue their activities unimpeded. Many of them also possess close connections to British intelligence services, to the extent

that at least some of them are reportedly intelligence informants and/or double agents.

4. Their intelligence connections appear to be related to their membership of extremist networks of strategic value to perceived British state interests abroad; both their intelligence connections and strategic value explain the reluctance of the state apparatus to prosecute them for their violations of British law.

In other words, British terrorism is not home-grown at all – rather in origin it is primarily alien to Britain, and to the British Muslim community. It is difficult to imagine how individuals such as the London bombers could have been radicalised in the absence of the originally non-British extremists whose presence the UK has been tolerated and whose activities have been facilitated by successive British Conservative and Labour governments.

## 8. Implications for National Security

British state policy at home and abroad has been radically different from the claims made for the Anglo-American 'war on terror' (now renamed 'the long war'). The British state has presided over the establishment, growth and consolidation of Islamist terrorist networks inside the UK. These networks have been used to manipulate and coopt associated networks in foreign regions of vital strategic interest. There is no doubt that this amounts to a form of collusion, similar in character to what was uncovered by the Stevens Inquiry concerning British state interpenetration with terrorist and criminal networks in Northern Ireland.[526]

Ironically, in the name of defending British national security, the state has continued to extend its powers in the form of unprecedented new forms of legislation purportedly to pursue the 'war on terror', but in practice simply increasing the ability of the state to operate with a minimum of accountability and a maximum of secrecy, outside the jurisdiction of public scrutiny. None of these measures that encroach on freedom of dissent, human rights and civil liberties, have in any way tackled the real causes of Britain's vulnerability to terrorism. That vulnerability exists principally due to the domestic and international policies of the state itself toward Islamist terrorist networks, policies that have systematically disrupted the ability of Britain's police and security services to function in accordance with their mandate to protect the British public. It is clear that the scale of this failure is such as to potentially amount, at the least, to a form of criminal negligence. The government's post-7/7 policies only confirm this. Rather than acknowledge the failures of senior policymakers in government, intelligence and police agencies, the state has done the opposite. It has demanded new powers for the dysfunctional national security apparatus in which the July bombings were incubated.

After 2001, the British state has followed the American strategy of expanded covert and open warfare in the Middle East and Central Asia. The promotion of British state and corporate power internationally has been a major priority for both Conservative and Labour governments, increasingly so under Prime Minister Blair. This overwhelming imperative has rarely been acknowledged and has never been adequately debated by the British public and its democratic representatives.

The British national security system has for too long operated not as a system to guarantee the security of British lives, but rather to guarantee the security of powerful vested interests to which the state appears irreparably beholden. This raises serious questions about the predicament of British democracy, the role of the state in the 'war on terror', the state as an instrument of corporate interest as opposed to public choice, and the ability of citizens to participate meaningfully in policymaking relevant to their own security. However, it is not within the scope of this investigation, which is ultimately only preliminary in nature, to explore the way forward from here in terms of what must be done to prevent further such terrorist attacks in the UK and elsewhere. Nevertheless, based on the facts and conclusions outlined so far, a number of basic but vital recommendations can be outlined whose necessity seems absolutely clear:

1. The British national security system, so beholden to the United States as well as powerful vested interests, needs not only to be reformed, but to be radically overhauled. The old adage of 'national security' justifying the unaccountable power and impenetrable secrecy of British intelligence policies can no longer be blindly accepted at face value. On the pretext of 'national security' the state has in fact systematically diluted the security of the British public, and it continues to do so post-7/7. The national security system therefore needs to be thoroughly and independently scrutinised in order that it can be entirely rehabilitated under a new mandate designed to serve the British public, not vested interests.

2. The state uses its unprecedented anti-terrorist powers selectively against peaceful dissidents, protesters and asylum-seekers, but refuses to act against the very real terrorist threat on British soil. Whatever one's view of the legitimacy of such legislation, the fact is that even

265

under common criminal law, genuine terrorist operatives in the UK can be easily charged and prosecuted. New anti-terrorist legislation thus has little practical meaning for real British security. Indeed, the shooting of Menezes demonstrates what unaccountable powers adopted in the name of 'national security' can mean for the British public. The real role of this legislation in relation to British state interests and the reasons for its selective applications, must be subject to independent investigation. Ultimately, the rationale and function of such legislation needs to be revised, and new, more meaningful, measures for security need to be established. Rather than increasing the power of the state over the public, new legislation must enable to the public to scrutinise and if necessary curb state policies. It is the state, not the general public that has acted decisively to undermine security, and therefore state policy that needs to be interrogated and reformed via a public process governed by the rule of law. Legislation to this effect must be considered.

3. The state-corporate system has constructed a foreign policy that runs parallel to mainstream claims about the war on terror. It has systematically brought the British state into collusion with criminal and terrorist networks in strategic regions. The hidden nexus that connects state, corporate, and intelligence policy, and the rationale behind it, therefore require independent investigation. The implications of this nexus for British democracy must also be considered. It is clear that extensive political reforms will be required to ensure that informed public opinion, rather than powerful vested interests, holds sway over policymaking. These ought to include two

core elements: firstly, that of information – the age of total secrecy to conceal the activities of the intelligence services from the public must be replaced by a new era of transparency represented by the national security apparatus being compelled to engage in a reasonably comprehensive disclosure; secondly, that of power – the ability of powerful and wealthy lobbies to influence the political process and to pressure decision-making must be drastically curtailed in order to establish the public interest at the heart of British foreign policy.

4. The extent of the advanced warning available to British intelligence services was clearly far more extensive and precise than officially conceded. The documentation gathered here suggests that it was sufficiently precise as to enable effective and efficient preventive action prior to the London bombings. In particular, huge question marks remain over why intelligence services failed to continue surveillance of the four 7/7 bombers despite their connections to a group planning terrorist attacks in London, including the Tube network, which was partially arrested in 2004. The fact that preventive action was not only entirely absent, but went almost in the opposite direction (such as the lowering of the threat level by the JTAC weeks before the bombings) demonstrates the need for the government to account fully and transparently for the 7/7 intelligence failure and its causes.

5. Such an accounting must be subject to impartial verification in relation to a host of related domestic and foreign policies. The impact of the state's foreign policies on its domestic policies toward Islamist terrorist networks associated with British foreign collusion, requires precise research and verification. The role of

intelligence informants and double agents in these networks and their involvement in the London bombings
must also be uncovered. It is plausible that such domestic
intelligence operations significantly hamper the ability
of security services to pursue terrorist operatives
considered in some manner useful for intelligence
purposes. Again, meaningful answers to such problems
can only be guaranteed on the basis of an independent
investigation.

In summary, there is no doubt that an independent public
inquiry into the events of 7/7, and the associated events of
21/7 and 22/7, is urgently required. This inquiry must be
independent in the sense that it must be free of state influence
or pressure. It must also be public in the sense that its objectives,
procedures, methods and processes are entirely transparent
and accountable, and moreover that rather than being
conducted in secret meetings behind closed doors where
information can be manipulated, it must be chaired by
genuinely independent experts in an open forum. These factors,
however, cannot mean anything in the absence of the legal
authority to compel the state to release information on the
London bombings and related issues.

The seriously compromised results of previous purportedly
'independent inquiries', such as the Hutton Inquiry, demonstrate the dangers inherent to launching such processes
without proper safeguards established to ensure independence.
Given the gravity, complexity, multi-dimensionality and international nature of the relevant issues, an independent public
inquiry into the London bombings should have a broad remit
to examine not merely those terrorist attacks, but a host of
related domestic and foreign policies pursued by the British

state over the last decade in alliance with the United States and several European states. Perhaps, then, such an inquiry ought to be not merely local to the UK, but international in scope.

An independent public inquiry is precisely what the British state is opposed to. There are obvious reasons for this, and they are mostly related to the state imperative to consolidate its current preoccupations, associated interests and strategies, even at the expense of democracy and security at home. Given the response of the government to 7/7, it is difficult to avoid the conclusion that the London bombings have been shamelessly exploited by the state to simply serve its own empowerment. Ultimately, an inquiry must be tied to the fundamental objective of holding government officials to account for the failures that facilitated the London bombings. The evidence in the public record suggests that government officials failed not because of a lack of information, bureaucratic bungling, or any other reasonably justifiable factors, but rather because a stark decision had been made: a decision to privilege a certain category of strategic and economic interests above the safety of British civilians. Although in the final analysis, this is a matter to be decided in an appropriate legal forum, in my view the public record establishes that the governmental failures behind the London bombings amount to criminal negligence. The officials and policymakers responsible for the key decisions that have paralysed the British national security system should no longer be permitted to hold office. They, and along with them the outmoded national security system over which they preside, should be removed by the British people.

# Afterword

On 11th May 2006 the British government published its two principal investigative reports on the London bombings, the first by the House of Commons Intelligence and Security Committee (ISC),[527] and the second being the government's own 'official account' of the bombings.[528]

The first problem with the official account is that it can hardly be considered an objective assessment. Written entirely by an anonymous civil servant, based on unspecified official intelligence sources, and edited by the government before final release, there was little prospect that it might contain serious and well-grounded criticism of the government's role.

Although at first glance the ISC report retains an air of independence as the output of a "Parliamentary inquiry", it is hardly more independent than Whitehall's own official narrative. All members of the ISC are appointed by the Prime Minister, and they report to him directly. He retains the power to censor the contents of the report on security grounds as he sees fit. Thus like the official account, its contents are subject to high-level government approval, and are similarly unlikely to offer an analysis that undermines the government's agenda.

These reports are fundamentally politicised – that is, written in the context of obvious political constraints, which limit their scope and shape their conclusions.

Even allowing for these constraints, the reports are guilty of a litany of omissions and serious factual inaccuracies. Read against what we know about the attacks from other sources, it is difficult to see how these reports offer anything at all of value. Virtually no new information is offered, and much of the material purportedly based on intelligence sources has already been widely reported in the media. The little new information there is pertains to specific details about the background of the bombers.

### Report of the Government's Official Account of the 7/7 London Bombings

Both reports gloss over or ignore the most serious inconsistencies in the previous official claims. The most pertinent assertions are about the organisation and planning behind the bombings. One of the most significant of these is that the bombings were relatively unsophisticated, requiring 'little expertise'. The reports claim the attacks were 'self-financed' with a relatively small amount of funds, and executed using easily available household ingredients in home-made bombs. 'Expert examination continues but it appears the bombs were homemade, and that the ingredients used were all readily commercially available and not particularly expensive. Each device appears to have consisted of around 2-5 kg of home-made explosive. The first purchase of material necessary for production so far identified was on 31st March 2005. No great expertise is required to assemble a device of this kind.'[529]

There are a number of ambiguities here that are difficult to make sense of. It seems that just under a year after the attacks, the government is still not a hundred percent certain of the composition of the bombs that went off in the London Underground on 7th July 2005. The official account says, for instance, that 'it appears' the bombs were home-made from cheap, household commodities, rather than confirming the matter decisively. The report notes that forensic analysis of the bombs continues, implying that the current conclusions about their composition is not complete and could change. Forensic science, however, is not normally so convoluted, and tends to provide unambiguous answers within a matter of hours and days. The idea that continuous examination over many months has failed to finish the job beggars belief. Either the government's forensic scientists are horrendously incompetent, or the government is being economical with the truth. The official account does not specify the explosive material used in the bombs, nor the household ingredients used to compose them. Instead it relies on the ISC report, which at least says that the bombs were made from home-made organic peroxide. The problem is that peroxide-based explosives produce explosions whose properties are inconsistent with the blasts that occurred in the Tube on 7/7 (see pp. 32-34).

The official account contradicts the statements made by intelligence and police officials, as well as forensic scientists, in the week after the attacks. According to multiple sources, the bombs were highly sophisticated devices composed of the military-grade plastic explosive C4, originally from the Balkans, traces of which were found by investigators at the bomb sites along with timing mechanisms (see pp. 23-26). There is no attempt to explain the inconsistency between the findings of forensic examination in the week after the attacks, and the tentative claims made months later. This is not an academic controversy. The forensic conclusions reported up to a week after 7/7 point unequivocally to the role of a wider support network linked to technologically competent criminal and terrorist groups in the Balkans. Throughout the 1990s, the British and American governments were deeply involved in manipulating al-Qaeda networks to control conflict and to secure regional hegemony. Rather than establishing once and for all that the bombs were home-made, the report retreats into inexplicable vagueness. A possible Balkan connection, with all its awkward implications, recedes from view.

The official account also states that: 'Current indications are that the group was self-financed. There is no evidence of external sources of income. Our best estimate is that the over-all cost is less than £8,000.'[530] Again, this assumption ignores reports suggesting that the 7/7 attacks were a far more techni-cally sophisticated operation than is now being admitted. Apart from the original police confirmations that the bombs were technically advanced and of military quality, numerous eyewitness accounts indicate that the bombs may have exploded from underneath the carriages, making this a far more difficult operation to plan and pull off successfully (see, pp. 37-39). Of course, these eyewitness accounts could be mistaken, but the official account does not even acknowledge their existence, let alone attempt to disclose any evidence that could provide a more convincing explanation of the police narrative.

The report also downplays the notion that the bombers operated as part of a wider al-Qaeda terrorist network, insist-ing that despite some tantalising circumstantial suggestions, there 'is as yet no firm evidence to corroborate this claim or the nature of al-Qaeda support, if there was any.'[531] Although speculating that some sort of cursory liaison with al-Qaeda members during visits to Pakistan seems likely, the report focuses on the role of Mohammed Sidique Khan in indoctri-nating and radicalising the group.[532] Although the report alludes vaguely to the fact that the bombers associated with a wider 'social network' consisting of various local 'Islamic groups', it avoids further details of the nature of this network, and instead perpetuates the image of the bombers as a largely self-radicalised cell, given that: 'The extent to which others may have been involved in indoctrinating the group, have known what they were planning, or been involved in the planning, is unknown at this stage.'[533]

This is perhaps the official account's most significant omission. The evidence discussed in this book demonstrates decisively that the London bombers had operated as part of a well established al-Qaeda terrorist network in Britain, whose key leadership is well known to British authorities. Amazingly, the official account fails to acknowledge the connection between the 7/7 cell and Haroon Rashid Aswat, believed by both British and US investigators to have been the senior al-Qaeda operative who masterminded the bombings, as established through records of telephone conversations between Aswat and the alleged chief bomber Sidique Khan. Although British authorities quickly backtracked on what they had confirmed to the press about Aswat's involvement in 7/7 after revelations from US intelligence sources that Aswat is an MI6 double agent, US and French investigators continue to describe Aswat as the London bombings mastermind (see pp. 144-151).

All four bombers were members of al-Muhajiroun, believed by American and Western intelligence services to be an al-Qaeda front organization that recruited British Muslims to participate in terrorist activity outside the UK. An abundance of evidence in the public record, including on-the-record admissions by al-Muhajiroun leaders and activists, confirms in detail the scope of al-Muhajiroun's terrorist activities before 7/7 (see pp. 72-82). Similar evidence suggests that the leader of al-Muhajiroun, Omar Bakri Mohammed, had advanced warning of the 7/7 attacks, and may even have had a specific role in radicalising the bombers as well as planning and facilitating their activities (see pp. 53-55, 57-58). Despite this, the British government never considered investigating or prosecuting him – and instead shielded him from legal scrutiny by allowing him to travel to Lebanon, outside UK jurisdiction. A large number of other individuals with documented connections to al-Qaeda are also simply excluded by the report. There is no mention, for instance, of the role of Abu Hamza in inspiring the bombers. His involvement has been repeatedly denied by British authorities but compelling evidence from a *Times* investigation (p. 56) is simply ignored. There is no mention of the role of senior al-Qaeda operatives such as Abu Faraj al-Libbi, who was directly involved in the planning of terrorist operations involving a network that included the four 7/7 bombers (see pp. 62-64, 124, 126-127). Although Hamza and Bakri are mentioned by name near the end of the official account, their relations to the 7/7 cell and the network in which it operated are ignored.

The official account also excludes the fact, reported shortly after the attacks, that British investigators had pinpointed the likely geographical location of al-Qaeda networks believed to be chiefly responsible for hatching the London attack plans, in Central Asia (e.g. Pakistan, Afghanistan, etc.), Northwest Africa (e.g. Algeria, Niger, etc.), and as noted above, the Balkans (pp. 27-28).

In systematically downplaying the undeniable role of al-Qaeda in the London bombings, the official account is attempting to draw public attention away from the fact that British authorities have tolerated the activities of an entrenched and burgeoning network of radical Islamists with terrorist connections inside the UK, for more than a decade. In doing so, the official account avoids acknowledging that many radical Islamists affiliated to al-Qaeda operated with impunity in Britain, and maintained a close relationship with British intelligence.

Haroon Rashid Aswat and his colleagues, Abu Hamza and Omar Bakri, were all used in an MI6 operation to recruit British Muslims to fight in Kosovo in the 1990s. British foreign policy in the Balkans meant that terrorists at home were permitted to run riot, and only this explains the reluctance of police and security services to prosecute individuals like Abu Hamza (who still has not been charged for numerous al-Qaeda linked terrorist activities in the UK). Disturbingly, the Balkans is not the only region where British foreign policy served to consolidate al-Qaeda activities. In both Central Asia and northwest Africa, British and American covert operations have collaborated with extremist Islamist terror networks affiliated to al-Qaeda in the pursuit of specific strategic and economic interests, largely to do with protecting corporate interests and controlling energy reserves. These networks are closely associated with the UK-based operatives linked to the London bombings (pp. 175-257) The role of western governments in systematically facilitating the activities of terrorist networks in the pursuit of foreign policy objectives in the Cold War and post-Cold War periods, until today, is completely ignored in the official account's Annex A, entitled 'The Evolution of the Modern International Terrorist Threat'. Similarly ignored are the numerous instances of British authorities turning a blind eye to open evidence of al-Qaeda terrorist activity in the UK by Bakri, Hamza and others with reported links to British intelligence. One notorious example is al-Muhajiroun's role in recruiting up to a thousand British Muslims to train in al-Qaeda camps in Pakistan and Afghanistan to fight on behalf of the Taliban, many of whom vowed to attack targets inside Britain upon return, a process that the government was aware of but inexplicably did nothing to stop (pp. 79-94).

The official account repeats many anomalous statements by the police about specific details of the bombings, including for instance the discovery of bombs in the car parked at Luton station, and of explosives residue at the alleged bomb-making factory in a flat in Leeds.[534] However, my examination of police accounts of these forensic findings at the time reveals considerable inconsistency in matters of detail. The number of bombs found in Luton, their composition, and even whether the Luton bombs were in fact found, have all varied in police statements. The official account does not explain the source of these inconsistencies, and instead pretends that they never occurred, providing little compelling reason to accept it as definitive (see pp. 43-44, 31-35).

Even minor details of the official account remain absurdly impossible, and it is difficult to see how competent and reliable intelligence organisations could fail to rectify them. For example, the report reiterates the mistaken claims by police officials about the chronology of the bombers' movements on the morning of 7th July 2005:

> '07.40: The London King's Cross train leaves Luton station.... 08.23: The train arrives at King's Cross, slightly late due to a delay further up the line. The 4 are captured on CCTV at 08.26am on the concourse close to the Thameslink platform and heading in the direction of the London Underground system.'[535]

Official Thameslink sources, along with Thameslink's own 'Actual Train Times' for the morning of 7/7, show that there was no 7:40AM train. There was, however, a 7:42AM train that arrived at Kings Cross at 8:39AM – after the bombers were caught on camera there. Worse still, police accounts have consistently disseminated two contradictory and mutually impossible versions of the bombers' movements to the press. Although the available data shows that the bombers might have taken an earlier train to arrive at King's Cross in time, the failure of the police, intelligence services and government to note the mistaken chronology and rectify the record speaks volumes about their investigative competence – and raises serious questions about the credibility of the official narrative (pp. 45-50).

This is not to assume that the government account is simply false. But these discrepancies and the government's refusal to release the evidence for their claims leave us little reason to take the report seriously. The case for an independent inquiry still stands.

### Report of the House of Commons Intelligence and Security Committee

The focus of the Parliamentary Intelligence and Security Committee report is, as would be expected, intelligence issues. The report's principal thesis, which complements the official account, is that:

'... none of the individuals involved in the 7 July group had been identified (that is, named and listed) as potential terrorist threats prior to July. We have also been told that there was no warning from intelligence (including foreign intelligence) of the plans to attack the London transport network on 7 July 2005.... We have been assured by the Agencies that there was no prior warning of the attacks that took place from any source, including from foreign intelligence services.'[536]

This is demonstrably false. On the contrary, extensive evidence in the public record derived from British, American, European and other security sources shows that the government had received a large number of advance warnings of an imminent attack on UK soil, specifically on the London Underground (pp. 121-135). The report singles out one warning in particular for debunking, from Saudi Arabia, which, it says, 'was examined by the Agencies who concluded that the plan was not credible. That information has been given to us: it is materially different from what actually occurred on 7 July and clearly not relevant to these attacks.'[537] The denial is, unfortunately, not credible, especially given that the ISC report avoids specifying the details of the alleged differences. Saudi sources state that they had warned specifically that an attack on the Underground would be conducted by an al-Qaeda terrorist cell of four individuals by July 2005. This is what happened. At the moment the report's conclusion, that no warning was received, remains mysterious (pp. 127-130).

Elsewhere, the ISC report justifies the decision by MI5's Joint Terrorism Analysis Centre to reduce the UK threat level in May 2005 because 'there was no intelligence of a current credible plot to attack the UK at that time (i.e. a group with established capability and current intent).' The ISC concludes that the decision 'was not unreasonable', as there was 'no specific intelligence of the 7 July plot nor of any other group with a current credible plot.'[538] In view of the numerous urgent and credible warnings received by British intelligence services in the years and months prior to 7/7 of an impending al-Qaeda terrorist attack in London, the ISC's position is simply indefensible, and demonstrates the grave problems in the government's entire approach to the London bombings investigation. Much of the intelligence available in advance of the attacks was detailed, precise, and when combined provided an increasingly coherent picture of what was soon to occur (pp. 121-135).

Furthermore, the ISC report's specific claims about the alleged failure to identify any of the London bombers before 7/7 are demonstrably false. Extensive evidence in the public record, again derived from Western security sources, shows that British intelligence had in fact identified all four bombers as members of a network of 13 presumed terrorists monitored under Operation Crevice, who were linked to plots to blow up several potential targets including West End nightclubs and the London Underground. The four bombers were among a total of five individuals out of these 13 who had managed to evade arrest (the others were successfully apprehended) but intelligence sources confirm that the five were allowed to escape for the very purpose of intensifying surveillance of their activities to uncover further evidence of terrorist activity. Sidique Khan, for instance, had been placed on a Scotland Yard 'target list' of terrorist suspects in 2004. The Yard had even opened a file on him, according to the *Sunday Times*. The ISC report ignores this and insists that he and the other bombers were only noticed on the periphery of a terrorist network, but never identified. Security sources told the *Mirror* that all four bombers were under surveillance by MI5 in the year prior to 7/7, as they were on a watchlist of about 100 people throughout the country considered to be Islamist fanatics capable of terrorist involvement. Again, this is not acknowledged by the ISC report. Perhaps an adequate explanation can be provided for these apparent discrepancies, but the report does not even attempt to give one. More seriously, British security officials expressed serious concern about the five individuals who had escaped arrest, and intelligence sources informed BBC News that they had wanted to place Khan on a higher level of investigation, but were prevented by senior officials (pp. 56-65). Again no explanation for this apparent lapse is given in the report. The ISC account does not even then adequately address what we already know from information available in the public record.

Ultimately, the report places the blame on a lack of sufficient resources to deal with the scale of the terrorist threat, which meant that intelligence officers were compelled to be selective in their choice of investigative targets. However, the lack of resources explanation comes in tandem with the notion that Khan and the other three bombers (although the ISC report does not even acknowledge that all four were under MI5 surveillance, only Khan and Tanweer) were not considered to be potential threats, justifying the diversion of resources to other more pertinent operations. But information from British, American and French intelligence sources confirms that the four bombers *were* known to the security services as terrorist suspects. Eight members of a network to which they belonged had already been arrested for plotting to bomb a number of targets including the London Underground. The decision to shut down further surveillance of Khan and the other would-be bombers was therefore a drastic intelligence failure that remains unexplained.

The issues raised here, dealt with in full detail in the main text of this book, are only a small sample of the many inconsistencies, errors and omissions contained in both the government's official account of the London bombings, and the report of the ISC. The implications are damning: the official narrative remains deeply questionable; the government has failed to deal with any of the salient controversies and complications that lie at the heart of its interpretation of events; the role of the British state in facilitating al-Qaeda terrorism both at home and abroad, and thereby corrupting its own anti-terrorist intelligence capabilities, is concealed from public understanding.

These two documents are little more than an insult to the intelligence of the British people. More than ever, it proves beyond doubt that an independent public inquiry into the London bombings and the events surrounding them is absolutely essential to discover precisely what happened on 7/7, how and why; and to ensure that the fundamental reforms necessary to rehabilitate the British national security system are implemented.

May 15th, 2006

# Acknowledgements

Thank you to Akeela for putting up with me during the hugely intensive time involved in the creation of this book, for her unwavering support and encouragement against the odds, and ultimately for her love, which keeps me alive. Thank you to Amina and Zainab for their endless patience, and even more endless and unquestioning love; their sweet defiance and ceaseless playful affection sets me free. Thank you to my Mum and Dad, for everything they've done and do for me, all without return; at the end of the day, I wouldn't have been able to write this book if it wasn't for them. Thank you to my Mum-in-law and Dad-in-law, for putting up with my tantrums and not kicking me out! Thank you to my agent Jonny Pegg for solid advice and help, and most of all for believing in my work. Thank you to my editor Dan Hind for the courage to take on this project, and for invaluable assistance throughout. Finally, thank you to all those who have supported my work over the years, and who work to make a better world not just possible, but real.

For more information and updates visit:
www.independentinquiry.co.uk

# Notes

1. Catriona Davies, Sally Pook and Nic Fleming, 'I saw a body and people with clothes blown off', *Telegraph* (8 July 2005)
http://www.telegraph.co.uk/news/main.jhtml?xml=/news/2005/07/08/nbomb408.xml.

2. Richard Alleyne, 'Tube bomb tore off side of train passing in the other direction', *Telegraph* (8 July 2005)
http://www.telegraph.co.uk/news/main.jhtml?xml=/news/2005/07/08/nbomb308.xml.

3. Sally Pook, Catriona Davies and Duncan Gardham, 'We were like sardines in there, waiting to die', *Telegraph* (8 July 2005)
http://www.telegraph.co.uk/news/main.jhtml?xml=/news/2005/07/08/nbomb108.xml.

4. Tom Leonard and Duncan Gardham, 'Bomber took his seat on bus and blew himself up', *Telegraph* (8 July 2005)
http://www.telegraph.co.uk/news/main.jhtml?xml=/news/2005/07/08/nbomb208.xml.

5. Tony Blair cited in *Financial Times* (11 July 2005)

6. Tony Blair, Statement to Parliament on the London Bombings (Westminster: Houses of Parliament, 11 July 2005)
http://www.number-10.gov.uk/output/Page7903.asp.

7. 'Police 'were consulted' over inquiry', *Daily Mail* (15 December 2005)
http://www.dailymail.co.uk/pages/live/articles/news/news.html?in_article_id=371778&in_page_id=1770.

8. Hannah K. Strange, 'UK government refuses 7/7 inquiry', United Press International (14 December 2005)
http://www.upi.com/InternationalIntelligence/view.php?StoryID=20051214-111222-1261r.

9. David Leppard, 'MI5 admits: we've run out of leads on bombers', *Sunday Times* (29 January 2006)
http://www.timesonline.co.uk/article/0,,2087-2014722_1,00.html.

10. Leppard, 'MI5 admits: we've run out of leads on bombers'op.cit

11. Nigel Morris, "London bombers had no help from al-Qa'ida, report concludes", Independent (12 April 2006)
http://news.independent.co.uk/uk/crime/article356828.ece.

12. Strange, 'UK government refuses 7/7 inquiry', op. cit.

13. Crispin Black, 'Contempt is the new sleaze: Let us emulate the Americans, and insist on an inquiry into the 7/7 attack', *Independent* (18 December 2005)

http://comment.independent.co.uk/commentators/article333786.ece.

14. Jeff Edwards and Chris Hughes, 'Exclusive: The Hunt', *Mirror* (9 July 2005)
http://www.mirror.co.uk/news/tm_objectid=15717499%26method=full%26siteid=94762%26headline=exclusive%2d%2d58%2d%2dthe%2dhunt-name_page.html.

15. Michael Taylor, 'Clues in Carnage: The path to bombers lies amid bits of debris', *San Francisco Chronicle* (9 July 2005)
http://www.sfgate.com/cgi-bin/article.cgi?file=/c/a/2005/07/09/MNG7CDLFL71.DTL.

The article explains the basic forensic procedures used to determine types of bombs and explosives at bomb scenes, citing James Crippin, a veteran of 25 years of bomb investigations for the Missouri State Highway Patrol and the Colorado Bureau of Investigation who is currently director of the Western Forensic Law Enforcement Training Center in Pueblo; and Michael Gleysteen, Assistant Special Agent-in-Charge of the San Francisco office of the Federal Bureau of Alcohol, Tobacco, Firearms and Explosives.

16. BBC News, 'Tube bombs 'almost simultaneous'' (9 July 2005)
http://news.bbc.co.uk/1/hi/uk/4666591.stm.

17. Don Van Natta Jr. and Elaine Sciolino, 'Timers Used in Blasts, Police Say; Parallels to Madrid Are Found', *New York Times* (7 July 2005)
http://www.nytimes.com/2005/07/08/international/europe/08intel.html?ex=1137214800&en=abdf0505464e6788&ei=5070.

18. Hugh Muir and Rosie Cowan, 'Four bombs in 50 minutes – Britain suffers its worst-ever terror attack', *Guardian* (8 July 2005)
http://www.guardian.co.uk/uk_news/story/0,,1523819,00.html.

19. ABC News, 'Officials: London Bus Body Could Be Bomber – Sources Tell ABC News Evidence of Timing Devices Also Found' (8 July 2005)
http://abcnews.go.com/WNT/print?id=918193.

20. Michael Evans, Sean O'Neill and Philip Webster, 'Terrorist gang 'used military explosives'', *The Times*, (12 July 2005)
http://www.timesonline.co.uk/article/0,,22989-1690391,00.html.

21. Jason Bennetto, 'Explosives used in bombs was of 'military origin'', *Independent* (12 July 2005),
http://news.independent.co.uk/uk/crime/article298515.ece.

22. *Financial Times* article. Cited in William Norman Grigg, 'London Bombings: More Balkans Blowback?' *New American* (1 August 2005)
http://www.thenewamerican.com/artman/publish/article_1955.shtml.

23. 'London bombers used 'military' explosives', United Press International (12 July 2005)
http://www.sciencedaily.com/upi/?feed=TopNews&article=UPI-1-20050712-07155500-bc-britain-explosions-explosives.xml.

24. Daniel McGrory and Michael Evans, 'Hunt for the master of explosives', *The Times* (13 July 2005).

25. UPI, 'London explosives have military origin' (13 July 2005)

http://www.sciencedaily.com/upi/?feed=TopNews&article=
UPI-1-20050713-07514000-bc-britain-explosions.xml.

26. Ibid.

27. Don Van Natta Jr. and Elaine Sciolino, "Military' quality bombs in London', *New York Times* (13 July 2005)
http://www.iht.com/articles/2005/07/12/news/london.php.

28. Sue O'Reilly, 'Explosives used in London bombings 'originated in the Balkans", *Irish Examiner*, (14th July 2005)
http://216.239.59.104/search?q=cache:5oGbhe1J9bkJ:www.examiner.ie/
pport/web/world/Full_Story/did-sg5ufWU0wu4m6sg7IQHSmeYhNE.
asp+london+bombings,Sue+O%27+Reilly,+military+ explosives&hl=en.

29. DEBKAfile, 'London police sources now believe the explosives used in Thursday's Tube blasts came from the Balkans' (8 July 2005).

30. DEBKAfile, 'London Terror Inquiry Heads Secretly to the African Sahara', *DEBKA-Net-Weekly*, No. 214 (18 July 2005)
http://www.debka.com/article.php?aid=1056.

31. Ibid.

32. Neil Mackay and David Pratt, 'Al-Qaeda chief has well-stocked teams in place', *Sunday Herald* (24 July 2005)
http://www.sundayherald.com/50952.

33. 'London bombs homemade from pharmacy ingredients', *Scotsman* (15 July 2005)
http://news.scotsman.com/uk.cfm?id=1610072005.

34. Dominic Kennedy and Issandr el Amrani, 'Police seek Egyptian chemist who had keys to bomb-maker's flat', *The Times* (15 July 2005)
http://www.timesonline.co.uk/article/0,,22989-1694945,00.html; CBC News, 'London bombing investigation spreads to Egypt, Pakistan' (15 July 2005)
http://www.cbc.ca/storyview/MSN/world/national/2005/07/15/
londonbombs050714.html.

35. Megan Lloyd Davies, 'El-Nashar: I challenge you to find bomb links', *Mirror* (19 July 2005)
http://www.mirror.co.uk/news/tm_objectid=15751877&method=
full&siteid=94762&headline=el-nashar-i-challenge-you-to-find-bomb-
links-name_page.html.

36. AFP, 'British police face doubts in Egypt over bombing role of Egyptian' (2004)
http://www.theallineed.com/news/0507/165607.htm.

37. Terry Kirby, 'Homemade explosives: the facts' *Independent* (16 July 2005)
http://news.independent.co.uk/uk/crime/article299443.ece.

38. Richard Evans, 'JCIT Briefing: Terrorist use of TATP explosive' (London: Janes Terrorism & Insurgency Centre, 22 July 2005)
http://www.janes.com/security/law_enforcement/news/jtic/
jtic050722_1_n.shtml.

39. Vikram Dodd and Rosie Cowan, 'Suicide bombs breakthrough gives police vital clues', *Guardian* (24 August 2005)
http://www.guardian.co.uk/attackonlondon/story/0,16132,1555215,00.html.

40. 'Terror police 'still to determine bomb type'', *Daily Mail* (19 July 2005)
http://www.dailymail.co.uk/pages/live/articles/news/
news.html?in_article_id=356259&in_page_id=1770.

41. Richard Evans, 'JCIT Briefing', op. cit.

42. Michael Evans, 'Explosives match al-Qaeda blueprint for bomb-making', *The Times* (16 July 2005)
http://www.timesonline.co.uk/article/0,,22989-1696035,00.html.

43. Jenny Hogan, 'Terrorist explosive blows up without flames', *New Scientist* (31 January 2005)
http://www.newscientist.com/article.ns?id=dn6925.
According to the authoritative website GlobalSecurity.org: 'In conventional high explosives such as TNT, each molecule contains both a fuel component and an oxidising component. When the explosive detonates, the fuel part is oxidised and as this combustion reaction spreads it releases *large amounts of heat*. The explosion of TATP involves entropy burst, which is the result of formation of one ozone and three acetone molecules from every molecule of TATP in the solid state. Just a few hundred grams of the material produce *hundreds of litres of gas in a fraction of a second*. The explosion of TATP is similar to the decomposition of azide, for example, which produces nitrogen gas *but little heat*, is used to fill airbags for cars.' See GlobalSecurity, 'Triacetone Triperoxide (TATP)' (viewed 24 January 2006)
http://www.globalsecurity.org/military/systems/munitions/tatp.htm.

44. 'Israeli invention detects TATP explosives', *Israeli Insider* (27 January 2005)
http://web.israelinsider.com/Articles/Briefs/4884.htm.

45. Ibid.

46. Interviews by Ann McFerran, 'The survivors', *Sunday Times Magazine* (4 December 2005)
http://www.timesonline.co.uk/article/0,,2099-1891957,00.html.

47. 'Where the bombers struck', *Guardian* (8 July 2005)
http://www.guardian.co.uk/terrorism/story/0,12780,1523850,00.html.

48. Interviews by Ann McFerran, op. cit.

49. 'Where the bombers struck', op. cit.

50. Jesse Hogan, et al., 'London bomb toll rises to 52', *Age* (8 July 2005)
http://www.theage.com.au/articles/2005/07/07/1120704533287.html.

51. BBC News, 'London bombing toll rises to 37' (7 July 2005)
http://news.bbc.co.uk/1/hi/uk/4661059.stm.

52. Jane Mingay, 'The London Bombings', *Digital Journalist* (August 2005)
http://www.digitaljournalist.org/issue0508/dis-mingay.html.

53. 'Freed chemist worried over return to UK', *Daily Mail* (10 August 2005)

http://www.dailymail.co.uk/pages/live/articles/news/
news.html?in_article_id=358768&in_page_id=1770.

54. Agence France Press, 'Britain clears Egyptian biochemist' (19 July 2005)
http://iafrica.com/news/us_terror/london/462801.htm.

55. Associated Press, 'Egyptian chemist knew two London attackers' (10
August 2005)
http://www2.chinadaily.com.cn/english/doc/2005-08/10/
content_467837.htm.

56. Richard Wood, David Leppard and Mick Smith, 'Tangled web that
still leaves worrying loose ends', *The Times* (30 July 2005)
http://www.timesonline.co.uk/article/0,,2087-1715122,00.html.

57. Valentine Spyroglou, 'French UCLAT Chief Notes Balkan Link to
London Bombings', Defense & Foreign Affairs Special Analysis
(Washington DC: Global Information System, 18 July 2005). This article is
not normally public domain, but was reprinted with permission online, at
http://www.slobodan-milosevic.org/news/dfasa071805.htm.

58. MPS Press Release, 'Metropolitian Police Service press conference at
11am 8 July', Metropolitan Police Service (8 July 2005)
http://cms.met.police.uk/news/major_operational_announcements/
terrorist_attacks/metropolitan_police_service_press_conference_
at_11am_8_july.

59. Jason Bennetto, 'Explosives', op. cit.

60. Mark Honinsbaum, 'Someone help me… please help me', *Guardian*
Audio Report (7 July 2005)
http://stream.guardian.co.uk:7080/ramgen/sys-audio/Guardian/
audio/2005/07/07/honisbaum_070705.ra.

61. Interviews by Ann McFerran, op. cit.

62. 'Where the bombers struck', op. cit.

63. CNN, 'Commuters recount subway horror' (15 July 2005)
http://edition.cnn.com/2005/WORLD/europe/07/07/
eyewitness.accounts.

64. 'I was in tube bomb carriage – and survived', *Cambridge Evening
News* (11 July 2005)
http://www.cambridge-news.co.uk/news/region_wide/2005/07/11/
83e33146-09af-4421-b2f4-1779a86926f9.lpf.

65. Sean O'Neill, Daniel McGrory, et. al., 'Police give warning that
bombers may strike again', *The Times* (9 July 2005)
http://www.timesonline.co.uk/article/0,,22989-1686680,00.html.

66. Daniel McGrory, 'Anxious mother's call led police to her bomber
son', *The Times* (13 July 2005)
http://www.timesonline.co.uk/article/0,,22989-1692028_1,00.html.

67. Sky News, 'Britain's suicide bombers' (13 July 2005)
http://www.sky.com/skynews/article/0,,30000-13385127,00.html.

68. Simon Jeffery, Mat Smith and agencies, 'London bombs were 'first
British suicide attacks'', *Guardian* (12 July 2005)

http://www.guardian.co.uk/attackonlondon/story/
0,16132,1526712,00.html?gusrc=rss.

69. BBC News, 'London bombers: Key facts' (21 July 2001)
http://news.bbc.co.uk/1/hi/uk/4676861.stm.

70. James Kirkup, 'Security services 'failed to arrest bombers last year'',
*Scotsman* (15 July 2005)
http://news.scotsman.com/uk.cfm?id=1398042005.

71. John Steele, 'Rucksack gang filmed at King's Cross "looked like the
infantry going to war" ' *Telegraph* (13 July 2005)
http://www.telegraph.co.uk/news/main.jhtml?xml=/news/2005/07/13/
ncctv13.xml&sSheet=/portal/2005/07/13/ixportaltop.html.

72. Mark McGiven, 'British born Muslim terrorists "who looked
completely normal" have "changed terrorist picture in Britain forever" ',
*Daily Record* (13 July 2005)
http://www.militantislammonitor.org/article/id/793.

73. MPS News Bulletin, 'One week anniversary bombings appeal'
(London: Metropolitan Police Service, 14 July 2005)
http://cms.met.police.uk/met/layout/set/print/content/view/full/1312.

74. 'Car could hold clues to London bombings', Leighton Buzzard
*Citizen/Observer* (14 July 2005)
http://www.leightonbuzzardonline.co.uk/
ViewArticle2.aspx?SectionID=1154&ArticleID=1085404.

75. James Button, 'London bomber slipped the net twice before', *Sydney
Morning Herald* (18 June 2005)
http://www.smh.com.au/news/world/
london-bomber-slipped-the-net-twice-before/2005/07/17/
1121538868658.html.

76. ABC News, 'Sources: July 7 Bomb Plot May Have Been Much Larger'
(20 January 2006)
http://abcnews.go.com/WNT/LondonBlasts/story?id=979905.

77. Jenny Booth, 'The deadly nail bombs meant for London commuters',
*The Times* (27 July 2005)
http://www.timesonline.co.uk/article/0,,22989-1710339,00.html.

78. Stephen Wright et. al., ''Primed bombs' could point to more suicide
cells', *Daily Mail* (18 July 2005)
http://www.dailymail.co.uk/pages/live/articles/news/
news.html?in_article_id=356180&in_page_id=1770.

79. Sean O'Neill and Stuart Tendler, 'Deadly device image leaked to US',
*The Times* (28 July 2005)
http://www.timesonline.co.uk/article/0,,22989-1711360,00.html.

80. CBC News, 'London police investigation: timeline' (11 August 2005)
http://www.cbc.ca/news/background/london_bombing/
investigation_timeline.html.

81. Jeff Edwards, 'Exclusive: Was it Suicide?' *Mirror* (16 July 2005)

http://www.mirror.co.uk/news/tm_objectid=15742951&method=full&siteid=94762&headline=was-it-suicide--name_page.html.

82. Philippe Naughton, et. al., 'CCTV picture shows London bomber', *The Times* (14 July 2005)
http://www.timesonline.co.uk/article/0,,22989-1693797,00.html.

83. http://www.timesonline.co.uk/printFriendly/0,,1-20749-1698044-20749,00.html.

84. 'Police appeal for bus bomber information', *Telegraph* (14 July 2005)
http://www.telegraph.co.uk/news/main.jhtml?xml=/news/2005/07/14/ubombings.xml&sSheet=/portal/2005/07/14/ixportaltop.html.

85. Amy Iggulden, 'If only we had been alert, say regulars on 7:48 to King's Cross Luton', *Telegraph* (14 July 2005)
http://www.expat.telegraph.co.uk/news/main.jhtml?xml=/news/2005/07/14/nluton114.xml.

86. Tina Susman, 'A city in silent grieving', Newsday (15 July 2005)
http://www.newsday.com/news/nationworld/world/ny-wobomb0715,0,7977248.story.

87. http://www.learning.channel4.co.uk/news/special-reports/special-reports-storypage.jsp?id=343.

88. 'Full police statement on London bombs', *The Times* (12 July 2005)
http://www.timesonline.co.uk/article/0,,22989-1691468,00.html.

89. Adam Nichols, 'Chemistry whiz linked to attack', *New York Daily News* (15 July 2005)
http://www.nydailynews.com/front/story/328394p-280543c.html.

90. 'Actual Train Times' for trains from Luton to Kings Cross on 7 July 2005, supplied by Marie Burnes, Thameslink Customer Relations (2005).

91. Ibid.

92. Jason Bennetto, 'Thirty key al-Qa'ida-linked terror suspects are identified by police', *Independent* (11 July 2005)
http://news.independent.co.uk/uk/crime/article298279.ece.

93. Charles Recknagel, 'London Bombings Investigators Seek Network Behind Suicide Attackers', Radio Free Europe/Radio Liberty (15 July 2005)
http://www.rferl.org/featuresarticle/2005/07/1590b0ca-2385-4fd4-87d1-b85e471657e2.html.

94. Craig Whitlock, 'Al-Qaeda Leaders Seen in Control', *Washington Post* Foreign Service (24 July 2005)
http://www.washingtonpost.com/wp-dyn/content/article/2005/07/23/AR2005072301052.html.

95. BBC News, 'Statement claiming London attacks' (7 July 2005)
http://news.bbc.co.uk/1/hi/uk/4660391.stm.

96. Yassin Mursharbash, 'What Does the Purported Al-Qaida Letter Actually Say', *Der Speigel* (7 July 2005)
http://service.spiegel.de/cache/international/0,1518,364134,00.html.
Al-Fagih's website is http://www.qal3ah.net.

97. Mark Tran and Donald MacLeod, 'Al-Qaida in Europe claims

responsibility for blasts', *Guardian* (7 July 2005)
http://www.guardian.co.uk/terrorism/story/0,12780,1523397,00.html.

98. Juan Cole, 'The time of revenge has come', *Salon* (8 July 2005)
http://www.salon.com/news/feature/2005/07/08/blowback/
index_np.html.

99. BBC News, 'Experts analyse bomber videotape' (3 September 2005)
http://news.bbc.co.uk/1/hi/uk/4210566.stm; NDTV, 'Al-Qaida claims
responsibility for London blasts' (2 September 2005)
http://www.ndtv.com/template/template.asp?template=
Londonblasts&slug=Al-Qaida+claims+UK+blasts&id=78227&callid=1.

100. Reuters, 'Militant cleric says attack on London 'inevitable'' (19 April
2004)
http://www.nzherald.co.nz/category/story.cfm?c_id=340&objectid=
3561379.

101. Sean O'Neil and Yakkov Lappin, 'Britain's online imam declares
war as he calls young to jihad', *The Times* (17 January 2005)
http://www.timesonline.co.uk/article/0,,2-1443903,00.html.

102. Interview with Glen Jenvey by David Storobin, Esq, 'UK Spy
Identifies Groups and People Behind London Bombings', Global Politician
(7 July 2005)
http://globalpolitician.com/articledes.asp?ID=960&cid=11&sid=60.

103. Sam Knight, 'Police defend Hamza inquiry as blame game begins',
*The Times* (8 February 2006)
http://www.timesonline.co.uk/article/0,,2-2030648,00.html.

104. BBC News, 'Row over French bomb arrest claim' (13 July 2005)

Section removed for
legal reasons

111. O'Neill, 'Radical Muslim leader', op. cit.

112. http://www.zwire.com/site/news.cfm?BRD=1861&dept_id=
152368&newsid=12730996&PAG=461&rfi=9

113. Jonathan Wald, 'N.Y. man admits he aided al Qaeda, set up jihad camp', CNN (11 August 2004)
http://www.cnn.com/2004/LAW/08/11/ny.terror.suspect/.

114. http://www.zwire.com/site/news.cfm?BRD=1861&dept_id= 152368&newsid=12730996&PAG=461&rfi=9

115. http://seattletimes.nwsource.com/html/nationworld/ 2002413851_london01.html

116. ABC News, 'London Bombers Have Ties to United States' (15 July 2005)

Section removed for
legal reasons

124. Black, 7/7, op. cit., p. 31.

125. Cited in Jamie Campbell, 'Why terrorist love Britain', *New Statesman* (August 2004)
http://www.newstatesman.com/site.php3?newTemplate= NSArticle_NS&newDisplayURN=200408090012.

126. Ibid.

127. Frank Gregory and Paul Wilkinson, 'Riding Pillion for Tackling Terrorism is a High-Risk Policy', Chatham House International Security Programme/National Security Challenge Briefing Paper (London: Royal Institute of International Affairs July 2005, No. 05/01) p. 2,
http://www.globalpolicy.org/empire/terrorwar/analysis/2005/ 0718ChathamHouse.pdf.

144. CNSNews.com,(24 May 2000).

145. Al-Sharq Al-Awsat (22 August 1998)

146. Laville, Sandra and Rozenberg, Gabriel, 'Al-Muhajiroun recruiting jihadis', *Telegraph* (17 September 2001).

147. Al-Muhajiroun Fatwa, 'Jihad Fatwa Against Israel' Case No. Israel/M/F50 (2 October 2000) available online at EmergencyNet News, Emergency Response and Research Institute, http://www.emergency.com/2000/fatwa2000.htm.

148. Shahar, Yael and Karmon, Ely, 'London-Based Islamic Group Issues Fatwa against Israel', International Policy Institute for Counter Terrorism, Herzlia (19 October, 2000) http://www.ict.org.il/articles/articledet.cfm?articleid=131.

149. Al-Muhajiroun Press Release, 'Advice and Warning to All Jews and Muslims in the UK' (17 October 2000). Also see Foster, Peter and Aldrick, Philip, 'Extremist backs 'kill Jews' poster', *Telegraph* (19 October 2000).

150. Reuters, 'Al-Muhajiroun issues fatwa against Musharraf' (18 September 2001).

151. *Asian Times*, 21 December 1999. Cited in *British Muslim Monthly Survey* (December 1999) 8 (12):9, http://artsweb.bham.ac.uk/bmms/1999/12December99.asp#Death%20threat%20against%20Yeltsin.

152. 'Bin Laden promises more suicide attacks', *The Times* (10 October 2001).

153. Andrew Dismore MP (Hendon), Hansard (Westminster: House of Commons (16 October 2001) 372 ( 31) http://www.parliament.the-stationery-office.co.uk/pa/cm200102/cmhansrd/vo011016/debtext/11016-15.htm.

154. *Sunday Telegraph* ( 23 September 2001).

155 *The Times* (22 September 2001).

156. *Daily Mail* (19 September 2001). Also see Whine, Michael, 'Al-Muhajiroun: The portal for Britain's suicide terrorists', International Policy Institute for Counter Terrorism, Herzliya (21 May 2003) http://www.ict.org.il/articles/articledet.cfm?articleid=484.

157. Alleyne, Richard and Bunyan, Nigel, 'Briton's boast of recruiting for bin Laden may lead to charges', *The Telegraph* (19 December 2001). http://www.opinion.telegraph.co.uk/news/main.jhtml?xml=/news/2001/12/19/nbut19.xml.

158. Demetriou, Danielle and Sawer, Patrick, 'Al-Muhajiroun say 1000 Brit Muslims have joined jihad', *This is London* (29 October 2001).

159. *Washington Post* (7 January 2002). Womack, Sarah and Alleyne, Richard, 'Police can't stop Muslim inciting terror in Britain', *The Telegraph* ( 8 January 2002).

http://www.telegraph.co.uk/news/main.jhtml?xml=/news/2002/01/08/nbutt08.xml.

160. Bamber, David, 'Hunt for 1,200 Britons who trained with al-Qa'eda', *Telegraph* (26 January 2003)
http://www.telegraph.co.uk/news/main.jhtml?xml=/news/2003/01/26/nalq26.xml&sSheet=/news/2003/01/26/ixnewstop.html&secureRefresh=true&_requestid=52048.

161. Banerji, Robin, 'Looking for Trouble', *Time Magazine* (8 December 2002)
http://www.time.com/time/europe/magazine/article/0,13005,901021216-397474,00.html.

162. Doyle, Neil, 'Al Qaeda uses Web sites to draw recruits, spread propaganda', *Washington Times* (11 September 2003).

143. Gertz, Bill, 'Islamists to honor 9/11 hijackers', *Washington Times* (30 August 2003)
http://www.washtimes.com/national/20030829-113829-1065r.htm.

164. Audrey Gillan and Duncan Campbell, 'Many faces of Bakri: enemy of west, press bogeyman and scholar', *Guardian* (13 August 2005)
http://www.guardian.co.uk/terrorism/story/0,12780,1548407,00.html.

165. Sandra Contenta, 'Jihad in London', *Toronto Star* (2 May 2004)
http://www.thestar.com/NASApp/cs/ContentServer?pagename=thestar/Layout/Article_PrintFriendly&c=Article&cid=1083535388730&call_pageid=968332188854.

166. Intel Report (Northern Virginia: Terrorist Research Center, 8 July 2005)
http://www.terrorism.com/modules.php?op=modload&name=Intel&file=index&view=649.

167. BBC News, 'Britain sheltering al-Qaeda leader' (8 July 8 2002)
http://news.bbc.co.uk/1/hi/uk/2115371.stm.
BBC News. 'Investigating Terror: People', 2001 (viewed 10 June 2004)
http://news.bbc.co.uk/hi/english/static/in_depth/world/2001/war_on_terror/investigation_on_terror/people_4.stm.
Cited in Watson, Paul Joseph, *Order Out of Chaos: Elite Sponsored Terrorism and the New World Order* (AEJ Productions, 2002).

168. BBC Radio 4, 'West London Terror Suspect' (19 October 2001)
http://www.bbc.co.uk/radio4/today/reports/politics/qatada.shtml.

169. British Treasury, Bank of England, 'Terrorist Financing: List of Suspects' (12 October 2001)
http://www.bankofengland.co.uk/sanctions/sanctionsconlistoct01a.pdf. Also see Watson, op. cit.

170. Harris, Paul, et. al., 'Britain's most wanted: How was the terrorist hunted for plotting terrorist attacks across Europe allowed to disappear in the UK', *The Observer* (5 May 2002)
http://observer.guardian.co.uk/focus/story/0,6903,710502,00.html.

171. Leppard, David, 'Terror links in Europe: MI5 knew for years of London mosque's role', *Sunday Times* (25 November 2001).

172. Ibid.

173. Terence McKenna, 'The Recruiters', CBC News (16 March 2004) http://www.cbc.ca/national/news/recruiters/qatada.html.

174. Emerson Vermatt, 'Mustafa Setmarian Nasar – A close friend of Bin Laden's and Al –Zarqawi's', *Militant Islam Monitor* (4 December 2005) http://www.militantislammonitor.org/article/id/1355.

175. Nick Fielding and Gareth Walsh, 'Mastermind of Madrid is key figure', *The Times* (10 July 2005) http://www.timesonline.co.uk/article/0,,2087-1688244,00.html.

176. WorldNetDaily, 'London bombings tied to Madrid attackers?' (7 July 2005) http://www.worldnetdaily.com/news/article.asp?ARTICLE_ID=45171.

177. Leppard, David, 'Terror links in Europe: MI5 knew for years of London mosque's role', *Sunday Times* (25 November 2001).

178. Townsend, et. al., 'The secret war', op. cit.

179. Lawrence Wright, 'The Terror Web', *New Yorker* (2 August 2004) http://www.newyorker.com/fact/content/?040802fa_fact.

180. AFP, 'Two Britons held over Morocco bomb', *Sydney Morning Herald* (3 August 2003) http://www.smh.com.au/articles/2003/08/03/1059849267388.html.

181. Mark Townsend, John Hooper, Greg Bearup, et. al., 'The secret war', *Observer* (21 March 2004) http://observer.guardian.co.uk/waronterrorism/story/0,1373,1174624,00.html.

182. AFP, 'Two Britons held over Morocco bomb', op. cit.

183. Townsend, et. al., 'The secret war', op. cit.

184. Jeremy Bradshaw, 'Who claims to be behind the London bombings?' Newsmax (12 July 2005) http://www.newsmax.com/archives/articles/2005/7/12/101248.shtml.

185. MIPT Terrorism Knowledge Base, 'Moroccan Islamic Combatant Group' (Oklahoma: National Memorial Institute for the Prevention of Terrorism, 8 January 2006) http://www.tkb.org/KeyLeader.jsp?memID=5885.

186. Daniel McGrory, 'Europe's police asked to step up hunt for Morocco-born scholar', *The Times* (8 July 2005) http://www.timesonline.co.uk/article/0,,22989-1686838,00.html.

187. Glenn Frankel, 'London subway blasts almost simultaneous, investigators concluded', *Washington Post* (10 July 2005) http://www.washingtonpost.com/wp-dyn/content/article/2005/07/09/AR2005070901248_pf.html.

188. Townsend, et. al., 'The secret war', op. cit.

189. Tapper, Jake, 'Muslim spy who infiltrated bin Laden's terror

network in London', *The Times* (16 January 2003)
http://www.timesonline.co.uk/article/0,,5041-544935,00.html.

190. Burke, Jason, 'How I was betrayed by the British', *The Observer* (18 February 2001)
http://www.observer.co.uk/focus/story/0,6903,439639,00.html.

191. Rotella, Sebastian and Sobart, Janet, 'British flex muscles in raid', *Daily Iowan* (21 January 2003)
http://www.dailyiowan.com/news/2003/01/21/Nation/
British.Flex.Muscles.In.Raid-347904.shtml.

192. Sweeney, John, 'Bin Laden connected to London dissident', BBC News (10 March 2002)
http://news.bbc.co.uk/1/hi/uk/1862579.stm.

193. O'Neill, Sean, 'Britain a perfect haven for Islamic radicals looking for recruits', *Telegraph* (11 September 2002)
http://www.telegraph.co.uk/news/main.jhtml?xml=/news/campaigns/
war/recruit.xml.

194. Greenslade, Nick, 'Who's afraid of al-Masari?' *Tribune* (27 February 2003)
http://www.tribweb.co.uk/greenslade21022003.htm.
[http://www.terrorismcentral.com/Library/Incidents/
USEmbassyKenyaBombing/Indictment/Introduction.html.]

195. Kenyan Embassy Bombing, op. cit.,
http://www.terrorismcentral.com/Library/Incidents/
USEmbassyKenyaBombing/Indictment/Introduction.html.

196. Sweeney, 'Bin Laden connected to London dissident', op. cit.

197. Fielding, Nick and Gadhery, Dipesh, 'Bin Laden called UK 260 times', *Sunday Times* (24 March 2002).

198. Kenyan Embassy Bombing, United States District Court, Southern District of New York, Indictment, *United States of America vs Usama Bin Laden, S(9) 98 Cr. 1023 (LBS)*,
http://www.terrorismcentral.com/Library/Incidents/
USEmbassyKenyaBombing/Indictment/Count1.html.

199. Nick Hopkins and Richard Norton-Taylor, 'Faulty intelligence', *Guardian* (29 November 2001)
http://www.guardian.co.uk/ukresponse/story/0,11017,608620,00.html.

200. Liberty Report, *Anti-Terrorism Legislation in the United Kingdom*, (Liberty: London, 2001)
http://www.liberty-human-rights.org.uk/resources/publications/
pdf-documents/anti-terrornew.pdf.

201. Don Mackay, Oonagh Blackman And Bob Roberts, 'They'll Attack Us This Week', *Mirror* (22 July 2005)
http://www.mirror.co.uk/news/tm_objectid=15766856&method=
full&siteid=94762&headline=they-ll-attack-us-this-week-name_page.html.

202. Mark Urban, 'Attack devices 'similar to 7 July'', BBC News (21 July

2005)
http://news.bbc.co.uk/1/hi/uk/4705419.stm.

203. Glenn Frankell, 'London Hit Again With Explosives', *Washington Post* Foreign Service (22 July 2005)
http://www.washingtonpost.com/wp-dyn/content/article/2005/07/21/AR2005072100474.html.

204. Paul Tumelty, 'Reassessing the July 21 London Bombings', *Terrorism Monitor* (Washington DC: Jamestowm Foundation, 8 September 2005, 3 (17))

205. 'London on high alert one month after blasts', *Daily Mail* (4 August 2005)
http://www.dailymail.co.uk/pages/live/articles/news/news.html?in_article_id=358138&in_page_id=1770.

206. Associated Press, 'British authorities question bombings suspect in Rome', *USA Today* (8 September 2005)
http://www.usatoday.com/news/world/2005-08-09-britain-suspect_x.htm.

207. Staff and agencies, 'Bomb suspects lodges extradition appeal', *Guardian* (26 August 2005)
http://www.guardian.co.uk/attackonlondon/story/0,,1557028,00.html.

208. Agenzia Giornalistica Italia, 'Hamdi Isaac, Judges: Was Involved in Preparation of Crimes' (Rome, 17 August 2005)
http://www.agi.it/english/news.pl.

209. This does not mean that, for instance, it is impossible to use flour to generate explosions – the point is that an explosion can only be generated using very specific ingredients in particular quantities, mobilised according to a precise procedure.

210. Tumelty, op. cit.

211. Audrey Gillan, 'Four suspects said to have worshipped at Finsbury Park mosque', *Guardian* (1 August 2005)
http://www.guardian.co.uk/religion/Story/0,,1540244,00.html.

212. Duncan Gardham and Philip Johston, 'Terror suspect is a convicted mugger', *Telegraph* (27 July 2005)
http://www.telegraph.co.uk/news/main.jhtml?xml=/news/2005/07/27/nbomb27.xml.

213. David Leppard, 'MI5 rebels expose Tube bomb cover-up' *The Times* (26 February 2006)
http://www.timesonline.co.uk/article/0,,2087-2059046,00.html.

214. Defence Intelligence Agency (DIA), 'Veteran Afghan Traveller's Analysis of Al Qaeda and Taliban's Exploitable Weaknesses' (Washington DC: Department of Defence, 24 September 2001); DIA, 'Veteran Afghanistan traveller's analysis of Al Qaeda and Taliban, military, political and cultural landscape and its weaknesses' (Washington DC: Department of Defence, 24 September 2001). Declassified in September 2003.

215. Frankel, 'London Hit Again With Explosives', op. cit.

216. Don Mackay, Oonagh Blackman and Bob Roberts, 'They'll attack us

this week', *Mirror* (22 July 2005)
http://www.mirror.co.uk/news/tm_objectid=15766856&method=
full&siteid=94762&headline=they-ll-attack-us-this-week-name_page.html.

217. 'A 'Strange' Al Qaeda Leader: 'I Don't Pray, I Drink Alcohol,''
*Journal of Turkish Weekly* [contributions from Turkish dailies, *Zaman* and
*Hurriyet*] (14 August 2005)
http://www.turkishweekly.net/news.php?id=17778.

218. 'Turkey arrests al Qaeda suspects,' BBC News (10 August 2005)
http://news.bbc.co.uk/2/hi/europe/4140210.stm.

219. Gun, Ercun, 'Sakra: I Dispatched Men to US and UK for Terrorist
Activity,' *Zaman* (15August 2005)
http://www.zaman.com/?bl=national&alt=&trh=20050815&hn=23056.

220. Jonathan Calvert and David Leppard, 'Police shot wrong man',
*Sunday Times* (24 July 2005)
http://www.timesonline.co.uk/article/0,,2087-1706793,00.html.

221. Ibid.

222. ITV News, 'Mistakes led to Tube shooting' (16 August 2003)
http://www.itv.com/news/index_1677571.html.

223. Vikram Dodd and Hugh Muir, 'De Menezes "shot for 30 seconds" ',
*Guardian* (26 August 2005)
http://www.guardian.co.uk/uk_news/story/0,3604,1556769,00.html.

224. Tony Thompson, Martin Bright , Gaby Hinsliff and Tom Phillips,
'Police knew Brazilian was not "bomb risk" ', *Observer* (21 August 2005)
http://observer.guardian.co.uk/uk_news/story/0,6903,1553440,00.html.

225. Rosie Cowan, Vikram Dodd and Richard Norton-Taylor, 'Met chief
tried to stop shooting inquiry', *Guardian* (18 August 2005)
http://www.guardian.co.uk/attackonlondon/story/0,16132,1551340,00.html.
In this context, it is difficult to understand how BBC *Panorama* reporter Peter
Taylor was able to vaguely speculate that 'it *appears* that the surveillance
officers finally made a positive identification before the bus that Jean was on
reached Stockwell… I *understand* that Commander Dick then *said something
like* "Are you absolutely sure", to which the answer *seems* to have been
"Yes" [my emphasis]', in Peter Taylor, 'Double tragedy of Stockwell
shooting', BBC *Panorama* (8 March 2006)
http://news.bbc.co.uk/1/hi/programmes/panorama/4782718.stm.

226. Stewart Tendler, 'Police tampered with log on dead Brazilian
"suspect" ', *The Times* (30 January 2006)
http://www.timesonline.co.uk/article/0,,22989-2016188,00.html.

227. 'Police who shot Brazilian on Tube "to escape charges" ', *Sunday
Times* (27 November 2005)
http://www.timesonline.co.uk/article/0,,2087-1892743,00.html.

228. Cowan, Dodd and Norton-Taylor, 'Met chief tried to stop shooting
inquiry', op. cit.

229. Richard Norton-Taylor, 'New special forces unit trailed Brazilian',

*Guardian* (4 August 2005)
http://www.guardian.co.uk/uk_news/story/0,3604,1542080,00.html.

230. James Cusick, 'An Innocent Man Shot Dead on the London Tube by Police', *Sunday Herald* (21 August 2005)
http://www.sundayherald.com/51372.

231. Sean Rayment, 'Britain forms new special forces unit to fight al-Qa'eda', *Telegraph* (25 July 2004)
http://www.telegraph.co.uk/news/main.jhtml?xml=/news/2004/07/25/nrsr25.xml.

232. Neil Mackay, 'Exclusive: confessions of a secret agent turned terrorist', *Sunday Herald* (23 June 2002)
http://www.sundayherald.com/25646.

233. Vikram Dodd, 'Seconds to decide if suspect is suicide threat' *Guardian* (23 July 2005)
http://www.guardian.co.uk/attackonlondon/story/0,16132,1534753,00.html.

234. Sophie Goodchild, 'Police chiefs urged secrecy over shoot-to-kill anti-terror tactics', *Independent on Sunday* (12 February 2006)
http://news.independent.co.uk/uk/crime/article344957.ece.

235. Dodd, 'Seconds to decide if suspect is suicide threat', op. cit.

236. BBC News, ''No impunity' for shoot-to-kill' (26 July 2005)
http://news.bbc.co.uk/2/hi/uk_news/4716645.stm.

237. John Gardner, 'Oxford Law Prof alarmed at "police's Mossad-style execution" of innocent suspect', *Bellaciao* (26 July 2005)
http://bellaciao.org/en/article.php3?id_article=7189.

238. Jason Bennetto, 'Police are given shoot-to-kill powers in domestic violence and stalking cases', *Independent* (25 October 2005)
http://news.independent.co.uk/uk/crime/article322021.ece.

239. Agence France-Presse, 'London police "suppressing" files on shot Brazilian' (5 March 2005).

240. Holden Frith, 'Police "had no warning" of terrorist attacks', *The Times* (7 July 2005)
http://www.timesonline.co.uk/article/0,,22989-1684588,00.html.

241. Robert Winnet and David Leppard, 'Leaked No 10 dossier reveals Al-Qaeda's British recruits', *The Times* (10 July 2005)
http://www.timesonline.co.uk/article/0,,2087-1688261,00.html.
Full dossier available on *The Times* website,
http://www.times-archive.co.uk/onlinespecials/cabinet1.pdf;
http://www.times-archive.co.uk/onlinespecials/cabinet2.pdf;
http://www.times-archive.co.uk/onlinespecials/cabinet3.pdf;
http://www.times-archive.co.uk/onlinespecials/cabinet4.pdf.

242. Jenny Booth, 'MI5 chief warns of terror threat facing Britons', *The Times* (8 November 2005)
http://www.timesonline.co.uk/article/0,,2-1349997,00.html.

243. Massoud Ansari, 'Al Qa'eda third in command "is running terror cells in the UK" ' *Telegraph* (19 September 2004)

244. UPI, 'Report: France and Saudi knew of 7/7 plans' (9 August 2005)

245. B. Raman, 'Repeat of Madrid in London', South Asia Analysis Group (7 July 2005, No. 1447)
http://saag.org/papers15/paper1447.html.

246. 'US intelligence may point to a link', Newsday (8 July 2005) available at
http://answers.google.com/answers/threadview?id=546199.

247. Brian Ross and David Scott, 'The Warning Before the Attack: Officials tell ABC News al-Qaeda leader warned of plans', ABC News (8 July 2005)
http://abcnews.go.com/WNT/LondonBlasts/story?id=922494.

248. Mushtak Parker, 'Police Warn of New Attack on London', Arab News (15 July 2005)
http://www.arabnews.com/?page=4&section=0&article=66976&d=15&m=7&y=2005.

249. Antony Barnett and Martin Bright, 'We warned MI6 of tube attack, claim Saudis', *Guardian* (4 September 2005)
http://www.guardian.co.uk/saudi/story/0,11599,1562436,00.html.

250. Hedges, 'Blast points to Al Qaeda', op. cit.

251. Martin Bright, et. al, 'Saudis warned UK of London attacks', *Observer* (7 August 2005)
http://observer.guardian.co.uk/uk_news/story/0,6903,1544263,00.html.

252. Toby Hamden, 'Al Qaeda in Saudi Arabia linked to London hits', *Washington Times* (7 August 2005)
http://washingtontimes.com/world/20050806-100648-8356r.htm.

253. Martin Bright, et. al, 'Saudis warned UK of London attacks', *Observer* (7 August 2005)
http://observer.guardian.co.uk/uk_news/story/0,6903,1544263,00.html.

254. Fielding and Walsh, 'Mastermind of key figure', op. cit.

255. Mark Oliver, "Al-Qaeda chief' held in Pakistan', *Guardian* (3 November 2005)
http://www.guardian.co.uk/spain/article/0,2763,1607660,00.html.

256. Edward Owen and Daniel McGrory, 'Madrid mastermind may plan UK attack', *The Times* (5 March 2005)
http://www.timesonline.co.uk/article/0,,3-1511134,00.html.

257. News24, 'Al-Qaeda ordered attacks' (11 July 2005)
http://www.news24.com/News24/World/Londonattacks/0,,2-10-1854_1735664,00.html.

258. Associated Press (7 July 2005). Cited in Stratfor, 'Israel Warned United Kingdom About Possible Attacks', Stratfor Consulting Intelligence Agency (7 July 2005)
http://fairuse.1accesshost.com/news2/stratfor-london.html.

259. Tom Kenny, 'Terrorism expert says at least one person tipped off to

attacks', Action News 36 (7 July 2005)
http://www.wtvq.com/servlet/Satellite?pagename=WTVQ/MGArticle/
TVQ_BasicArticle&c=MGArticle&cid=1031783713979&path=.

260. Arutz Sheva, 'Report: Israel Was Warned Ahead of the First Blast',
Israel National News (8 July 2005)
http://www.israelnationalnews.com/news.php3?id=85346.

261. 'Mossad tells Brits: Same explosive likely used in Tel Aviv and
London blasts', *Israeli Insider* (11 July 2005)
http://web.israelinsider.com/Articles/Security/5997.htm.

262. Stratfor, 'Israel Warned United Kingdom About Possible Attacks',
Stratfor Consulting Intelligence Agency (7 July 2005)
http://fairuse.1accesshost.com/news2/stratfor-london.html.

263. 'City centre hit by bomb scare', *South Wales Echo* (4 July 2005)
http://icwales.icnetwork.co.uk/capitalcity/news/tm_objectid=
15697676&method=full&siteid=50082&headline=
city-centre-hit-by-bomb-scare-name_page.html.

264. 'Bomb scare ahead of G-8 Summit', *Evening Telegraph* (5 July 2005)
http://www.eveningtelegraph.co.uk/output/2005/07/05/
story7304397t0.shtm.

265. Sean O' Neill and Daniel McGrory, 'Abu Hamza and the 7/7
bombers', *The Times* (8 February 2006)
http://www.timesonline.co.uk/article/0,,2-2030129,00.html.

266. Interview with Glen Jenvey by David Storobin, Esq, 'UK Spy
Identifies Groups and People Behind London Bombings', op. cit.

267. Black, *7-7: What Went Wrong?* op. cit., p. 40-41.

268. Simon Freeman, 'Leaked security services memo says Britain was
safe', *The Times* (19 July 2005)
http://www.timesonline.co.uk/article/0,,22989-1700121,00.html.

269 Black, *7-7: What Went Wrong?* op. cit., p. 38-39.

270. Ibid., p. 44.

271. 'The reconstruction: 7/7 – what really happened?' *Independent* (20
January 2006)
http://news.independent.co.uk/uk/crime/article299674.ece.

272. Daniel McGrory, Michael Evans and Dominic Kennedy, 'Killer in
the classroom', *The Times* (14 July 2005)
http://www.timesonline.co.uk/article/0,,22989-1693463,00.html.

273. Peter Finn and Glen Frankel, 'Al Qaeda Link to Attacks in London
Probed', *Washington Post* (1 August 2005)
http://www.washingtonpost.com/wp-dyn/content/article/2005/07/31/
AR2005073100624.html.

274. ITN News, ''Detained Briton' in bomb phone link' (21 July 2005)
http://216.239.59.104/search?q=cache:kjTSuhYqW0gJ:www.itn.co.uk/news/
962650.html+%27Detained+Briton%27+in+bomb+phone+link+ITN&hl=en.

275. Zahid Hussain, Daniel McGrory and Sean O'Neill, 'Top al-Qaeda

Briton called Tube bombers before attack', *The Times* (21 July 2005)
http://www.timesonline.co.uk/article/0,,22989-1702411,00.html.

276. Richard Woods, David Leppard and Mick Smith, 'Tangled web that still leaves worrying loose ends', *The Times* (30 July 2005)
http://www.timesonline.co.uk/article/0,,2087-1715122,00.html.

277. Ibid.

278. Tony Harney, "Batley man' linked to bin Laden and bombers', Leeds *Today/Yorkshire Evening Post* (30 July 2005)
http://www.leedstoday.net/ViewArticle2.aspx?SectionID= 39&ArticleID=1101334.

279. Simon Freeman, 'British al-Qaeda suspect facing extradition to the US', *The Times* (8 August 2005)
http://www.timesonline.co.uk/article/0,,22989-1726513,00.html.

280. Associated Press, 'London bombing suspects formally charged' (8 August 2005)
http://sify.com/news/fullstory.php?id=13913208.

281. Woods, et. al., 'Tangled web that still leaves worrying loose ends', op. cit.

282. Ibid.

283. Interview with John Loftus by Mike Jerrick, 'The Links of Terror Suspect to MI6', Fox News (29 July 2005); Complete transcript (Montreal: Center for Research on Globalization, 1 August 2005)
http://www.globalresearch.ca/index.php?context=viewArticle&code= 20050801&articleId=783.

284. Christopher Berry-Dee, 'London Bombing ringleader, Haroon Rashid Aswat – double agent for MI6?', *New Criminologist* (23 August 2005)
http://www.newcriminologist.co.uk/news.asp?id=1124824797.

285. Berry-Dee, 'Haroon Aswat…FBI agent threatens former USDA federal agent, now staff reporter for The New Criminologist', *New Criminologist* (25 September 2005)
http://www.newcriminologist.co.uk/news.asp?id=-1677497717.

286. BBC News, 'Briton facing extradition to US' (5 January 2006)
http://news.bbc.co.uk/2/hi/uk_news/4583520.stm.

287. BBC News, 'Briton 'facing Guantanamo spell'' (22 December 2005)
http://news.bbc.co.uk/2/hi/uk_news/4552652.stm.

288. Jason Bennetto and Ian Herbert, 'London bombings: the truth emerges', *Independent* (13 August 2005)
http://news.independent.co.uk/crime/article305547.ece.

289. Interview with John Loftus by Mike Jerrick, 'The Links of Terror Suspect to MI6', op. cit.

290. Andrew Dismore MP (Hendon), Hansard (Westminster: House of Commons, 16 October 2001, Vol. 372, No. 31)
http://www.parliament.the-stationery-office.co.uk/pa/cm200102/ cmhansrd/vo011016/debtext/11016-15.htm.

291. Sean O'Neill, 'Abu Hamza 'boasted of Bosnia action'', *The Times* (17

January 2006)
http://www.timesonline.co.uk/article/0,,2-1988689,00.html.

292. Barnett, Anthony, et. al., 'MI5 wanted me to escape, claims cleric', *Observer* (21 October 2001).

293. Barnett, 'Bin Laden mastermind "still hiding in Britain" ', *Observer* (5 May 2002)
http://observer.guardian.co.uk/uk_news/story/0,6903,710330,00.html.

294. Harris, Paul, 'Britain's most wanted', op. cit.

295. Crumley, Bruce, 'Sheltering a Puppet Master?', *Time*,(7 July 2002)
http://www.time.com/time/world/article/0,8599,300609,00.html.

296. McGrory, Daniel and Ford, Richard, 'Al-Qaeda cleric exposed as an MI5 double agent', *The Times* (25 March 2004)
http://www.timesonline.co.uk/article/0,,3-1050175,00.html.

297. Open Judgement of Mr Justice Collins (Chairman), Special Immigration Appeals Commission, January 2004, pp. 11-12,
http://www.channel4.com/news/ftp_images2/2004/03/week_4/23_document.pdf.

298. Gillan, Audrey, 'Detained Muslim cleric is spiritual leader to militants, hearing told', *Guardian* (20 November 2003).

299. Richard Ford and Daniel McGrory, 'Blunkett fury as Privy Councillors attack terror laws', *The Times* (19 December 2003).

300. Associated Press, 'Cleric charged with incitement in Britain', ABC News (19 October 2004)
http://abcnews.go.com/International/print?id=178869.

301. Sean O'Neill, 'Police viewed imam's terror book years before he was seized', *The Times* (18 January 2006)
http://www.timesonline.co.uk/article/0,,2-1990799,00.html.

302. Sam Knight, 'Police defend Hamza inquiry as blame game begins', *The Times* (8 February 2006)
http://www.timesonline.co.uk/article/0,,2-2030648,00.html.

303. John Steele and George Stone, 'CPS twice refused to prosecute Abu Hamza', *Telegraph* (9 February 2006)
http://www.telegraph.co.uk/news/main.jhtml?xml=/news/2006/02/09/nhamz09.xml&sSheet=/news/2006/02/09/ixnewstop.html.

304. Jason Burke, 'How I was betrayed by the British', *Observer* (18 February 2001)
http://observer.guardian.co.uk/focus/story/0,6903,439639,00.html.

305. Jake Tapper, 'The Spy Who Came in From the Mosque', *Weekly Standard* (13 January 2003, Vol. 8, No. 7)
http://www.weeklystandard.com/Content/Public/Articles/000/000/002/077wgbzn.asp?pg=1.

306. Dhaika Dridi and Chris McGann, 'Infiltrator links men at Oregon ranch to al-Qaida', *Seattle-Post Intelligence* (30 July 2002)
http://seattlepi.nwsource.com/local/80576_terror30.shtml.

307. Press Association, 'CPS defends Hamza evidence handling',

*Scotsman* (8 February 2006)

http://news.scotsman.com/latest.cfm?id=201922006.

308. Alan Cowell, 'Cleric asserts British once asked his aid on terror', *New York Times* (20 January 2006)

http://www.nytimes.com/2006/01/20/international/europe/20cnd-hamza.html?ex=1138856400&en=5dd8a0a697b862ed&ei=5070.

309. Burke, 'How I was betrayed by the British', op. cit.

310. Sean O'Neill, 'Why France lived in fear of "Londonistan" ', *Telegraph* (13 October 2001)

http://www.telegraph.co.uk/news/main.jhtml?xml=/news/2001/10/13/nmosq13.xml.

311. Jason Burke, 'AK-47 training held at London mosque', *Observer* (17 February 2002)

http://observer.guardian.co.uk/islam/story/0,1442,651748,00.html.

312. Jamie Doward and Diane Taylor, 'Hamza set up terror camps with British ex-soldiers', *Observer* (12 February 2006)

http://observer.guardian.co.uk/uk_news/story/0,,1708002,00.html.

313. Sean O' Neill, Daniel McGrory, Philip Webster, 'Police had Hamza "murder evidence" 7 years ago', *The Times* (9 February 2006)

http://www.timesonline.co.uk/article/0,,2-2031812,00.html.

314. Mukherjee, Subroto, 'Omar Sheikh: Profile of a Kidnapper,' *South Asian Outlook* (March 2002)

http://www.southasianoutlook.com/sao_back_issues/march_2002/omar_sheikh.htm.

315. Stock, Jon, 'Inside the mind of a seductive killer', *The Times* (21 August 2002) archived at

http://www.cooperativeresearch.org/timeline/2002/londontimes082102.html.

316. Ibid.

317. Bamber, David, et. al., 'London house linked to US plot', *The Telegraph* (30 September 2001)

http://news.telegraph.co.uk/news/main.jhtml?xml=/news/2001/09/30/nhunt30.xml.

318. For extensive documentation and cross-referencing on Sheikh Saeed's involvement in 9/11 on behalf of both al-Qaeda and Pakistani intelligence services, see Nafeez Mosaddeq Ahmed, *The War on Truth: 9/11, Disinformation and the Anatomy of Terrorism* (London: Arris, 2005) pp. 137-146. Sources on the transfers to Atta ordered by Gen. Ahmad in his then capacity as head of Pakistani military-intelligence include the *Times* of India (New Delhi), *Dawn* (Karachi) and the *Wall Street Journal* (Washington) quoting Indian, Pakistani and American government and intelligence officials.

319. CNN, 'Suspected Hijack Bankroller Freed by India in 99' (6 October 2001)

http://www.cnn.com/2001/US/10/05/inv.terror.investigation.

320. Hirschkorn, Phil, 'Embassy Bombing Trial Revealed bin Laden Links,' CNN (16 October 2001)
http://www.cnn.com/2001/US/10/16/inv.embassy.bombings.connections/.

321. Michael Meacher, 'Britain now faces its own blowback', *Guardian* (10 September 2005)
http://www.guardian.co.uk/comment/story/0,3604,1566916,00.html.

322. 'Did Pearl die because Pakistan deceived CIA?,' *Pittsburg Tribune-Review* (3 March 2002)
http://www.pittsburghlive.com/x/tribune-review/opinion/datelinedc/s_20141.html.

323. Klaidman, Daniel, 'US officials are eager to try the main suspect in Daniel Pearl's murder,' *Newsweek* (13 March 2002)
http://www.msnbc.com/news/723527.asp.

324 Swami, Praveen, 'A Sheikh and the money trail,' *Frontline* (13-26 October 2001, 18 (21))
http://www.frontlineonnet.com/fl1821/18210150.htm.

325. *New York Times* (15 March 2002).

326. CNN (28 February 2002).

327. 'Did Pearl die because Pakistan deceived CIA?,' *Pittsburg Tribune-Review*, op. cit.

328. Hussain, Zahid and McGrory, Daniel, 'London schoolboy who graduated to terrorism', *The Times* (16 July 2002)
http://www.timesonline.co.uk/newspaper/0,,171-357086,00.html.

329. Williams, David, 'Kidnapper-Guy Hotmail.com', *Daily Mail* (16 July 2002) archived at
http://www.cooperativeresearch.org/timeline/2002/dailymail071602.html.

330. Press Trust of India, 'UK Move To Allow Entry To Ultra Alarms Abducted Britons' (3 January 2000) archived at
http://www.cooperativeresearch.org/timeline/2000/pti010300.html.

331. Anson, Robert Sam, 'The Journalist and the Terrorist', *Vanity Fair* (August 2002) archived at
http://www.cooperativeresearch.org/timeline/2002/vanityfair0802.html.

332. BBC News, 'Profile: Omar Saeed Sheikh' (16 July 2002)
http://news.bbc.co.uk/2/hi/uk/1804710.stm.

333. BBC News, 'Militant free to return to UK' (3 January 2000)
http://news.bbc.co.uk/1/hi/uk/588915.stm.

334. 'Did Pearl die because Pakistan deceived CIA?,' op. cit.

335. Meacher, 'Britain faces its own blowback', op. cit.

336. See for instance Intelligence Services Act 1994 at
http://www.opsi.gov.uk/acts/acts1994/Ukpga_19940013_en_1.htm.

337. Yaakov Lappin, 'British Muslim group declares new jihad', Ynetnews (19 October 2005)
http://www.ynetnews.com/Ext/Comp/ArticleLayout/CdaArticlePrintPreview/1,2506,L-3156809,00.html

338. For extensive documentation largely from newly declassified secret

British Foreign Office files, see Mark Curtis, *The Ambiguities of Power: British foreign policy since 1945* (London: Zed, 1995).

339. Vesna Peric Zimonjic, 'Fears rise over support to terrorists', Inter Press Service (25 July 2005)
http://www.ipsnews.net/africa/interna.asp?idnews=29625.

340. ISN Security Watch, 'British in Bosnia to Probe 7 July Terror Link' (15 January 2006)
http://www.isn.ethz.ch/news/sw/details.cfm?id=14359.

341. Defense & Foreign Affairs Special Analysis, 'Despite Firm Linkages to 9/11, Madrid, and London Attacks, Bosnian Jihadist Networks Remain "Out of Bounds",' (13 July 2005). Cited in Spyroglou, op. cit.

342. O'Neill, Brendan, 'How we trained al-Qa'eda', *The Spectator* (13 September 2003).

343. Aldrich, Richard J., 'America used Islamists to arm the Bosnian muslims: The Srebrenica report reveals the Pentagon's role in a dirty war', *Guardian* (22 April 2002)
http://www.guardian.co.uk/yugo/article/0,2763,688327,00.html.

344. Wiebes, Cees, *Intelligence and the War in Bosnia 1992-1995*, Lit Verlag (2003, pp. 159–62)
http://213.222.3.5/srebrenica.

345. Ibid., p. 167.

346. Cited in Chossudsky, Michel, 'Osamagate', Centre for Research on Globalisation, Montreal (9 October 2001)
http://www.globalresearch.ca/articles/CHO110A.html.

347. Ibid., p. 207.

348. Bodanksy, Yossef, *Some Call It Peace: Waiting for War in the Balkans*, International Media Corporation, London (1996, Chapters 3 and 9). An online version is available at:
http://members.tripod.com/Balkania/resources/geostrategy/bodansky_peace.

349. Chossudovsky, Michel, 'Osamagate,' Centre for Research on Globalisation, Montreal (9 October 2001)
http://globalresearch.ca/articles/CHO110A.html.
Chossudovsky has taught as Visiting Professor at academic institutions in Western Europe, Latin America and Southeast Asia, has acted as economic adviser to governments of developing countries and has worked as a consultant for several international organisations, including the United Nations Development Program (UNDP), the African Development Bank, the United Nations African Institute for Economic Development and Planning (AIEDEP), the United Nations Population Fund (UNFPA), the International Labour Organization (ILO), the World Health Organisation (WHO), the United Nations Economic Commission for Latin America and the Caribbean (ECLAC).

350. Wiebes, op. cit., Chapter 4.

351. Michael Meacher, 'Britain now faces its own blowback', *Guardian*

(10 September 2005)
http://www.guardian.co.uk/comment/story/0,3604,1566916,00.html.

352. *New York Times* (17 June 1993).

353. *New York Times* (17 June 1993).

354. Ibid.

355. Cutileiro, Jose, 'Pre-war Bosnia', Letter to *The Economist* (9-15 December 1995).

356. *New York Times* (17 June 1993); Silber, Laura, 'Serbs confident they can end war and keep spoils', *Financial Times* (21 May 1993); 'Bosnia, genocide in broad daylight', *Impact International* (August-September 1992). For further discussion see Sonyel, Salahi R., *The Muslims of Bosnia*, op. cit.

357. Charles G. Boyd, *Foreign Affairs* (September/October 1995). His declarations refer particularly to Fikret Adbic's autonomous government.

358. See for example 'CIA agents training Bosnian army', *Guardian* (17 Nov 1994); 'America's secret Bosnia agenda', *Observer* (20 Nov 1994).

359. This was reported by the British press in November 1994 in newspapers such as the *Guardian*, the *Observer* and the *Independent*, as well as by the French and German press.

360. Flounders, Sara, 'Bosnia Tragedy: The unknown role of the Pentagon', op. cit.

361. *The Nation* (30 January 1995).

362. See *Toronto Star* (16 July 1995); *Washington Post* (16 February 1994); 'Call that safe?', *Economist* (15–21 July 1995).

363. Dobbs, Michael and Smith, R. Jeffrey, 'New Proof Offered of Serb Atrocities', *Washington Post* (28 October 1995).

364. Gutman, Roy, 'UN's Deadly Deal', *Newsday* (29 May 1996).

365. Judah, Tim, *The Serbs: History, Myth and the Destruction of Yugoslavia* (Yale, 1997, pp. 300f.)

366. US Ambassador Warren Zimmerman in an interview with the Croatian daily *Danas* (12 January 1992).

367. Tim Judah, Kosovo: War and Revenge (New Haven: Yale University Press, 2002, p. 120).

368. Grigg, William Norman, 'Behind the Terror Network,' *The New American* (5 November 2001, 17 (23))
http://www.thenewamerican.com/tna/2001/11-05-2001/vo17no23.htm.

368. *Scotsman* (29 August 1999). Cited in Chossudovsky, 'Osamagate', op. cit.

370. *Sunday Times* (12 March 2000).

371. *The Herald* (27 March 2000).

372. Craig, Larry E., *The Kosovo Liberation Army: Does Clinton Policy Support Group with Terror, Drug Ties?: From 'Terrorists' to 'Partners'*, (United States Senate Republican Policy Committee, Washington DC, 31 March 1999)
http://www.fas.org/irp/world/para/docs/fr033199.htm.

373. Seper, Jerry, 'KLA rebels train in terrorist camps', *Washington Times* (4 May 1999).

374. EU General Affairs Council cited in *Agence Europe*, (9 December 1998, 7559); Little, Alan, 'Moral Combat: NATO At War', BBC2 Special (12 March 2000); 'How Nato was sucked into Kosovo conflict', *Sunday Telegraph* (27 February 2000); *Current History* (March 2000). Sources cited in Chomsky, Noam, *A New Generation Draws the Line: Kosovo, East Timor and the Standards of the West* (Verso, London, 2000).

375. Judah, Tim, *Kosovo: War and Revenge* (Yale University Press, New Haven, 2000, p. 178).

376. Cited in Chomsky, *A New Generation*, op. cit.

377. Opinion of the Upper Administrative Court at Münster, (24 February 1999) (Az: 14 A 840/94,A); opinion of the Upper Administrative Court at Münster, (11 March 1999 (Az: 13A 3894/94.A). Internal German documents cited in Eric Canepa, Brecht Forum, New York (28 April 1999). All these reports can be read online at
http://www.suc.org/kosovo_crisis/documents/ger_gov.html.
Also see *Junge Welt*, (24 April 2000)
http://www.jungewelt.de/1999/04-24/011.shtml
where these documents were originally featured and examined in German, and the newspaper's commentary at
http://www.jungewelt.de/1999/04-24/001.shtml.

378. *The New York Times* (8 April 1999).

379. Zimonjic, Vesna Peric, Inter Press Service (IPS) (23 March 1999); Agence France Press (AFP) (23 March 1999).

380. To evaluate the full Rambouillet text visit the following website, where it is available for complete perusal,
http://www.state.gov/www/regions/eur/ksvo_rambouillet_text.html.
*Interim Agreement for Peace and Self-Government in Kosovo* (23 February 1999); reproduced in *Le Monde Diplomatique* (17 April 1999).

381. Neil Clark, 'How the battle lines were drawn', *Spectator* (14 June 2003)
http://www.antiwar.com/spectator/spec15.html.

382. 'NATO Attacks', *Sunday Times* (28 March 1999).

383. BBC News (19 April 1999).

384. BBC News, 'Kostunica warns of fresh fighting' (29 January 2001)
http://news.bbc.co.uk/1/hi/world/europe/1142478.stm.
Also see Beaumont, Peter, et al., 'CIA's bastard army ran riot in Balkans, backed extremists', *Observer* (11 March 2001)
http://observer.guardian.co.uk/international/story/0,6903,449923,00.html.

385. *Sunday Times* (18 March 2001). Cited in Chossudovsky, Michel, 'NATO invades Macedonia' (Montreal, Ottawa: Centre for Research on Globalisation, 22 August 2001)
http://www.globalresearch.ca/articles/CHO108C.html.

386. Bisset, James, op. cit.

387. Taylor, Scott, 'Macedonia's Civil War: "Made in the USA" ', Randolph Bourne Institute (20 August 2001)
http://www.antiwar.com/orig/taylor1.html.

388. Szamuely, George, 'Happy Days, Here Again', *New York Press*, (15 (6): 6–12 February 2002)
http://www.nypress.com/15/6/taki/bunker.cfm.

389. Deliso, Christopher, 'European Intelligence: The US Betrayed Us in Macedonia', Randolph Bourne Institute (22 June 2002)
http://www.antiwar.com/orig/deliso46.html.

390. Dettmer, Jamie, 'Al-Qaeda's Links in the Balkans', *Insight on the News* (1 July 2002).

391. Ibid.

392. Taylor, Scott, 'Signs point to a bin Laden-Balkan link', *Halifax Herald* (29 October 2001)
http://www.balkanpeace.org/hed/archive/oct01/hed4292.shtml. .

393. Cited in CPB Report, 'Bin Laden's Balkan Connection', Centre for Peace in the Balkans, Toronto (September 2001)
http://www.balkanpeace.org/our/our09.shtml.

394. *Neue Zürcher Zeitung* (25 October 2001). Cited in Pascali, see note 91.

395. CPB Research Analysis, 'Balkan – Albania – Kosovo – Heroin – Jihad', Center for Peace in the Balkans, Toronto (May 2000)
http://www.balkanpeace.org/our/our03.shtml.

396. Cited in Pascali, Umberto, 'Bin Laden Puppet Masters Smoked Out in the Balkans', *Macedonia TV* (9 November 2001)
http://www.makedonija.tv/bin_laden_puppetmasters_smoked_o.htm.
Pascali is a veteran journalist based in Macedonia who writes for the respected daily *Dvnenik*.

397. Cited in Pascali, 'US Protects Al-Qaeda Terrorists in Kosovo', Centre for Research on Globalisation, Montreal (21 November 2001)
http://globalresearch.ca/articles/PAS111A.html.

398. Cited in Pascali, 'Bin Laden Puppet Masters', op. cit.

399. FBI Most Wanted Terrorists, 'Ayman al-Zawahiri' (viewed 11 June 2004)
http://www.fbi.gov/mostwant/terrorists/teralzawahiri.htm.

400. Foden, Giles, 'The hunt for 'Public Enemy No 2': Egyptian may now be running terror operations from Afghanistan', *Guardian* (24 September 2001)
http://www.guardian.co.uk/international/story/0,3604,556872,00.html.

401. Ibid.

402. Sachs, Suan, 'Egyptian Raised Terror Funds in US in 1990s', *New York Times* (23 October 2001) p. B4. Also see Williams, Lance, 'Top bin Laden aide toured California', *San Francisco Chronicle* (11 October 2001).

403. 'Bin Laden had US terror cell for a decade', *Sunday Times* (11 November 2001).

404. Bodansky, Yossef, 'US Trade: Mubarak for S-For Safety?', *Defense and Foreign Affairs Strategic Policy* (January 1998). Available online as Bodansky, 'The Price of Washington's Bosnia Policy', Freeman Center for

Strategic Studies, Houston, (February 1998)
http://www.freeman.org/m_online/feb98/bodansky.htm.

405. Bodansky, 'US Trade', op. cit.

406. Dyson, Mark and Lehrer, Jim, 'Terrorist Attack', PBS *Newshour* Transcript (17 November 1997)
http://www.pbs.org/newshour/bb/middle_east/july-dec97/egypt_11-17.html.

407. Bodansky, Yossef, *Bin Laden: The Man Who Declared War On America* (Prima Publishing, Roseville, CA, 1999, 2001, p. 213).

408. Philip Johnston, 'Al-Qa'eda link hides multitude of suspects', *Telegraph* (8 July 2005)
http://www.telegraph.co.uk/news/main.jhtml?xml=/news/2005/07/08/nterr08.xml.

409. CNN (26 August 2003).

410. Mark Thompson, 'How the Mean US Fighting Machine Lost its "Lean",' *Time* (5 January 2001)
http://www.time.com/time/world/article/0,8599,93858,00.html

411 . *New York Times* (1 February 1999) Cited in Lahaye, Marie-Pierre, *Yugoslavia: How Demonizing a Whole People Serves Western Interests.*

412. Schwartz, Benjamin and Layne, Christopher, 'The Case Against Intervention in Kosovo', *The Nation* (19 April 1999).

413. Lelyveld, Michael, 'Caucasus: US Military Presence In Caspian Appears Inevitable', Radio Free Europe/Radio Liberty, Boston (4 February 1999)
http://www.rferl.org/

414. Lelyveld, 'Caucasus: US Military Presence In Caspian Appears Inevitable', op. cit.

415. BHHRG Report, *NATO Targets Yugoslavia: Report of a visit to Belgrade, 10th-13th May, 1999* (London: British Helsinki Human Rights Group, 22 May 1999)
http://www.bhhrg.org/CountryReport.asp?ReportID=170&CountryID=20.

416. Abrahams, Fred, 'Macedonia', *Foreign Policy In Focus* (April 1998, 3 (7)).

417. *Sole 24 Ore* [Italian daily] (13 April 1999). Cited in Collon, Michel, *Monopoly – L'Otan à la Conquête du monde*, EPO (March 2000, p. 96).

418. Monbiot, George, 'A Discreet Deal in the Pipeline', *Guardian* (15 February 2001).

419. See information at Alexander Gas and Oil Connections, (October 2000)
http://www.gasandoil.com/goc/news/nte04224.htm.

420. Cited in Monbiot, George, 'A Discreet Deal in the Pipeline', op. cit.

421. US Congress, Testimony of Frank J. Cilluffo , Deputy Director, Global Organized Crime, Program director to the House Judiciary Committee (13 December 2000). Cited in Chossudovsky, 'Osamagate', op. cit.

422. Colin Freeman, 'US 'disappointed' at British failure to stem opium trade', *Telegraph* (17 July 2005)

http://www.telegraph.co.uk/news/main.jhtml?xml=/news/2005/07/17/wafg17.xml&sSheet=/news/2005/07/17/ixworld.html.

423. BBC News, 'Afghanistan retakes heroin crown', (3 March 2003) http://news.bbc.co.uk/2/hi/business/2814861.stm.

424. B. Raman, 'Assassination of Haji Abdul Qadeer in Kabul' (South Asia Analysis Group, 7 August 2002, Paper No. 489) http://www.saag.org/papers5/paper489.html.

425. Ibid.

426. John K. Cooley, *Unholy Wars: Afghanistan, America and International Terrorism* (London: Pluto, 2000, p. 180)

427. Scott, Peter Dale, *Drugs, Oil and War: The United States in Afghanistan, Colombia and Indochina* (New York: Rowman & Littlefield, 2003); Scott, 'Al-Qaeda, US Oil Companies, and Central Asia', op. cit.

428. National Commission on Terrorist Attacks, *The 9/11 Commission Report: Final Report of the National Commission on Terrorist Attacks Upon the United States* (New York: W. W. Norton, 2004, p. 58).

429. Scott, 'Al-Qaeda, US Oil Companies, and Central Asia', op. cit.

430. David Leppard, Paul Nuki and Gareth Walsh, 'BP accused of backing 'arms for oil' coup', *Sunday Times* (26 March 2000); 'BP Linked to the Overthrow of Azerbaijan Government,' *Drillbits and Trailings* (17 April 2000, 5 (6))
http://www.moles.org/ProjectUnderground/drillbits/5_06/1.html.

431. Moscow News (13 September 2000); Associated Press (14 November 1999).

432. Yossef Bodansky, Defense & Foreign Affairs: Strategic Policy (October 1999); Nair Aliyev, *Ekho* [Russian-language daily in Azerbaijan] (1 September 2001).

433. Bronwen Maddox, 'Bush's officers parade policy contradiction', *The Times* (5 December 2003)
http://www.timesonline.co.uk/printFriendly/0,,1-3-919746,00.html.

434. FCO Press Release, 'Foreign Secretary Meets the President of Azerbaijan' (London: Foreign & Commonwealth Office, 14 December 2004) http://www.fco.gov.uk/servlet/Front?pagename=OpenMarket/Xcelerate/ShowPage&c=Page&cid=1007029391638&a=KArticle&aid=1101394807368.

435. Bodansky, Yossef, 'The Great Game for Oil', *Defense & Foreign Affairs Strategic Policy* (June/July 2000).

436. Levon Sevunts, 'Who's calling the shots? Chechen conflict finds Islamic roots in Afghanistan and Pakistan', *Gazette* (26 October 1999).

437. Soner Cagaptay and Alexander Murinson, 'Good Relations between Azerbaijan and Israel: A Model for Other Muslim States in Eurasia?', Policy Watch (Washington DC: Washington Institute for Near East Policy, 30 March 2005, No. 982)
http://www.washingtoninstitute.org/templateC05.php?CID=2287.

438. Amirouche, Hamou, 'Algeria's Islamist Revolution: The People Versus Democracy?', *Middle East Policy* (January 1998, 5 (4)).

439 Addi, Lahouari, 'Algeria's Tragic Contradictions', *Journal of Democracy* (1996, 7 (3): 94–107).

440. Lombardi, Ben, 'Turkey: The Return of the Reluctant Generals', *Political Science Quarterly*, (Summer 1997, 112 (2)).

441. Entelis, John P., *Democracy Denied: America's Authoritarian Approach Towards the Maghreb – Causes & Consequences* (XVIIIth World Congress of the International Political Science Association, Quebec, 1–5 August 2000).

442. *The Guardian* (8 April 2004).

443. 'Armed Islamic Group: Algeria, Islamists' in *Terrorism: Questions & Answers* (Council on Foreign Relations: Washington DC, 2004) http://cfrterrorism.org/groups/gia.html.

444. Cited in Hiel, Betsy, 'Algeria Valuable In Hunt For Terrorists,' *Pittsburgh Tribune-Review* (18 November 2001).

445. Kjeilen, Tore, 'GIA', *Encyclopedia of the Orient* (1996–2004) http://i-cias.com/e.o/gia.htm.

446. Boudjemaa, M., 'Terrorism in Algeria: Ten Years of Day-to-Day Genocide' in Cilliers, Jakkie and Sturman, Kathryn (ed.), *Africa and Terrorism: Joining the Global Campaign* (Institute for Security Studies Monograph No. 74, Pretoria, July 2002) http://www.iss.co.za/PUBS/MONOGRAPHS/No74/Chap6.html.

447. Robinson, Colin, 'Armed Islamic Group a.k.a. Groupement Islamique Arme' (Center for Defense Information: Washington DC, 5 February 2003) http://www.cdi.org/terrorism/gia_020503.cfm.

448. Office of the Attorney-General, Australia, in ABC Asia Pacific, 'Cause & Effect: Terrorism in the Asia Pacific Region' (2004) http://abcasiapacific.com/cause/network/armed_islamic.htm.

449. Gunaratna, Rohan and Hirschkorn, Phil, et. al., 'Blowback', Jane's *Intelligence Review* (13 (8) 1 August 2001).

450. Amirouche, Hamou, 'Algeria's Islamist Revolution: The People Versus Democracy?', *Middle East Policy* (5 (4) January 1998).

451. *Paris Match* (9 October 1997).

452. *Independent* (30 October 1997).

453. *Sunday Times* (16 July 2000).

454. *Independent* (30 October 1997).

455. Chinade, M., 'Not so secret terrorist junta', *Impact International* (February 1998, 28 (2).

456. Television Swiss Romande (TSR), Switzerland (January 1998).

457. Sweeney, John, 'Seven monks were beheaded. Now the whistleblower has paid with his life', *Observer* (14 June 1998).

458. Lounis Aggoun and Jean-Baptiste Rivoire, *Françalgérie: crimes et mensonges d'Etats* (Paris: La Découverte, 2004).

459. Simon, Daniel Ben, 'Arabs Slaughter Arabs in Algeria', *Ha'aretz* (20 April 2001). Also see Hadjarab, Mustapha, 'Former Officer Testifies To Army Atrocities', *Algeria Interface* (9 February 2001). Souadia, for instance,

admits accompanying commandos from the army's 'anti-terrorist' squad to Lakhdaria, an alleged rebel stronghold 50 miles from Algiers. The squad disguised themselves as bearded fundamentalists. 'All the suspects of course ended up being killed. We arrested people, we tortured them, we killed them and then we burned their bodies.' In that region alone, 'I must have seen at least 100 people liquidated'. (*Guardian*, 14 February 2001). See Souadia, Habib, *The Dirty War: The testimony of a former officer of the special forces of the Algerian army, 1992-2000*, (La Decouverte: Paris, 2001).

460. Cited in Italian Anti-Terrorist Judge Ferdinando Imposimato's Foreword to Souadia's book, *The Dirty War*, ibid.

461. Review of Samraoui's book, *A Chronicle of the Years of Blood: How the Secret Services Manipulated Islamic Groups*, Denoel, 2003, in *Sueddeutsche Zeitung* (15 March 2004).

462. Naima Bouteldja, 'Who really bombed Paris?' *Guardian* (8 September 2005)
http://www.guardian.co.uk/comment/story/0,,1564933,00.html.

463. Sweeney, John, 'We accuse 80,000 times', *Observer* (16 November 1997).

464. Bone, Alistair, 'The running man', *New Zealand Listener* (189 (3301) 16–22 August 2003).

465. Sweeney, 'We accuse 80,000 times', op. cit.

466. Norton-Taylor, Richard, 'Terrorist case collapses after three years', *Guardian* (21 March 2000).

467. 'The Providential Fog of London', *Le Figaro* (3 November 1995).

468. *Le Parisien* (4 November 1995).

469. Colvie, Marie, 'Britain plans Algerian arms deal despite ethical policy', *Sunday Times* (16 July 2000).

470. Reuters, 'Qatar confirms British arms to go to Algeria', (19 July 2000)
http://edition.cnn.com/2000/WORLD/meast/07/19/arms.qatar.reut.

471. Strategic Export Controls, *Annual Report 1999*, (Foreign and Commonwealth Offices: London, 2000); Strategic Export Controls, *Annual Report*, (Stationery Office: London, 2001).

472. Aldridge, Bob, *Understanding the 'War on Terrorism': The Oil & Gas Interests Part 2 – (Africa)*, (Pacific Life Research Center: Santa Clara, CA, 1 February 2003, p. 6–7)
http://www.plrc.org/docs/030201.pdf. .

473. Ciment, James, 'The Battle of Algiers', *In These Times* (December 1997).

474. Cooley, John K., *Unholy Wars: Afghanistan, America and International Terrorism*, (Pluto Press: London, 1998, pp. 205–6).

475. Richard Labévière, *Dollars for Terror: The US and Islam* (New York: Algora, 2000), pp. 182–9.

476. Sweeney and Doyle, 'Algeria Regime Responsible for Massacres', op. cit.

477. Sweeney, 'We accuse 80,000 times', op. cit.

478. 'Algeria', United States Energy Information Administration (February 1999)
http://www.eia.doe.gov/emeu/cabs/algeria.html.

479. Ritt Goldstein, 'Africa: Oil, al-Qaeda and the US Military', Asia Times (30 March 2004)
http://www.atimes.com/atimes/Front_Page/FC30Aa02.html.

480. Douglas Farah, 'The African Pipeline Expands. The Brotherhood Returns to Sudan' (26 January 2006)
http://www.douglasfarah.com.

481. Emily Hunt, 'Al-Qaeda's North African Franchise: The GSPC Regional Threat', *Policy Watch* (Washington DC: Washington Institute for Near East Policy, 28 September 2005, No. 1034)
http://www.washingtoninstitute.org/templateC05.php?CID=2379.

482. Africa Report, 'Islamist Terrorism in the Sahel: Fact or Fiction' (Brussells: International Crisis Group, 31 March 2005, p. 7)
http://www.tecom.usmc.mil/caocl/Africa/Pan-Sahel/Readings/Islamist%20Terrorism%20in%20the%20Sahel-Fact%20or%20Fiction.pdf

483. Salima Mellah and Jean-Baptiste Rivoire, 'Who Staged the Tourist Kidnappings? El Para, the Maghreb's Bin Laden', *Le Monde Diplomatique* (February 2005)
http://mondediplo.com/2005/02/04algeria.

484. Hamid Ould Ahmed, 'Algeria Jails Top Islamic Desert Militant for Life', Reuters (26 June 2005)
http://www.tiscali.co.uk/news/newswire.php/news/reuters/2005/06/26/world/algeriajailstopislamicdesertmilitantforlife.html.

485. Jason Motlag, 'US takes terror fight to Africa's "Wild West",' *San Francisco Chronicle* (27 December 2005)
http://www.sfgate.com/cgi-bin/article.cgi?file=/c/a/2005/12/27/MNGISGDLR91.DTL.

486. Jeremy Keenan, 'Terror in the Sahara: the Implications of US Imperialism for North & West Africa', *Review of African Political Economy* (September 2004, 31 (101): 475–486). Keenan reviews a wealth of evidence in excruciating detail. Also see his two other briefings which contain more extensive background analysis demonstrating a US-Algerian intelligence deception in relation to the GSPC: Keenan, 'Americans & 'Bad People' in the Sahara-Sahel', *Review of African Political Economy* (March 2004, 31 (99): 130–9); 'Political Destablisation and 'Blowback' in the Sahel', *Review of African Political Economy* (December 2004, 31(102): 691–703).

487. Christopher Deliso, 'West Africa: Where the empire will come to ruin', (27 September 2004)
http://antiwar.com/edmonds/?articleid=3658.

488. *L'Expression* [Algerian daily] (6 June 2004).

489. Douglas Farah, 'Salafists, China and West Africa's Growing Anarchy' (Washington: International Assessment and Strategy Centre, 7

December 2004)
http://www.strategycenter.net/research/pubID.55/pub_detail.asp.

490. Tony Karon, 'Why Africa Has Become a Bush Priority', *Time* (7 July 2003)
http://foi.missouri.edu/evolvingissues/whyafrica.html.

491. Keenan, 'Terror in the Sahara', op. cit., p. 491.

492. Ambassador Cofer Black, 'The Prevention and Combating of Terrorism in Africa', Remarks at the Second Intergovernmental High-Level Meeting on the Prevention and Combating of Terrorism In Africa, Algiers (Washington DC: US Department of State, 13 October 2004)
http://www.state.gov/s/ct/rls/rm/2004/37230.htm.

493. Motlag, 'US takes terror fight to Africa's "Wild West" ', op. cit.

494. Salima Mellah and Jean-Baptiste Rivoire, 'Who Staged the Tourist Kidnappings?' op. cit.

495. Pierre Abramovici, 'United States: the new scramble for Africa', *Le Monde* (July 2004)
http://mondediplo.com/2004/07/07usinafrica.

496. Salima Mellah and Jean-Baptiste Rivoire, 'Who Staged the Tourist Kidnappings?' op. cit.

497. Mark Curtis, *Web of Deceit: Britain's Real Role in the World* (London: Vintage, 2004, p. 70).

498. US Department of State Press Release, 'US Promotes Development and Governance in Africa to Counter Terrorism – State Dept. official outlines key programs that bind continent to America' (16 April 2004).

499. African Oil Policy Initiative Group (AOPIG), 'African Oil: A Priority for US National Security and African Development' (2002) p. 4.

500. Friends of the Earth Press Release, 'The New West African Gas Pipeline' (Montreal, Ottawa: Centre for Research on Globalization, 9 September 2005)
http://www.globalresearch.ca/index.php?context=viewArticle&code=FRI20050909&articleId=912.

501. Douglas Farah (*Washington Post* reporter), 'Terrorist Responses to Improved US Financial Defences', Testimony in Hearing before Subcommittee on Oversight and Investigations of the Committee on Financial Services, US House of Representatives (Washington DC: US Government Printing Office, 16 February 2005, No. 109-3: 23–6, 41–57)
http://financialservices.house.gov/media/pdf/109-3.pdf.

502. Douglas Farah, 'Al Qaeda Cash Tied to Diamond Trade', *Washington Post Foreign Service* (2 November 2001, p. A01).

503. Associated Press, 'Al-Qaeda bought diamonds before 9/11', *USA Today* (7 August 2004)
http://www.usatoday.com/news/world/2004-08-07-al-qaeda-diamonds_x.htm.

504. Douglas Farah, 'Report Says Africans Harbored Al Qaeda Terror

Assets Hidden In Gem-Buying Spree', *Washington Post* (29 December 2002) p. A01.

505. Douglas Farah Press Release, 'Blood from Stones: The Secret Financial Network of Terror' (May 2004)
http://www.douglasfarah.com/reviews/press-release.shtml.

506. Ibid.

507. Newsweek, cited in Nafeez Mosaddeq Ahmed, *The War on Truth: 9/11, Disinformation and the Anatomy of Terrorism* (London: Arris, 2005).

508. Bryan Bender, 'Liberia's Taylor gave aid to Qaeda, UN probe finds', *Boston Globe* (4 August 2004)
http://www.boston.com/news/nation/washington/articles/2004/08/04/liberias_taylor_gave_aid_to_qaeda_un_probe_finds/.

509. Ibid.

510. Edward Harris (AP), 'Hezbollah extorting funds from West Africa's diamond merchants, US officials say', *San Francisco Chronicle* (29 June 2004)
http://www.sfgate.com/cgi-bin/article.cgi?f=/news/archive/2004/06/29/international1421EDT0643.DTL.

511. Douglas Farah Press Release, 'Blood from Stones', op. cit.

512. Jean-Philippe Rémy, 'The Trafficker Viktor Bout Lands US Aid for Services Rendered in Iraq', *Le Monde* (18 May 2004)
http://www.globalpolicy.org/security/issues/iraq/contract/2004/0518bout.htm.

513. Douglas Farah, 'Arrest Aids Pursuit of Weapons Network', *Washington Post Foreign Service* (26 February 2002)
http://www.washingtonpost.com/ac2/wp-dyn?pagename=article&node=&contentId=A2005-2002Feb25&notFound=true.

514. Curtis, *Web of Deceit*, op. cit., p. 71.

515. BBC News, 'Peace without justice in Sierra Leone' (10 February 2000) http://news.bbc.co.uk/1/hi/world/africa/636696.stm.

516. John Pilger, 'Our soldiers aren't in Sierra Leone for the sake of morals or democracy. They are there for the control of diamonds', *New Statesman* (29 May 2000)
http://www.newstatesman.com/200005290013.

517. UN Panel of Experts, Report of the Panel of Experts Appointed Pursuant to Security Council Resolution 1306 (2000), Paragraph 19, in Relation to Sierra Leone (December 2000, Part 1)
http://www.globalpolicy.org/security/issues/sierra/report/001220.htm.

518. Cited in Pilger, 'Our soldiers aren't in Sierra Leone for the sake of morals or democracy', op. cit.; and 'In the service of diamond firms', *Socialist Worker* (20 May 2000, No. 1697).

519. Ibid.

520. Kenneth Roth (HRW Executive Director), 'UK Arms May go to Abusive Forces in Sierra Leone', Letter to Hon. Robin Cook, Secretary of State for Foreign and Commonwealth Affairs, and Hon. Geoff Hoon,

Secretary of State for Defense, United Kingdom (New York: Human Rights Watch, 25 May 2000) http://www.hrw.org/press/2000/05/sleone0525.htm.

521. *Telegraph* (21 May 2000).

522. Ambrose Ganda, 'Intervention, Recolonisation or Facilitation', *Focus on Sierra Leone* (London, 18 March 2001)
http://www.focus-on-sierra-leone.co.uk/
Intervention_Recolonisation_Facilitation.htm.

523. Mark V. Kollie, 'Corruption, Greed, Injustice And Humanitarian Assistance In Sierra Leone: The Slpp Government A Case Under Review' (Freetown: Africa Analysis International, 26 November 2002, No. 7)
http://www.theperspective.org/aai.html.

524. Mark Malan and Sarah Meek, 'Extension of Government Authority and National Recovery', in Mark Malan, Sarah Meek, Thokozani Thusi, et al. (eds), *Sierra Leone: Building the Road to Recovery* (Institute for Security Studies, March 2003, No. 80, Chapter 7)
http://www.iss.co.za/Pubs/Monographs/No80/Chap7.html.

525. Donald Temple, 'Sierra Leone: An Obscure Battlefield in the War on Terrorism', Terrorism Monitor (Washington DC: Jamestown Foundation, 20 December 2005, 3 (24))
http://www.jamestown.org/terrorism/news/article.php?articleid=2369857.

526. See Paul Larkin, *A Very British Jihad: Collusion, Conspiracy & Cover-Up in Northern Ireland* (Belfast: Beyond the Pale, 2004).

527. House of Commons Intelligence and Security Committee, "Report into the London Terrorist Attacks on 7th July 2005" (May 2006).

528. "Report of the Official Account of the Bombings in London on 7th July 2005" (London: Stationary Office, 11 May 2006)

529. Ibid., p. 23.

530. Ibid., p. 23

531. Ibid., p. 21

532. Ibid., p. 16-17.

533. Ibid., p. 17.

534. Ibid., p. 22.

535. Ibid., p. 4.

536. House of Commons ISC, "Report into the London Terrorist Attacks", op. cit., p. 13.

537. Ibid., p. 13.

538. Ibid., p. 20.